MARKETING:
AN INTRODUCTION

ROGER W. HUTT

Associate Professor of Management
Arizona State University West

WILLIAM A. STULL

Professor of Marketing Education
Utah State University

SB05BB
PUBLISHED BY
SOUTH-WESTERN PUBLISHING CO.
CINCINNATI, OH   DALLAS, TX   LIVERMORE, CA

Acquisitions Editor: Eve Lewis
Developmental Editor: Nancy A. Long
Production Editor: Thomas N. Lewis
Senior Designer: Darren K. Wright
Photo Researcher: Mike O'Donnell
Marketing Manager: Donald H. Fox

COVER PHOTO: © Guy Motil/Westlight

ISBN: 0-538-60820-X

Library of Congress Catalog Card Number: 90-62769

8 9 MT 9

Printed in the United States of America

CONTENTS

PREFACE v

▰ UNIT 1
THE WORLD OF MARKETING 1

CHAPTER   1   Overview of Marketing 2

            2   Marketing Functions and Activities 25

            3   Marketing Careers 48

▰ UNIT 2
ANALYZING THE MARKETPLACE 81

CHAPTER   4   Obtaining and Using Marketing Information 82

            5   Understanding the Products and Services You Market 104

            6   Consumer Buying Behavior 128

            7   Organizational Buying Behavior 150

            8   Dividing a Market into Segments 170

▰ UNIT 3
PROMOTION AND SELLING 193

CHAPTER   9   Overview of Promotion 194

           10   Promotion: Personal Selling 214

iii

	11	Promotion: Advertising	234
	12	Promotion: Visual Merchandising, Sales Promotion, and Public Relations	262

UNIT 4
PRICING AND DISTRIBUTION 287

CHAPTER	13	Pricing	288
	14	Marketing Channels and Intermediaries	310
	15	Physical Distribution	334

UNIT 5
MARKETING AND YOU 355

CHAPTER	16	Special Topics in Marketing	356
	17	Obtaining Your First Job in Marketing	380
	18	Getting Off to the Right Start in Marketing	402

GLOSSARY	421
INDEX	445

PREFACE

Marketing: An Introduction, Second Edition, presents marketing as a creative, competitive, and dynamic activity that impacts the lives of millions of consumers and employees. Indeed, the United States' vast marketing system has no equal anywhere in the world. The people, companies, and other institutions that perform marketing activities in an efficient and timely manner deserve much of the credit for our standard of living.

As defined by the American Marketing Association, marketing is the process of planning and executing the conception, pricing, promotion, and distribution of ideas, goods, and services to create exchanges that satisfy individual and organizational goals. Marketing, then, includes all those activities that provide products and services for the satisfaction of consumer needs and wants.

Marketing: An Introduction, Second Edition, is designed for an introductory course in marketing. The goals of this text-workbook are to:

1. Expose students to the various career opportunities in marketing and acquaint them with the career development process.
2. Help students develop an understanding of marketing, in both profit and nonprofit organizations, and its important role in the free enterprise system.
3. Introduce students to the basic marketing functions, activities, and institutions.
4. Help students develop an appreciation for the *marketing concept* and the importance of this concept to organizations.
5. Expose students to the four Ps of marketing, their interrelationship, and their importance to the field of marketing.
6. Provide students with an opportunity to develop the basic social, marketing, and personal skills that are required for successful employability in marketing.

New Features

New features contained in *Marketing: An Introduction, Second Edition*, include:

- Expanded coverage of selected topics, such as organizational markets, marketing trends, and pricing, to reflect the latest marketing practices.
- Glossary of key marketing terms.
- Content that is consistent with Marketing's National Curriculum Framework and Core Competencies.
- Examination of marketing by nonprofit organizations, in addition to profit-oriented organizations.

- Discussion of marketing as it applies to both products and services.
- Marketing Insight, a new end-of-chapter activity that consists of a short case drawn from the real world of marketing.

Important Features

Marketing: An Introduction, Second Edition, will provide most students with their first opportunity to study marketing and understand the role it plays in the overall economy. The text-workbook is also a means for acquiring the necessary skills for employment in—at a minimum—entry-level marketing jobs. Important features of each chapter are:

- Realistic and clearly stated learning objectives.
- Key marketing terms printed in boldface type.
- Examples based on actual marketing practices and situations.
- Emphasis on marketing subject matter as well as on the development of skills required for successful employment in marketing occupations.
- End-of-chapter activities that make use of various methods to reinforce learning:

    a. *Applying Marketing Terms.* Students demonstrate their knowledge of key terms by matching each term with an application of that term.
    b. *Mastering Key Concepts.* Students write short answers to demonstrate their understanding of key concepts.
    c. *Developing People Skills.* Students use problem-solving skills to develop solutions for case studies that focus on interpersonal relations.
    d. *Marketing Project.* Students use creativity and marketing knowledge to complete these projects. Many of these will require students to practice their oral and written communication skills.
    e. *Marketing Insight.* Students make use of their critical thinking, reasoning, and decision-making skills to analyze a case based on real world marketing practices.

Organization

Marketing: An Introduction, Second Edition, consists of eighteen chapters grouped into five units.

Unit 1 The World of Marketing: Unit 1 is an overview of marketing. Students are introduced to the marketing concept, types of businesses, utility, and marketing functions. The unit concludes with an overview of the various occupations open to students preparing for careers in marketing.

Unit 2 Analyzing the Marketplace: Students learn the importance of obtaining and using various types of information to make wise marketing decisions. The importance of understanding the products or services you market, as well as the buying behavior of your customers, is discussed. Consumers and organizations, the two large groups into which buyers can be divided, are each examined in a separate chapter. Students are also introduced to the practice of dividing mass markets into segments.

Unit 3 Promotion and Selling: The focus of this unit is on the important role promotion and selling play in the overall marketing process. Personal selling, advertising, visual merchandising, sales promotion, and public relations are each discussed.

Unit 4 Pricing and Distribution: This unit examines various pricing methods, marketing channels, and physical distribution methods that organizations use to deliver products and services to the location where they are needed.

Unit 5 Marketing and You: The final unit shows students how marketing can fit into their plans for the future. Some special topics and trends in marketing are presented, including demographic trends, international events, and the environmental movement. Guidance is offered to help students search for and obtain their first jobs. The unit concludes with some straightforward advice on getting off to the right start in a marketing career.

The time and effort invested in learning about marketing will be worth it. In fact, there are at least five reasons why the study of marketing is important. First, marketing provides satisfaction to consumers by creating utility. Utility, or usefulness, is added to products and services by the millions of people who hold marketing occupations. Second, marketing stimulates the economy. Marketing is a vital force that keeps national and world economies operating. Third, marketing offers career opportunities. Nearly one-third of our nation's labor force is engaged in marketing. Fourth, marketing is the cornerstone of entrepreneurship. Entrepreneurs, the people who take the risks of starting and managing businesses, use marketing skills to determine the needs and wants of consumers. Fifth, by learning how marketing works you can become a better-informed consumer. Even if you do not select marketing as your career, you will spend the rest of your life as a consumer.

Roger Hutt
William Stull

UNIT 1
THE WORLD OF MARKETING

1   OVERVIEW OF MARKETING

2   MARKETING FUNCTIONS AND ACTIVITIES

3   MARKETING CAREERS

CHAPTER 1
OVERVIEW OF MARKETING

After you read this chapter and complete the activities at the end, you will be able to:

1. **Define marketing.**
2. **Explain the three parts of the marketing concept.**
3. **Discuss the role of marketing in nonprofit organizations.**
4. **Describe the five major types of businesses.**
5. **Identify the five types of utility.**
6. **Explain why it is important to study marketing.**

Mark had a successful career as the sales manager for a distributor of office furniture. As he described it, his salary was "in the high five figures." He also had a liberal expense account and was permitted personal use of his company car. Several large office buildings were under construction or in the planning stage, indicating the probability of a steady stream of potential buyers of office furniture for some time to come. Mark, however, had lost interest in his job and had decided to do what he had always wanted to do. He opened his own business.

Mark formed a company to sell personal computers and accessories, mainly printers. He believed that most of his customers would be law firms, accounting firms, banks, and insurance companies. As Mark said, "I successfully managed a sales force that sold office furniture to these kinds of firms and I intend to be just as successful in selling personal computers and printers to them." Using the proceeds of a loan as well as some personal savings and money provided by two investors, Mark purchased a large inventory of computers and accessories. While the items were in their original unopened cartons, most were discontinued by their manufacturers. Mark intended to sell to those buyers who were more interested in a low price than in having the latest model of a computer.

He thought that in less than five years the sales volume of his new company would exceed that of his former employer. "I don't know much about computers, but I do know that if you can sell office furniture, you can sell anything."

After he had been in business for more than four months, Mark realized there was a problem. His company was not reaching the sales volume he knew it would need to succeed. His sales people were making sales calls, but they were not making sales. Why? Mark did not find out the type of computers and printers his potential customers preferred before buying the inventory. In other words, he did not pay enough attention to marketing.

MARKETING DEFINED

Marketing is the performance of activities that provide products and services for the satisfaction of consumer needs and wants.[1] As depicted in Figure 1-1, marketing is like a link in a chain. It connects those who provide a product or service with those who buy and use it. Marketing involves finding out what products and services consumers need and want and then making those items available.

Figure 1-1   A link in a chain.

Consumer Needs and Wants

Ultimate consumers are persons or households that buy products or services for personal or family use. (For convenience, the term **consumers** will be used when referring to ultimate consumers.) This makes everyone a consumer. As consumers we all have needs and wants. **Needs** are things we must have—food, clothing, and shelter.

---

[1]The American Marketing Association defines marketing as "the process of planning and executing the conception, pricing, promotion, and distribution of ideas, goods, and services to create exchanges that satisfy individual and organizational goals."

Wants are things we can live without but which make our lives easier or more comfortable. Sports cars and designer clothes are examples of wants.

Products and Services

Everything you purchase is either a product or a service. **Products,** also called **goods,** are tangible items. They are things you can touch. Look around your home and you will see different kinds of products or goods. You will find some items that are called **durable goods** because they are made to last for several years. Furniture, cars, refrigerators, and television sets are examples of durable goods.

You will also see some items that are called **nondurable goods** because they last only a short time. They are used quickly and are replaced often. Food, clothing, cosmetics, and cleaning supplies are examples of nondurable goods.

Services are tasks or activities that we pay others to do or provide for us. They are intangible which means that you cannot touch them, nor can you see, hear, smell, or taste them.

You use services regularly. When you pay someone to cut your hair, dry-clean your clothes, or repair the transmission in your car, you are buying a service. You are also using services when you make a telephone call, watch a movie on cable television, rent a car, have your teeth cleaned, or buy an insurance policy.

THE MARKETING CONCEPT

When a business follows the **marketing concept,** its goal is to satisfy customers and do so at a profit. Although this is a simple idea, it is not followed by all firms. Recall how you have been treated by some salespersons. Perhaps you have walked into a store where a salesperson tried to sell you something that you did not want. This is called the **sales concept,** which means trying to sell something before learning what customers want. By following the marketing concept, however, a business finds out first what customers want and then makes it available.

The marketing concept has three parts:

1. A customer concept.
2. A total company effort.
3. Profit as a goal.

Illustration 1-1   The goal of the marketing concept is to satisfy customers and make a profit.

Customer Concept

A **customer concept** means doing what the customers want, not what the business wants. Some stores are open evenings and weekends for their customers' convenience. Many restaurants have separate eating areas for smokers and nonsmokers. These are provided because nonsmoking customers want it that way. Practices such as these may be inconvenient for businesses, but what the customers want is more important.

Business people should use the customer concept when choosing a product or service to sell. Once it was enough for a company to make a product and figure out how to sell it. Now managers must ask, "What products should we be making and to whom should we be selling them?"

Total Company Effort

Total company effort means that all parts of the business work together. Unfortunately, all companies do not function this way. Have you ever thought that one part of a business did not know what another part was doing? Have you ever gone to a store to buy an audio cassette tape or a compact disc that the store advertised? The salespeople are not aware of the advertisement, the item is not in the store, and it will not be available for at least two weeks. You are upset that you wasted your time going to the store. You were misled because total company effort was lacking. You were frustrated because you could not buy what you wanted.

You may decide that you will never go to that store again. The store has lost a customer. But this did not have to happen. You would have been a satisfied customer if the store had stocked the advertised product. You may have become a regular customer. And this is what marketing is all about—doing what is necessary to make people want to do business with a company again and again.

◤ Profit as a Goal

Profit is the difference between the income generated by the business and the cost of running that business. Profit should be a goal of the business. Even nonprofit firms must earn more revenue than they spend, or they cannot exist for long. Once a company knows what customers want, managers must find out if the company can satisfy those wants and earn a profit at the same time. Some people say that sales should be the goal. But a huge sales volume alone does not guarantee success. Many companies have failed even though they had millions of dollars in sales. Companies with sales of more than one billion dollars a year have gone out of business. In the 1980s and 1990s, some of the nation's largest airlines have been struggling to survive.

◤ MARKETING AND NONPROFIT ORGANIZATIONS

Marketing is not a business activity limited to firms that sell video cassette recorders, gasoline, airline travel, and other products and services. **Nonprofit organizations,** those that do not have profit making as their primary goal, also use marketing practices. Examples of nonprofit organizations include museums, charities, and political parties. The goal of a museum may be to increase the number of people who visit its exhibits each year. The charity may seek to obtain increased cash contributions, as well as the assistance of volunteers to help in carrying out its work. One of a political party's goals may be to encourage citizens to vote for its candidates. All of these organizations use marketing practices to communicate with their consumers and achieve their goals.

▰ MARKETING AND AMERICAN BUSINESS

Marketing is the energy that drives our economy. It brings the products and services that we need and want to the marketplace, the place of exchange. Marketing thrives in every part of the American business system.

Business firms can be classified according to the kind of business activity they engage in. Generally, there are two kinds of business activities: industrial and commercial. **Industrial business activity** refers to the production of goods. **Commercial business activity** includes marketing products made by other companies and providing financing and other services.

Businesses can also be classified by type. There are five major types of businesses: (1) extractors, (2) manufacturers, (3) wholesalers, (4) retailers, and (5) service businesses. Extractors and manufacturers are involved in industrial business activities; wholesalers, retailers, and service organizations are engaged in commercial business activities. The five major types of businesses are explained in the following paragraphs.

▰ Extractors

Extractors grow products on farms or remove raw materials from where they are found in nature. Think of the different extractors who provide products you use every day. The farmer who grew the grain for your breakfast cereal is one. The cotton growers who provide the raw material for your jeans and shirts and the company that pumps crude petroleum from the ground for gasoline are two other important extractors. Those who mine coal, dig gravel, or harvest timber are also important.

Extractors usually sell products directly to other companies. However, when farmers sell fresh vegetables from their roadside stands, they have direct contact with consumers. The product is not shipped a long distance and there is little need for advertising. In this case, marketing is a simple process.

Sometimes an extractor's product will change hands many times before it reaches the customer. Instead of operating a roadside stand, a farmer may decide to sell tomatoes to a company that buys from many growers and sells in large quantities to a food processor. The food processor, in turn, changes the tomatoes into tomato sauce and packs it into cans. Once the tomato sauce is on the store shelf, the customer can buy and use it to make spaghetti sauce. In this instance, marketing has become a complicated process.

◢◣ Manufacturers

Manufacturers take materials and parts and combine them into products that customers can use. Someone who wants a car is not interested in sheets of steel, plate glass, paint, belts, and hoses. These items have no value until they are combined to make an automobile.

Textile mills and clothing producers are examples of manufacturers. Textile mills take cotton, spin it into yarn, and make the yarn into cloth. After it has been dyed or printed with designs, clothing producers buy the cloth and make it into shirts, slacks, and dresses.

Sometimes a manufacturer sells products to other manufacturers. A maker of electrical wire sells it to a company that uses it in microcomputers. A company that makes windshield glass sells it to one of the large automakers.

◢◣ Wholesalers

Although manufacturers turn out thousands of different products, these items are of no use to anyone unless they are available when and where someone wants to buy them. Much of what we buy is obtained through wholesalers. **Wholesalers** are business organizations that buy large quantities of goods from extractors and manufacturers and sell them to other companies. Your breakfast cereal probably passed through a wholesaler organization on its way from the food processor (manufacturer) to your supermarket.

Manufacturers and large service organizations buy parts and supplies from wholesale firms. Appliance manufacturers purchase large quantities of parts to make refrigerators, stoves, microwave ovens, toasters, and so on. Hospitals purchase supplies and equipment—sheets, pillows, beds, medicine—to meet the needs of patients. Schools buy paint, floor wax, and cleaning supplies from local wholesalers.

Supermarkets stock more than 8,000 different items on their shelves. Without wholesalers, supermarket managers would have to buy directly from hundreds of food processors and manufacturers. This buying process would take all their time, leaving no time for the daily operation of the store.

Wholesalers make it easier for extractors and manufacturers to distribute their products. Instead of selling to a hundred different supermarkets, a food packer can sell a thousand cases of canned soup to one wholesaler. The wholesaler can then sell ten cases to each supermarket.

Most wholesalers handle just one line of product. One may carry groceries while another stocks only hardware, electrical supplies, or auto parts.

Some wholesalers sell only to organizations that do not resell the items in the same form. Examples are wholesalers of equipment for hospitals, dental offices, and restaurants, and chemicals used in manufacturing.

Retailers

Retailers are businesses that buy products from extractors, manufacturers, or wholesalers and sell them to persons who will actually use them. Retailers, therefore, buy for resale to the ultimate consumers.

What is a retail business? If you are like most people you will probably say it is a store where you shop and buy food, clothes, or other items. Selling goods in a store is called **over-the-counter retailing.** It is only one of four forms of retailing. The other three are mail order, direct, and vending machine retailing.

Mail order retailing involves selecting products from catalogs or advertisements and placing orders by mail or telephone. The products are sent directly to the consumer. Many personal, household, or gift items can be bought without leaving home. Mail order is one of the fastest growing segments of retailing in the United States.

In **direct retailing,** sellers take the product to the customer; that is, customers are contacted directly. Door-to-door selling of cosmetics or cleaning supplies is a familiar example. People who sell home-grown produce in neighborhoods is another example.

In **vending machine retailing,** customers deposit coins in a machine and receive goods immediately. Many products are sold through coin-operated machines that automatically dispense merchandise. Soft drinks, candy, snacks, cosmetics, film, small toys, stamps, and road maps are sold this way. Insurance policies are sold through vending machines at airports.

Service Businesses

Service businesses perform tasks or activities for their customers. They comprise the fastest growing segment of business activity. In the United States today, more people work in service businesses than in manufacturing firms. Hundreds of different services are available. The Yellow Pages of your telephone directory lists service businesses such as auto repair shops, driving schools, dry cleaners, cable television companies, and miniature golf courses. Businesses and organizations also use a number of services, including those provided by accountants, lawyers, architects, trucking companies, and advertising agencies.

THE IMPORTANCE OF MARKETING

Because it is a part of the fabric of our society, it is important to understand marketing and the role it plays. Five important reasons you should study marketing are that it (1) provides satisfaction to consumers by creating utility, (2) stimulates the economy, (3) offers career opportunities, (4) is the cornerstone of entrepreneurship, and (5) can help you become a better-informed consumer.

Marketing Creates Utility

The goal of every person who works in marketing is to add value to products and services. This added value is called **utility,** which means usefulness.

In order to understand marketing, you should become familiar with the five kinds of utility: form utility, place utility, time utility, possession utility, and information utility. Each type of utility contributes something essential to making a product or service useful. If any utility is missing, you would not buy the product or service because it would not fulfill your needs.

Form Utility. Beneath the soil of Texas lie vast reserves of crude petroleum. But after the substance is pumped from the ground, it is not useful because it cannot be used in an automobile in that form. However, in Houston a refinery will process crude petroleum into gasoline and oil. When a raw material is changed into a useful form, it has gained **form utility.** Form utility has a cost which includes all the expenses of processing or manufacturing.

Courtesy of Conoco

Illustration 1-2

When crude petroleum is processed into gasoline and oil, it gains form utility.

Form utility is added by a production process, not a marketing process. However, a business uses marketing to find out what products consumers need and want and how much they are willing to pay. In this way marketing and manufacturing work together to create form utility.

Place Utility. Refined oil is canned and shipped from Houston to a service station near your home. This has added value to the oil. It is now useful to you. When a product or service is available in a convenient location, it has gained **place utility.** The cost of place utility is the cost of shipping the product and having it available to customers at a convenient place.

Illustration 1-3   When refined oil is transported to a service station near your home, it gains place utility.

MOBIL OIL CORPORATION

Time Utility. You may not need oil right now, but you will when your car is due for an oil change. Having a product available when the customer needs it creates **time utility.** The cost of time utility is the cost of having products on hand when customers wish to buy them.

Possession Utility. Possession utility means that a transaction has been completed. The buyer now owns the product or service and has the right to use it. You now own the can of oil and can use it in your

Illustration 1-4   Having oil available when the customer needs it creates time utility.

car. As with the other utilities, costs are involved in possession utility. The business must have employees to assist you with your purchase, accept your cash, or fill out a charge account form. The product may also have to be brought from the stockroom or warehouse (a building for the storage of merchandise).

Information Utility. Marketing creates **information utility** by providing informative messages to buyers of their products as well as to those who may become buyers. Examples of these messages are advertisements, such as those that appear in newspapers and on television, and instructional materials that accompany products. Buyers cannot buy products or services unless they know where they are available and at what price. Likewise, buyers may have difficulty using some products, such as a camcorder, unless they have the necessary information available to them in a manual or instruction booklet. The cost of information utility is the company's total cost for providing all of its informative messages.

Illustration 1-5   When you purchase a can of oil, it gains possession utility.

Location courtesy of Wooster Pike Auto Parts, Cincinnati, Ohio

Illustration 1-6

Providing
descriptive
brochures
creates
information
utility.

Marketing Stimulates the Economy

Marketing is the "lubricant" that helps to keep the economy operating. Our nation's **gross national product (GNP),** a measure of the total dollar value of goods and services produced, continues to rise year after year. It is the task of marketing to handle this mountain of goods and services which make up the bulk of the GNP. Experts believe that the economy will continue to grow in the years ahead and that marketing will play an even more important part in that growth.

Figure 1-2 shows the circular flow of money and products or services. As shown in the upper loop of Figure 1-2, people exchange their economic resources (land, labor, capital, and entrepreneurial ability) with businesses for income. Land is exchanged for rent; labor is exchanged for wages, salaries, and benefits; capital is exchanged for interest; and entrepreneurial ability is exchanged for profit. The lower loop shows that, in their role as consumers, people spend their income to buy the products and services which are marketed by businesses.

Figure 1-2   Circular flow of money and products or services.

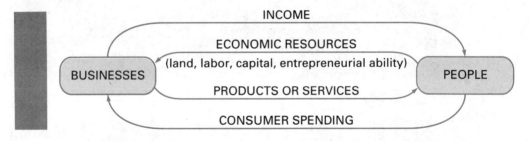

The circular flow will not work without marketing. That is, if firms do not sell their products and services, they will not be able to provide income to employees. If employees do not have income, they will not be able to buy products and services as consumers. These flows go on simultaneously and repeatedly.

Marketing Offers Career Opportunities

Marketing is an exciting and dynamic career field offering opportunities to work mostly with people rather than things. Chances are that you and many of your classmates will have careers in marketing. That's because marketing provides employment to nearly one of every three workers in the United States.[2]

Included are employees in wholesale, retail, service, transportation, and storage companies. Job opportunities also exist in the marketing departments of extractive, manufacturing, and construction businesses. The demand for marketing personnel often remains strong when the employment outlook in other areas of the work force is dim.

Marketing jobs provide job security, chances for advancement, and excellent wages and salaries. Frequently, a salesperson's pay is directly linked to the volume of sales made; higher sales mean higher individual earnings.

Because marketing skills involve working with people and determining their needs and wants, these skills last a lifetime and can be used in other career fields. You will even be able to use marketing skills when you are ready to start your career; that is, you will market yourself to obtain the job you want.

In the United States, marketing executives are often chosen as the chief executive officers (CEO) of major industrial and commercial businesses. In fact, more CEOs have had backgrounds in marketing or sales than in any other area.[3]

Marketing is the Cornerstone of Entrepreneurship

An **entrepreneur** is a person who attempts to earn a profit by taking the risk of starting and managing a business enterprise. The process of starting and managing a business enterprise is called **entrepreneurship.**

Entrepreneurs try to satisfy consumers by improving existing products and services or creating new products and services. Marketing is the cornerstone of entrepreneurship because entrepreneurs use marketing skills to determine the needs and wants of consumers.

---

[2]Robert F. Lusch and Virginia N. Lusch, *Principles of Marketing* (Boston: Kent Publishing Company, 1987), p. 6.

[3]Maggie McComas, "Atop the Fortune 500: A Survey of the C.E.O.s," *Fortune* (28 April 1986), p. 26.

◢◣ Marketing Can Help You Become a Better-Informed Consumer

Understanding how marketing works can make you a better-informed consumer. You are involved in the marketing process every time you read a newspaper advertisement, watch a television commercial, or buy a product or service. You probably engage in one or more of these activities each day. Therefore, it is important to understand marketing and what individual firms are trying to accomplish through their marketing efforts. By being able to answer questions about which products generally have higher prices, which are heavily advertised or receive little or no advertising, you will become a better-informed consumer.

Thus, marketing is an important topic of study and well worth the time and effort invested in learning about it. It provides satisfaction to consumers by creating utility, stimulates the economy, and offers career opportunities. Because of its emphasis on the customer concept, it is the cornerstone of entrepreneurship. Finally, the study of marketing can help you become a better-informed consumer.

APPLYING MARKETING TERMS

Name _____

Match each term with the statement that best describes an application of that term. Write the letter in the space provided.

a. time utility
b. possession utility
c. customer concept
d. form utility
e. total company effort

f. information utility
g. profit
h. place utility
i. gross national product (GNP)
j. nonprofit organizations

_____ 1. Wood, nails, and glue changed into furniture.

_____ 2. The pediatrician's office is open until 9:00 P.M., three nights a week for working parents.

_____ 3. The supermarket has bread on the shelf when you need it.

_____ 4. Employees in the shipping department know what the people in the advertising department are doing.

_____ 5. Advertisements and instructional materials are sent to consumers.

_____ 6. Red Cross, Girl Scouts, and Boy Scouts.

_____ 7. You have purchased some lettuce and carrots and are going to make a salad.

_____ 8. The company's self-service gasoline stations are conveniently located throughout the city.

_____ 9. A goal of the business.

_____ 10. Includes the dollar value of every item you buy.

MASTERING KEY CONCEPTS

Name _____

Answer each of the following questions in the space provided.

1. What is the difference between needs and wants?

2. Identify and describe the three parts of the marketing concept.

3. Explain the difference between the marketing concept and the sales concept.

4. "Marketing is useful only to those organizations seeking to make a profit." Do you agree or disagree with this statement? Why?

5. What is commercial business activity?

6. List the five major types of businesses and give an example of each.

7. Explain the five kinds of utility and identify the cost involved with each kind of utility.

8. Why is it important to study marketing?

Read the following description of a human relations situation. Then complete your answers on a separate piece of paper.

Fashionable Home Furniture Store

For the past few weeks, Ann and Alberto have been shopping for a sofa for their family room. Finally, they found the one they wanted at the Fashionable Home Furniture Store. The sale price of the sofa was fifteen percent off the regular price, and it could be delivered within the next week.

While they were trying to decide whether to buy the sofa, they began talking to one of the salespeople. Ann commented, "We were so happy to find a furniture store in this town open in the evening." The salesperson answered, "We're open in the evening because it's our policy to make shopping for furniture as convenient as possible for our customers. Most of our customers are people like you, people who have nine-to-five jobs and are not able to shop for furniture during the day." Ann and Alberto liked the store because of its policy of serving customers' needs. They decided to buy the sofa.

The store's delivery coordinator called the next day and told Ann the sofa could be delivered between 9:00 A.M. and 5:00 P.M. on the following Wednesday. Ann mentioned that both she and her husband worked during the day and would not be at home to receive delivery. The delivery coordinator explained that deliveries were made only during those hours and asked if Ann or Alberto could stay home from work to receive the delivery. Ann replied, "Your delivery hours do not agree with your store's policy of making shopping for furniture as convenient as possible for your customers." The delivery coordinator said, "I'm not familiar with the policy stated by the salesperson, but I can assure you that it is our delivery policy to deliver the furniture between 9:00 A.M. and 5:00 P.M. weekdays."

Ann was upset, but she didn't want to cancel the order. She said, "I'll be at home Wednesday waiting for the delivery." Ann would miss a day of work for which she would not be paid.

1. Does Fashionable Home Furniture conduct its business according to a customer concept? Why or why not?
2. A part of the marketing concept is a total company effort. Does this accurately describe Fashionable Home Furniture? Explain.
3. Assume that many other customers of Fashionable Home Furniture have had the same experience as Ann and Alberto. What would you do if you were the new manager of the store and you wanted the store to follow the marketing concept?

MARKETING PROJECT 1

Use your own paper to complete this project.

The Marketing Concept at Work

1. Name a product you bought recently.
   a. Where did you buy the product?
   b. Would you say that the business where you bought the product follows the marketing concept or the sales concept? Explain your answer using specific examples of how the business was following one concept or the other.
   c. How would you describe the reputation this business has in the community?
2. Name a service you bought recently.
   a. Where did you buy the service?
   b. Would you say that the business where you bought the service follows the marketing concept or the sales concept? Explain your answer using specific examples of how the business was following one concept or the other.
   c. How would you describe the reputation this business has in the community?
3. Based on your contact with the businesses described above, what can you conclude about how a firm's reputation is determined by whether it practices the marketing concept?

Read the following description of real-life marketing practices. Then complete your answers on a separate piece of paper.

Automatic Teller Machines

American consumers were first introduced to automatic teller machines (ATMs) more than twenty years ago. Using ATMs, which are freestanding, self-service electronic terminals, people are able to perform simple banking transactions without the aid of a teller. The heaviest users of ATMs are those people who are mobile, better educated, and on the go.

Convenience is one of the major attractions of ATMs. They are generally available 24 hours a day, seven days a week at many bank and nonbank locations. Bank locations include both walk-up and drive-up ATMs on a bank's premises. Nonbank locations include supermarkets, amusement parks, convenience stores, shopping centers, airports, hotels, college campuses, and other high-traffic sites.

In addition to being conveniently located, ATMs are easy to use. Consumers insert their ATM cards, which are issued by their banks, and then enter their personal identification numbers at the terminal. The machine responds by allowing them to determine the balances in their bank accounts, withdraw cash from checking or savings accounts, deposit money, or perform other simple transactions. In most cases, ATMs are performing the same functions they performed when they were introduced two decades ago. Specifically, they are used mostly to dispense cash, just as they were then.

Nevertheless, ATMs have changed and more changes are expected. Today, for example, more than 75,000 ATMs are tied together into regional and national networks. This means that you can be hundreds of miles from your bank and still be able to withdraw cash from your bank account.

According to an article in *The Wall Street Journal*, "Banks are just beginning to experiment with non-cash transactions, and marketers say it's too early to tell which ones will catch on." In one city, consumers may obtain monthly bus and railroad passes from an ATM, while in other selected cities they may obtain gift certificates, postage stamps, or grocery coupons the same way. In Phoenix, Arizona, a savings and loan association offers discount movie tickets through its ATMs.

When banks find new uses for their ATMs, they are actually finding new ways to serve their customers. They are also obtaining additional sources of revenue. Usually a small fee is charged to the customer who uses an ATM card from one bank at other banks' machines. Because a fee is charged on a portion of the estimated five billion ATM transactions each year, banks have a source of income that did not exist twenty years ago. In addition, banks may collect a fee from those organizations who distribute tickets, coupons, or other items through their ATMs.[4]

1. Other than those previously mentioned above, what other items could be distributed through ATMs? Justify your answer.
2. Which type(s) of utility do banks create by making ATMs available at convenient locations for their customers? Explain.
3. Banks are expanding the types of non-cash transactions or items available on their ATMs. Explain how these actions demonstrate that the banks are following the marketing concept.

---

[4]Christopher J. Chipello. "Banks Start Spicing Up Their ATM Menus," *The Wall Street Journal* (5 October 1989), p. B1.

CHAPTER 2
MARKETING FUNCTIONS AND ACTIVITIES

After you read this chapter and complete the activities at the end, you will be able to:

1. **Define the eight marketing functions.**
2. **Identify the four parts of the marketing mix.**
3. **Describe the marketing environment.**

Teresa drove into the parking lot at 7:40 A.M. Her workday did not start until 8:00 A.M., but she didn't want to be late. It was the first day of her marketing internship. Because of her good grades, she was selected to participate in the internship program, which would provide her with a salary for the summer. Teresa didn't know too much about the medium-sized company, but she did know that she would be working in the marketing department. She was assigned to work for Mr. Thomas Baker, the vice president for marketing.

Mr. Baker welcomed Teresa to the company and to the marketing department. After a brief discussion in Mr. Baker's office, Teresa accompanied him to a conference room for the weekly meeting of managers and assistant managers in the marketing department.

Teresa was surprised to see so many people in the room. She thought there would be just a few executives in the marketing department; instead, there were eleven, including Mr. Baker. Mr. Baker asked the people to introduce themselves, giving their job titles and a brief description of their responsibilities. Teresa learned that there were five separate areas in the marketing department, each with a manager and an assistant manager: product planning, sales, advertising and sales promotion, market research, and distribution. Teresa realized that there was more to marketing than she had first thought.

MARKETING FUNCTIONS

The marketing process can be divided into eight tasks, called **marketing functions,** that are performed as products and services flow from producer to consumer. The marketing functions are (1) product or service planning, (2) purchasing or buying, (3) physical distribution, (4) promotion and selling, (5) pricing, (6) financing, (7) obtaining and using marketing information, and (8) risk management.

Product or Service Planning

Product or service planning is deciding which products or services the company will develop and offer to its customers. Products, or goods, are tangible items, while services are tasks or activities that we pay others to do or provide for us.

The simplest approach is to market only one product or service. However, most companies offer more than one. For example, each of the soups offered by the Campbell Soup Company is a different product. Even a business that cleans homes, whose service appears to be only cleaning, probably offers an array of services. For example, does the customer wish to have the house cleaned every week or every other week? Does the customer want the windows washed? The home cleaning business actually offers several services, each with a different price. The sum of all the products and/or services offered by a business is its **product or service mix.**

The product or service planning function also includes branding and packaging decisions. One of the major ways organizations identify and differentiate their products is by the brand. Think of all the different brands you know. A **brand** is a name, design, or symbol, or a combination of these, that identifies the products of a seller or a group of sellers. Chevrolet, Coca-Cola, and Crest are brand names. McDonald's golden arches, the hood ornament on a Mercedes Benz automobile, and Apple Computer Company's rainbow-colored apple that has a bite out of it are brand marks.

The popularity of self-service retailing has made packaging an important part of marketing. **Packaging** is designed to physically protect the product, provide product information, and establish a symbolic image. Information on the package may include detailed instructions for using the product as well as a description of its nutritional value. Depending on how it looks, a package may convey symbolic meanings or images to buyers. A package with a pleasing appearance (e.g., those used for higher priced perfumes) can be very effective in attracting the attention of shoppers and in building favorable attitudes toward the product.

Purchasing or Buying

The terms purchasing and buying have similar meanings. However, the appropriate term to use in a particular situation is determined by industry practice. **Purchasing** is the act of selecting and obtaining the kind, quality, and quantity of products and services used in manufacturing and service businesses. Examples include purchasing raw materials, parts, or legal services. **Buying** is the act of selecting and obtaining the kind, quality, and quantity of products to be sold by wholesale and retail businesses. A wholesaler buying computer paper from a manufacturer to be resold to a retailer or a retailer buying computer paper from a wholesaler to be resold to consumers are examples. Neither of these two terms should be confused with **consumer buying,** which is the process of buying products or services for personal or family use.

Every business does some purchasing or buying. Wholesalers need goods for retailers to buy. Retailers need goods for their customers to buy. Manufacturers need equipment, raw materials, and supplies to make finished products. Service businesses need supplies to operate from day to day. For example, dry cleaners use various fluids to clean clothing and draperies. Insurance agents use file cabinets, stationery, office supplies, and microcomputers. Farmers need seed, fertilizer, and harvesting equipment.

Purchasing or buying involves more than simply choosing needed products and services. It also means making decisions on quality and quantity. The right quality is not necessarily the highest quality. For example, a furniture manufacturer will use high quality wood to make fine furniture that people will buy for their homes. Low quality wood, however, is used to reinforce the cartons for shipping the furniture to stores.

Companies must also buy the correct quantities of goods and services. A restaurant must buy enough fresh meat to feed the expected number of guests, but not so much that it spoils before it can be used. An auto assembly plant must have sufficient tires for the number of cars it is producing, but not so many that there's no place to store them.

Physical Distribution

Physical distribution includes all the activities required to efficiently move finished products from producers to customers. Transportation and storage are the two components of the physical distribution function.

Transportation is the movement of goods from where they are produced or stored to where they are sold. Because it makes products available in locations convenient for the buyer, transportation creates place utility.

Products may be transported by motor trucks, railroads, airplanes, waterways, and pipelines. Some products are moved from place to place using a combination of transportation methods. **Pig-**

gyback freight is a good example of a combination transportation method; goods are loaded onto truck trailers and then shipped on railroad flatcars. When the train reaches its destination the trailer is removed, hooked up to a truck tractor, and driven to the customer's location.

Storage means stocking goods for future use. This marketing function is important because goods are not always sold at the time they are produced. Therefore, storing products helps a business meet the needs of customers. Retail stores provide a service for customers when they buy goods from many sources and store them in refrigerated units, stockrooms, and on shelves. Thus, goods are available when customers are ready to buy them. Breakfast cereal, frozen vegetables, canned soup, and toothpaste are shipped to warehouses and stores all over the country. Customers are able to buy these products whenever they wish. By having products available when customers want to buy them, businesses create time utility.

Promotion and Selling

Promotion and selling includes seeking markets and then communicating product and service information to those markets to influence customer buying. This marketing function is important because the goal of every profit-seeking organization is to sell its products or services. Automakers must sell their cars, restaurants must serve (sell) meals, and movie theaters must sell tickets. Businesses create possession utility when they sell a product to a customer; that is, they transfer possession or ownership of the product to the customer.

Customers must be informed of the goods and services available in stores. This is accomplished by various means designed to promote products and services. Promotion and selling informs customers of goods and services and helps persuade them to purchase these offerings. By promoting products, whether through personal selling, advertising, visual merchandising, sales promotion, or publicity, information utility is created. Promotion and selling are discussed in detail in Unit 3.

Pricing

Pricing is the process of determining the exchange value of a good or service. This exchange value is the price and it is usually expressed in dollars and cents. To marketers, of course, this means deciding how much to charge for their products and services.

Setting prices can be an extremely complicated process because it is affected by so many factors outside the control of the company. For example, before setting a price on a product you are selling you should know how much your customers are willing and able to pay and how much your competitors are charging for the same product. You should also find out if there are any trends in product sales. For example, compared to what consumers have purchased in recent years, are they now buying more, less, or the same amount of the product?

◤ Financing

Financing is granting credit to customers so that they can buy the company's products or services. Buying on credit has almost become a way of life. Homes, cars, appliances, furniture, and services are often purchased on credit. Many people like to buy what they want today and pay for it later. Because of this trend toward buying on credit, financing has become an essential marketing function. **Consumer credit** permits people to obtain products and services now for personal or family use and pay for them later. Some stores have their own charge account plans and accept only the credit card issued by their stores. Others honor the major bank credit cards.

Trade credit is financing provided by suppliers, manufacturers, and wholesalers to their customers—that is, to other businesses. For instance, a supplier of raw materials extends credit to a manufacturer who uses the materials to make a product. The manufacturer, in turn, extends credit to a wholesaler who buys a large quantity of the product for resale. Finally, the wholesaler extends credit to retailers who sell the product to consumers. Thus, providing credit opportunities creates possession utility.

◤ Obtaining and Using Marketing Information

A business firm needs marketing information in order to plan and carry out its marketing activities. Specifically, marketing information is used to answer questions such as these:

1. Who are the customers for the product or service?
2. How many potential customers are there?
3. What are the needs and wants of the customers?
4. What price are customers willing to pay?
5. What do customers like about the business and its products or services? What do they dislike?

The kind of marketing information needed by a company often depends on the type of business in which it is engaged. For example, a local meat-packing company that sells beef in bulk would be interested in knowing the number of households that own home freezers. A manufacturer of nursery furniture, such as baby beds and high chairs, would probably want to learn the birthrates in various cities. A bank may want to find out how many potential customers it has for its credit card.

Risk Management

Risk taking is a part of being in business. Clothing retailers always take a risk when they buy a large quantity of what they believe is going to be the "in" fashion of the coming season. As you have probably observed, some of these fashions catch on, while others do not. Likewise, for every successful novel, record album, or movie, there are many others that lose money. No matter what the product or service, the risk of failure is always a possibility. However, even risk can be managed.

Risk management is the process of analyzing risks to the company and then developing ways to handle them. While there are various ways of handling risk, it is unlikely that it can be eliminated completely. Clothing retailers, such as those discussed above, can protect themselves to some extent from the risk of stocking the wrong fashion items by hiring expert managers and also by obtaining and using market information. The risk of loss due to shoplifting by customers can be managed by hiring security personnel and training employees to be alert for shoplifters. Risks of losses due to fire or flood damage or the death of key employees can be managed through the use of insurance.

MARKETING MIX — THE FOUR Ps OF MARKETING

Two primary activities of any business enterprise are production and marketing. In a broad sense **production** is the creation of something that can satisfy a need or want. It includes the activities of extractors, manufacturers, builders, and all businesses that provide services. Marketing consists of all the activities needed to make those products and services available to satisfy customers.

Marketers follow the customer concept; they try to see things as their customers see them. A specific group of customers that a company wants to serve is called its **target market.** A business may have several target markets, one for each of its products or services. Instead of trying to meet everyone's needs with just one model, automobile manufacturers produce several models. Each model is designed with a specific target market in mind. Some people want large luxury cars, while others prefer small, economy models. Several choices between these two models are also available.

Once a company has defined its target market, it is ready to select the appropriate marketing mix to reach that market. The **marketing mix** is a blending of product or service, price, promotion, and place decisions. These are often referred to as the four Ps of marketing. **Managers** get work done through other people. Therefore, it is their job to see that marketing tasks are performed efficiently. **Marketing management** plans, implements, and controls the marketing mix to satisfy the company's chosen target market. As shown by the target on the left in Figure 2-1, all four elements of the marketing mix must be planned with the target market in mind.

Figure 2-1   The product or service, price, promotion, and place decisions must be coordinated to reach the target market.

THIS   NOT THIS

Product or Service Decisions

Product or service decisions are involved in the development of the right product or service for the target market. When developing a product, many factors other than the tangible item must be considered. Guarantee, brand name, packaging, installation, and alterations are a few of the factors that accompany the production of a new item. A product may be defined as a "bundle of values" for which a customer pays a price. This bundle of values might include a number of things. For example, when you buy a car you are probably buying more than transportation. A car can be a symbol of status, taste, and achievement. It may also show that you are thrifty, especially if you buy an economy model.

Consumers buy more than the physical or tangible aspects of a product. In fact, you could even say that people do not buy "things" at all; rather they buy solutions to problems. One person illustrated this idea by explaining why people buy quarter-inch drill bits: "They

Illustration 2-1   Customers buy microwaves for the convenience they provide in meal preparation.

do not want quarter-inch bits. They want quarter-inch holes." Likewise, the consumer who shops for a microwave oven is not interested in the appliance itself but in convenience and the ability to serve meals requiring little preparation time. A person who buys a membership in a health club is interested in good health, youthfulness, and the chance to be part of a group devoted to physical fitness.

Price Decisions

Price decisions involve setting prices for products or services that are acceptable to customers and profitable to the company. As a consumer, you have probably noticed that people do not buy on the basis of quality only. They compare prices and quality and then choose the best product for their use.

Assume that you are a marketing manager. What price should you charge for your product or service? A price low enough to attract a lot of customers but high enough to cover all costs and provide a profit!

In most cases there is an acceptable price range, not a single ideal price. Think of the price range as the area between the ceiling and the floor. The ceiling is the maximum price consumers would be willing to pay for a product or service. The floor is the lowest price that will cover all the firm's costs and still earn a profit. It is the job of the marketing manager to set prices within the acceptable price range while considering the prices charged by other businesses.

Price signals the value of a product or service. The product or service must be worth the price charged. A company's target market helps determine the image the business must present to its customers. Pricing (and the other parts of the marketing mix) should always be pointed toward building and maintaining this image. Customers often judge a business and its products or services by the prices charged. For example, prices charged by a fine restaurant reflect a different image from those charged by a fast food establishment.

Promotion Decisions

Promotion decisions are concerned with ways to inform members of a target market about a product or service and influence them to buy it. Promotion is probably the most dynamic and aggressive element in the marketing mix.

Promotion is the communication mechanism of marketing. **Communication** is the exchange of information. Promotion includes all communication by a firm with customers, potential customers, and sales staff for the purpose of increasing the sales of products or services.

Specifically, promotion is communication designed to gain attention, inform, teach, remind, persuade, or reassure people about a product or a service. Promotion can be thought of as a process of sending messages. For example, television commercials are usually used to send a message informing consumers of a new breakfast cereal. But promotion is not limited to advertising. Methods of promotion include personal selling, advertising, visual merchandising, sales promotion, and public relations or publicity. These various methods of promotion are discussed in Unit 3.

Place Decisions

Where do customers expect to buy certain items? Answers to this question help marketing managers make **place decisions;** that is, they must decide where to sell products and services. Products are then transported from the locations where they are produced or stored to the place of sale.

Some items are sold in a variety of places. For example, you can buy flashlight batteries at a supermarket, a convenience store, a drugstore, a service station, a hardware store, and possibly from a vending machine. Batteries are available at these locations because consumers expect to find them at these places.

MARKETING ENVIRONMENT

Marketing does not occur in a vacuum. It is surrounded by factors or forces that influence it. The **marketing environment** includes all factors that may affect marketing directly or indirectly. The following four factors are of particular importance: (1) competition, (2) laws and government, (3) the economy, and (4) society and culture. Marketing managers have no control over these factors, but must consider them when making marketing decisions.

Competition

Rarely is a product or service sold by only one business. Usually several sellers offer the same or similar products or services. Sellers may try to attract customers by setting their prices lower than or comparable to those of other firms serving the same target market. These sellers are called competitors. **Competition** is the effort of two or more businesses acting independently to sell their products and services to the same consumers. Each business is trying to get a share of the market.

One company may compete with other companies by lowering its prices. It may offer something new that will better satisfy consumer needs or add features that competing products do not have. The result is rivalry among companies to make products and services more attractive to consumers.

A business is sometimes forced to change its marketing mix because of the actions of one or more competitors. Until federal laws were changed in the 1980s, American Telephone and Telegraph Co. (AT&T) was the only company providing long distance telephone service in the United States. Then competitors entered the marketplace. Two of those competitors, MCI Communications and U.S. Sprint Communications, attracted customers away from AT&T with lower rates. AT&T responded to the competition by changing its marketing mix. More than 5,000 employees were transferred into sales jobs, emphasis was placed on selling service to business customers, prices were reduced on long distance service, and a variety of

Illustration 2-2

Competition means you have choices when you shop.

new services, such as a feature that displays an incoming caller's phone number, were introduced.[1]

The effects of competition can also be seen in other areas of the American economy. A package delivery company began overnight delivery service to all parts of the country. Competing businesses soon offered the same service. Several airlines lowered their fares after a competitor acquired passengers and publicity by doing so. Because of competition among computer manufacturers, consumers can buy microcomputers that have a large number of features at attractive prices.

Competition is beneficial for consumers and the nation. It forces businesses to offer new products, improved products and services, and wide selections at reasonable prices. As a result, customers have varied goods and services to choose from. Were it not for competition, consumers would have to accept products and services as offered or do without.

◣ Laws and Government

Every business, large or small, must deal with various aspects of the government. Most laws and agencies affecting marketing are at the Federal government level. Figure 2-2 is a partial list of federal agencies whose regulations affect a firm's marketing mix.

Figure 2-2   Many federal agencies establish regulations that affect a firm's marketing mix decisions.

FEDERAL AGENCY	AREA OF RESPONSIBILITY
Consumer Product Safety Commission (CPSC)	Establishes product safety standards and governs product recalls.
Federal Communications Commission (FCC)	Regulates the nation's airwaves (television, radio, and long-distance telephone).
Food and Drug Administration (FDA)	Establishes standards for food and drugs, approves new drugs, oversees product labeling.
Interstate Commerce Commission (ICC)	Regulates railroads, pipelines, interstate motor trucks, and inland water carriers.
Patent and Trademark Office (PTO)	Issues patents for new product ideas and registers trademarks.

---

[1]Janet Guyon, "Stung by Rivals, AT&T is Fighting Back," *The Wall Street Journal* (30 June 1989), p. B1.

Over the years Congress has passed a group of laws known as antitrust laws. **Antitrust laws** are designed to protect competition by preventing one company from gaining an unfair advantage over another. The Sherman Antitrust Act of 1890 prevents businesses from acting with intent to restrict trade. The act also prohibits establishing monopolies. A **monopoly** exists when one organization has control over the entire market for a product or service. The firm is the sole seller of a product or service for which there are no close substitutes. Monopolies are illegal in the United States except in special circumstances, such as companies that provide electricity or natural gas. These types of companies, however, are usually heavily regulated.

In 1914, Congress passed the Clayton Act which was intended to strengthen the Sherman Antitrust Act by prohibiting additional practices that were considered threats to competition. One of the practices prohibited by this act is called a tying agreement. In a **tying agreement,** a business, in order to obtain certain products, has to agree to buy other products from the same seller. In many cases, the buyer did not want to buy these other products, but was forced to do so. Another provision of the Clayton Act restricts firms from merging with or buying out other businesses that deal in the same line of products if this would substantially lessen competition or result in the creation of a monopoly.

The Federal Trade Commission Act, also passed in 1914, established a government agency called the Federal Trade Commission (FTC). The FTC was given the authority to prohibit the use of unfair methods of competition and to protect consumers from unfair or deceptive business practices in interstate commerce. The FTC investigates companies that are accused of unfair methods of competition, such as misleading advertising.

The marketing environment is controlled by many laws and government agencies, a few of which have been described in this section. To be effective, business managers must be familiar with all laws and agencies, federal, state, and local, that affect their marketing activities.

The Economy

History shows that the American economy experiences long periods of growth, or upswings, at times interrupted by declines. Like a roller coaster traveling up and down its track, the economy travels through cycles of fluctuations that have an impact on marketing. A **business cycle** consists of alternating periods of expansion and contraction of economic activities such as production, employment, and income. Each business cycle usually has four phases: prosperity, recession, depression, and recovery.

Prosperity is a period of relatively high economic activity. Profits, consumer confidence, capital investment (money invested in a business), and employment are high. Interest rates are at low or moderate levels.

During a **recession** there is a marked decline in the level of economic activity. Business firms begin to delay expansion plans. As unemployment increases, buying power decreases. Confidence in the economy declines. Consumers cut down on their purchases of major items such as houses, cars, and appliances.

The lowest level of economic activity in a business cycle is called a **depression.** Unemployment and the number of business failures are very high. Consumers are unwilling, and perhaps unable, to buy products and services. Investment is low.

Recovery is a business cycle phase in which the economy moves from recession or depression toward prosperity. There is an increase in business activity. Firms begin to invest money in new plants and equipment and to hire employees. Consumers become more confident in the economy. Thus, consumer spending, especially for expensive items such as houses and cars, increases. Banks become willing to make loans and investment increases.

Marketing cannot escape the effects of the business cycle. Products and services are affected by economic change in various ways. For example, during economic declines consumers become more value and price conscious. Instead of buying new cars, they have their old cars repaired. As the economy improves, consumers begin to purchase such items as furniture, second color television sets, vacation cruises, and recreational equipment.

Another important economic factor that has an impact on marketing is inflation. **Inflation** is a general rise in the price of products and services. Prices rise more rapidly than incomes; therefore, consumer buying power declines. Because inflation reduces purchasing power, consumers become more price conscious. Managers must consider this when planning a marketing mix. For example, supermarket managers may find that when inflation is high, consumers are more interested in price and less interested in the quality of products.

Society and Culture

Society and culture affect marketing decisions. A **society** is a community, nation, or broad grouping of persons with common traditions, institutions, activities, and interests. A society usually provides protection, security, and a national identity. The wants of individuals and families within a society change as tastes, preferences, and living styles change. Changes in tastes, preferences, and living styles reflect changes in the culture of a society. **Culture** is the sum of all ideas and structures, including social norms, customary beliefs, and values, that a society develops in order to cope with its environment and provide for the control of members' behavior. People think and act according to the rules of their culture. **Values** are defined as the ideas and principles that we consider correct, desirable, or important. Our values determine what we want from life and how to turn those wants into reality. Members of a society measure their behavior according to the values of their culture.

   Society and culture affect all areas of marketing. The following examples illustrate the effect of social and cultural change on the marketing of products and services.

- The post-World War II baby boom generation is moving into the prime buying years. They are major purchasers of homes, furniture, and cars.
- America is shifting from a youth-oriented society to a nation of middle-aged and elderly people—many of them affluent. Marketing people are aware of this trend and are directing their promotional techniques toward this segment of society. For example, middle-aged couples and elderly people are often featured in television commercials and other advertisements for everything from appliances to frozen food.

Illustration 2-3

The expanding middle-aged and elderly segments of American society are increasingly the focus of marketing efforts.

- Pediatricians in various parts of the country have office hours at night and on weekends for the convenience of working parents.
- Clothing styles have become informal. Manufacturers and retailers have altered their clothing lines in order to supply the casual apparel that customers want.

Thus, society and culture are very important influences in the marketing environment. Marketing managers must be up-to-date on cultural and social changes in order to adjust the marketing mix and provide the products and services that customers want.

APPLYING MARKETING TERMS

Name _____

Match each term with the statement that best describes an application of that term. Write the letter in the space provided.

a. recovery
b. transportation
c. target market
d. purchasing or buying
e. marketing environment

f. promotion and selling
g. product or service planning
h. monopoly
i. financing
j. risk management

_____ 1. Illegal in the U.S. except in special circumstances.

_____ 2. Helps create possession utility.

_____ 3. The right quality is not necessarily the highest quality.

_____ 4. Influences purchase behavior.

_____ 5. After World War II, consumer spending increased dramatically.

_____ 6. Hire expert managers and obtain market information.

_____ 7. Marketing does not occur in a vacuum.

_____ 8. Creates place utility.

_____ 9. Includes branding and packaging.

_____ 10. One for each of the firm's products or services.

Answer each of the following questions in the space provided.

1. What are the eight marketing functions?

2. Why is packaging an important part of marketing?

3. Name the two components of the physical distribution function.

4. What are the four elements of the marketing mix?

5. The only way to manage business risks is by purchasing insurance. Explain why you agree or disagree with this statement.

6. How does competition affect a firm's marketing mix?

7. What type of business would have more than one target market?

8. Explain how marketing is affected by the business cycle.

DEVELOPING PEOPLE SKILLS

Read the following description of a human relations situation. Then complete your answers on a separate piece of paper.

The Overdrawn Checking Account

Rose assumed she had overdraft protection on her checking account. Commonly known as a bounced check, an overdraft is when you write a check for more money than you have on deposit in your checking account. Overdraft protection is an arrangement whereby the bank gives you an automatic loan to cover the amount of the overdraft.

Rose had several extraordinary expenses recently and she used every cent in her checking account. Thinking she had overdraft protection, she continued writing checks. However, within a day or two she was getting calls from people who said the bank would not honor her checks. She was embarrassed and, as far as she was concerned, it was the bank's fault.

Rose was angry when she went to the bank to discuss the overdrawn checks. A customer service representative told her that her account did not have overdraft protection. Rose responded with contempt, "Why doesn't my account have it? I thought you got it automatically."

The bank employee answered, "You don't get it automatically. Obtaining overdraft protection involves filling out a loan application that must be approved by our loan department. You have a good credit rating and I believe your application would be approved."

Rose's answer was, "Because of your bank's stupid rules, I wrote bad checks to my dentist and to several stores in town. How can I face those people again?"

1. Was Rose angry at the bank or was she actually angry at herself? Explain your answer.
2. Realizing that she was angry, how should Rose have prepared herself to discuss the problem in a businesslike manner with the bank employee?
3. Describe the extent to which the bank employee acted in a businesslike manner. Give an example.
4. If you were one of Rose's friends, would you give her any advice on the way she talked to the bank employee? What advice would you give her?

MARKETING PROJECT 2

Use your own paper to complete this project.

The Marketing Mix Memo

Assume that you have just been hired to be the marketing manager of a new chain of quick oil change and lube shops. You are to write a memo to the president of the company, an individual who knows very little about marketing, explaining what the marketing mix is. The purpose of your memo is to convince the president of the importance of selecting the appropriate marketing mix for your company.

MARKETING INSIGHT

Read the following description of real-life marketing practices. Then complete your answers on a separate piece of paper.

Telemarketing Static

Telemarketing refers to a selling approach that is conducted entirely by telephone. Outbound telemarketing involves a telemarketer using the telephone to contact customers. The cost of each customer contact is lower than the cost of making personal visits to customers' homes or businesses. Auto and home insurance, carpet cleaning service, and water softeners are just a few of the products and services that have been sold this way.

With inbound telemarketing, customers call the company to make purchases or to obtain information about products or services. Companies often provide a toll-free 800 number for customers to use with inbound telemarketing.

The vast majority of telemarketers are honest business people. However, some dishonest individuals have been attracted to the industry, particularly to outbound telemarketing. Consumers have been complaining to their legislators, at both the state and national levels, about unethical and fraudulent practices of some telemarketers. For example, there are the low priced vacations that are sold over the telephone. It turns out that consumers end up paying substantial additional sums of money to get the vacations. Among federal laws being considered is one allowing customers to return the goods within three days if they change their minds. Another law would require telemarketers to be licensed by the state.

Think about the number of times you answer the telephone and hear the caller promoting a product or service. Some consumers take the opportunity to make a purchase. Others complain that their privacy is being invaded. Several states are considering legislation which would identify in the telephone book those people who do not want to receive sales calls with an asterisk (*).[2]

1. Describe your personal experiences, if any, with telemarketing.
2. What could telemarketers do to achieve a better public image?
3. What consumer products do you believe can be sold effectively by outbound telemarketing? Why?
4. What consumer products do you believe can be sold effectively by inbound telemarketing? Why?

---

[2]Cyndee Miller, "Lawmakers Eager to Crack Down on Telemarketing Fraud," and "Telemarketing Foes: Don't Reach Out to Us," *Marketing News* (3 July 1989), pp. 1, 14.

CHAPTER 3
MARKETING CAREERS

After you read this chapter and complete the activities at the end, you will be able to:

1. **Describe the different types of businesses and organizations that offer marketing career opportunities.**

2. **Name marketing occupations that are expected to offer increased employment opportunities in the near future.**

3. **Identify the different specialty areas included in marketing and give examples of businesses that employ persons in each of these areas.**

4. **Discuss the five different levels of marketing occupations.**

5. **Find out more about marketing careers.**

6. **Plan for your future career by examining your interests, abilities, and personality and compare these qualities with the competencies required in various marketing careers.**

We are all affected by marketing every day of our lives. When you got up this morning, you probably showered, washed and dried your hair, brushed your teeth, and groomed yourself using popular brands of toiletries. Maybe you had a breakfast of orange juice from Florida, cereal produced in Michigan, milk delivered by a local dairy, and toast made from wheat grown in Nebraska. Perhaps you watched the early morning news on TV, where you were exposed to a national advertising campaign promoting the purchase of a certain brand of automobile.

As you drove to school, you probably listened to your favorite music on the car radio. Or, if you rode the school bus, you may have listened to your Walkman® radio. In either case, the music you listened to was undoubtedly followed or interrupted by a commercial, perhaps advertising a sale at a local supermarket or promoting a political candidate running for office in your local community. At lunch, maybe you had a burger and fries sold to you by a national chain of fast food restaurants that has an outlet in your school cafeteria. After lunch, perhaps you visited the school store to stock up on a few supplies that you had been meaning to purchase.

After school and on Saturdays you are employed as a part-time salesperson in the catalog office of a large department store. You really like your job because it is interesting and it gives you spending money for purchasing clothes, renting videos, and making payments on your car insurance. On your way to work, you remember that you need to stop and pick up some items for your parents from the local pharmacy and also the dry cleaning. The road you take to your job crosses a busy railroad track. Today you waited for a long freight train. Perhaps you wondered what was loaded in each of those freight cars. So goes the day.

All of the products and services that you came in contact with on this typical day were made available by people employed in different marketing occupations. These occupations are found along the channels of distribution, the paths that goods or services follow as they move from manufacturers or producers to the point of consumption. Before any of these products or services were made available, someone conducted marketing research to determine their chances for success in the marketplace. Someone was responsible for promoting and distributing these items. Each had to follow a distribution channel. For example, the Walkman® radio was sold by its manufacturer to a wholesaler who, in turn, sold it to the specialty store where it was purchased. Salespeople were available at this store to assist in the buying decision. Thus, all the activities required to provide these products and services were performed by people in marketing careers.

MARKETING OCCUPATIONS

Marketing consists of many different types and levels of occupations. They are not limited to the familiar occupations found in the marketing of consumer goods and services but are also found in production or manufacturing businesses, marketing businesses, service businesses, and in nonprofit organizations.

Production Businesses

A business that manufactures, constructs, extracts, or grows products that are marketed in order to achieve the goals of the company is called a **production business**. Manufacturers, extractors, and other production businesses employ people who specialize in the various marketing functions, including product or service planning, purchasing or buying, physical distribution, promotion and selling, pricing, financing, obtaining and using marketing information, and risk management.

Marketing Businesses

A business that buys products for resale is called a **marketing business**. Wholesalers and retailers are primary examples of marketing businesses. Wholesalers buy goods in large quantities from companies that produce them and then market these products in smaller quantities to retailers and other businesses. Retailers buy products from wholesalers and other companies and sell them to ultimate consumers. The majority of marketing industries are retail businesses.

Service Businesses

The fastest growing segment of the business community, in terms of the number of businesses involved and of employment opportunities, is composed of **service businesses**. Service businesses market intangible products to consumers or organizational markets. The marketing of services is diversified, includes many different types of firms, and provides numerous employment opportunities. Examples of service businesses include the following:

1. Hotels, motels, restaurants, and amusement parks that provide lodging, food service, and recreation.
2. Advertising agencies, display specialists, and transportation firms that perform services for just about every type of organization.
3. Banks and other financial institutions, credit agencies, insurance and real estate companies, and travel agencies that provide services to consumers and businesses.
4. Automobile service and repair shops and dry cleaning and laundry establishments that perform services on the possessions of their customers.
5. Beauty salons, barbershops, photography studios, and health clubs that provide personal services for customers.

Nonprofit Organizations

Marketing occupations have also experienced a rapid growth in nonprofit organizations. A **nonprofit organization** can be defined as an organization, either private or public, that is involved in providing

Illustration 3-1   Service businesses are the fastest growing segment of
the business community.

a product or service without using profit as its goal. Nonprofit organizations generally have two major groups that they serve: (1) their
clients (users of their services) and (2) their funders (those who provide the financial support required). Examples of nonprofit organizations include colleges and universities, public and private nonprofit
hospitals, political parties, foundations such as the Ford Foundation,
religious organizations, the Salvation Army, the American Red
Cross, United Way, and the American Cancer Society. Most large
nonprofit organizations use very systematic marketing procedures to
accomplish their goals.

Employment Opportunities in Marketing

According to the U.S. Department of Labor (Bureau of Labor Statistics), by the year 2000 the labor force of the United States will be
141.1 million persons. This represents an increase of 16 percent over
the number employed in 1988.

Over two-thirds of the nation's workers are currently employed in service and marketing businesses—transportation, communications, public utilities, finance, insurance, real estate, wholesale and retail firms, and government. Production businesses—agriculture, mining, construction, and manufacturing—employ less than one-third of the country's labor force. Since marketing positions are found in service, marketing, and production businesses, it is difficult to estimate the exact number of workers who are or will be employed in the marketing occupations. A conservative estimate, however, indicates that 47 million workers, or one-third of the labor force, will be employed in marketing jobs by the year 2000.

Figure 3-1 contains employment data for 24 occupations typically classified as marketing occupations. An employment figure and an estimate of employment growth for the period 1988–2000 are provided for each job title. The occupations showing the greatest expected growth generally fall into the service business category. Examine the data given in the table to determine which marketing jobs offer the greatest opportunity for employment.

Figure 3-1   Employment prospects vary from occupation to occupation.

EMPLOYMENT DATA FOR SELECTED MARKETING OCCUPATIONS 1988–2000

JOB TITLE	EMPLOYMENT	PROJECTED RATE OF GROWTH 1988–2000
Advertising clerks	18,000	Faster than average
Buyers	207,000	Slower than average
Cashiers	2,310,000	About as fast as average
Counter and rental clerks	241,000	Faster than average
Flight attendants	88,000	Much faster than average
Food and beverage service workers	4,500,000	Faster than average
Hotel and motel clerks	113,000	Faster than average
Hotel managers and assistants	96,000	Faster than average
Insurance sales workers	423,000	About as fast as average
Manufacturer and wholesale sales reps	1,883,000	Faster than average

(continued)

EMPLOYMENT DATA FOR
SELECTED MARKETING OCCUPATIONS
1988–2000

JOB TITLE	EMPLOYMENT	PROJECTED RATE OF GROWTH 1988–2000
Marketing, advertising, public relations managers	406,000	Faster than average
Market research analysts	36,000	Faster than average
Property and real estate managers	225,000	About as fast as average
Public relations specialist	91,000	About as fast as average
Purchasing agents	458,000	About as fast as average
Real estate agents, brokers, and appraisers	422,000	About as fast as average
Reservation and transportation ticket agents	133,000	Faster than average
Restaurant and food service managers	524,000	Faster than average
Retail sales workers	4,571,000	Faster than average
Securities and financial services sales workers	200,000	Much faster than average
Service sales reps	481,000	Much faster than average
Stock clerks	2,200,000	About as fast as average
Traffic, shipping, and receiving clerks	535,000	Slower than average
Travel agents	142,000	Much faster than average

Source: Adapted from U.S. Department of Labor, Bureau of Labor Statistics, *Occupational Outlook Handbook*, Bulletin No. 2350. (1990–1991 ed.), Washington: U.S. Government Printing Office, April, 1990.

LOOKING AT MARKETING OCCUPATIONS

Marketing occupations can be examined by studying the marketing functions performed by a business or by observing the institutional environment or setting in which these functions are carried out. Marketing occupations can also be classified by occupational specialty area.

Marketing Functions

The most commonly performed marketing functions are (1) product or service planning, (2) purchasing or buying, (3) physical distribution, (4) promotion and selling, (5) pricing, (6) financing, (7) obtaining and using marketing information, and (8) risk management. Some of these functions must be performed whether the product involved is an article of clothing, a beverage, a box of cereal, real estate, a vacation trip to Florida, or a multimillion dollar piece of industrial equipment. Depending on the product or service being marketed, these functions or tasks may be simple or complex. In a small business with a limited product or service line, one person usually handles all these activities. In large firms with numerous or complex product or service lines, employees often specialize in a particular marketing function.

Marketing functions are performed in a number of different institutional environments or settings. They may occur in retail or wholesale businesses, other marketing businesses, service businesses, nonprofit organizations, or production businesses. Some firms perform all the foregoing marketing functions; others need to complete only a few. A small retail business, for example, usually must complete all the marketing functions. Likewise, a large manufacturing business that markets the goods it produces often undertakes most of these functions. On the other hand, a real estate business or advertising agency may perform only a limited number of marketing functions.

Marketing Specialty Areas

The U.S. Department of Education has identified and classified the different occupations included in the marketing career field. These occupations are grouped into **occupational specialty** areas. Figure 3-2 on pages 55–58 defines some of these specialty areas. It also provides a listing of the different types of businesses that employ persons prepared in each area.

Figure 3-2   Specialty areas in marketing.

CLASSIFICATION OF MARKETING BUSINESSES BY OCCUPATIONAL SPECIALTY AREA

SPECIALIZED MARKETING AREAS	EXAMPLES OF TYPICAL BUSINESS
Apparel and Accessories Marketing. People employed in this area perform marketing functions and tasks for retail businesses, and manufacturing firms involved in the marketing of clothing and related articles for personal wear and adornment.	Apparel and accessories manufacturers Clothing departments of department and discount stores Gift shops Jewelry stores Men's clothing stores Shoe stores Wholesale clothing outlets Women's clothing stores
Business and Personal Services Marketing. People employed in this area perform marketing functions for firms that (1) provide service for other businesses or (2) provide personal services for consumers.	*Business Services Marketing* Advertising agencies Display service businesses Employment agencies Marketing research and consulting firms Newspapers and broadcasting companies *Personal Services Marketing* Beauty salons and barbershops Fitness and health care centers Funeral homes Homes maintenance firms Maintenance firms Photography studios Shoe repair shops Video rental stores
Entrepreneurship. People employed in this area perform management and marketing functions relative to managing or owning a small business.	All smaller retail, wholesale, or service businesses Usually not associated with any national organization

(continued)

CLASSIFICATION OF MARKETING BUSINESSES BY OCCUPATIONAL SPECIALTY AREA

SPECIALIZED MARKETING AREAS	EXAMPLES OF TYPICAL BUSINESS
Financial Services Marketing. People employed in this area perform marketing functions and tasks for various types of financial businesses.	Commercial banks Consumer finance companies Credit agencies Credit bureaus Credit departments of various firms Credit unions Savings and loan associations
Floristry Marketing. People employed in this area perform tasks resulting in the sale of plants, cut flowers, floral arrangements, and related items.	Florists Garden stores and departments Greenhouses Wholesale greenhouses
Food Products Marketing. People employed in this area perform marketing functions and tasks for retail and wholesale firms and food processing and manufacturing firms that deal primarily with food and beverage products.	Beverage distributors Convenience stores Food manufacturers Institutional food distributors Specialty food stores Supermarkets Wholesale food distributors
Retail Marketing Operations. People employed in this area perform marketing functions and tasks for retail businesses that market a wide variety of products and related customer services. These firms sell products that are included in other specialty areas.	Catalog stores Discount department stores Full- and limited-line department stores Variety stores

(continued)

CLASSIFICATION OF MARKETING BUSINESSES BY OCCUPATIONAL SPECIALTY AREA

SPECIALIZED MARKETING AREAS	EXAMPLES OF TYPICAL BUSINESS
Home and Office Products Marketing. People employed in this area perform marketing functions and tasks for retail, wholesale, and manufacturing firms that deal in (1) hardware, building materials, and equipment used for furnishing and maintaining homes, or (2) products, equipment, and supplies used in public or private business offices.	Appliance stores Carpet and floor covering stores Computer stores Furniture stores Home repair centers Lumber companies Office equipment and supply stores Paint stores and home decorating centers Wholesalers and manufacturers of these products
Hospitality and Recreation Marketing. People employed in this area perform marketing functions and tasks for businesses concerned with helping people satisfy their desire to make productive and enjoyable use of their leisure time.	Convention centers Fast food restaurants Full-service restaurants Hotels and motels Private and public recreation centers Resorts Sporting goods stores Time share condominiums
Insurance Marketing. People employed in this area perform marketing functions and tasks related to the sale and placement of insurance contracts with carriers.	Accident and health insurance companies Insurance underwriting firms Life insurance agencies Life insurance companies Local agencies for all types of insurance companies
Health Products and Services Marketing. People employed in this area perform marketing functions and tasks related to the sale of health products and services.	Hospitals Nursing homes Health care equipment sales and rentals Drug stores and pharmacies Manufacturers of health care products

(continued)

CLASSIFICATION OF MARKETING BUSINESSES BY OCCUPATIONAL SPECIALTY AREA

SPECIALIZED MARKETING AREAS	EXAMPLES OF TYPICAL BUSINESS
Real Estate Marketing. People involved in this area perform marketing functions and tasks related to the buying, selling, appraising, renting, managing, and leasing of property.	Real estate agencies Real estate appraisal firms Residential and commercial management companies
Tourism and Travel Marketing. People involved in this area perform functions and tasks for firms engaged in passenger and freight transportation, travel services, warehousing, and other services dealing with transportation, storage, travel, or tourism.	Airlines Bus lines Freight companies Package delivery services Steamship companies Taxicab companies Trains Travel agencies Trucking companies Warehouses
Vehicle and Petroleum Marketing. People involved in this area perform functions and tasks for retail or wholesale businesses involved in the distribution of petroleum products, or for retail, wholesale, manufacturing, and service businesses engaged in the marketing of cars, vans, trucks, mobile units, boats, recreational vehicles, and farm vehicles and implements. The marketing of related parts, accessories, equipment, and services required to maintain the above vehicles and implements is also included.	Automobile and truck dealerships Automotive parts stores Farm implement outlets Petroleum wholesalers Recreational vehicle dealerships Service stations Vehicle rental agencies Wholesale part distributors

Source: Adapted from National Center for Education Statistics, *A Classification of Instructional Programs*, U.S. Department of Education, December, 1989.

◣ LEVELS AND DIVERSITY OF MARKETING OCCUPATIONS

There are hundreds of different occupational titles which can be classified under marketing. There are also many different levels of occupations in marketing—some relatively simple, others more complex. Marketing occupations can be described as entry level, career sustaining, specialized, supervisory, and managerial/entrepreneurial.[1] As an employee moves from the entry level through the career-sustaining level to the managerial level, jobs become more complicated, usually requiring more training and experience.

In addition to training and experience, other factors determine the classification of a job. For example,

1. *Nature of employment.* Is the position full- or part-time? Are there any educational or training requirements for a person functioning at this level?
2. *Knowledge of products or services.* How much product or service knowledge is required of a worker in this position?
3. *Supervisory responsibilities.* Is the person holding this position responsible for supervising others?
4. *Marketing techniques.* Does the position require knowledge of, or skills in, marketing functions? How much knowledge or what level of skill is needed?
5. *Decision making.* What is the level of responsibility in this position? Are decision-making skills required? Is the worker responsible for the success or profitability of the business?

Figure 3-3 depicts the various levels of marketing occupations, ranging from entry level to managerial/entrepreneurial.

Figure 3-3   Levels of marketing occupations.

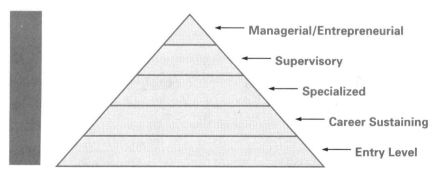

- Managerial/Entrepreneurial
- Supervisory
- Specialized
- Career Sustaining
- Entry Level

---

[1] Adapted from *National Curriculum Framework and Core Competencies*, Marketing Education Resource Center, Columbus, Ohio, 1987.

▲ Entry-Level Marketing Occupations

Entry-level occupations in marketing require little specialized training or experience and involve routine duties. Many entry-level jobs provide only part-time employment. An employee at this level is not usually expected to use many decision-making skills. Examples of job titles in this category are food salesperson, part-time retail salesperson, gift wrapper, hotel bellhop, theater ticket agent, supermarket bagger, baggage porter, and automobile service station attendant. A **job description** is a brief statement listing what a worker does in a specific job. Typical job descriptions for several entry-level occupational titles follow:

- *Stock clerk.* Keeps track of supplies and equipment. Receives, unpacks, and stores incoming merchandise and reports damaged or spoiled goods. Keeps track of items in storage and issues equipment and supplies. Checks outgoing items for quality and quantity. Organizes and marks items for inventory with prices or codes. Employed by any organization that keeps large quantities of goods on hand.
- *Automobile service station attendant.* Services automobiles and other motor vehicles with fuel, lubricants, and accessories. Fills fuel tank with gasoline or diesel fuel. Checks level of oil in crank-

Illustration 3-2   A part-time retail salesperson requires little specialized training or experience.

case and amount of water in radiator and adds oil and water if necessary. Lubricates vehicle and changes oil. Replaces parts such as tires, air filters, and lights. Washes and waxes vehicles. Collects payment from customer, operates cash register, and handles charge card sales.

- *Supermarket customer service clerk.* Bags groceries in sack or carton and loads groceries in customer's car. Collects shopping carts from parking area and returns carts to store. Replaces supplies used at checkout counter. May price and stock food items on shelves.
- *Food salesperson.* Serves customer at fast food, ready-to-eat restaurant. Takes customer's order, relays order to food preparation area, delivers food on trays to customers. Fills containers with coffee, tea, and other beverages. Receives payment from customer, operates cash register, and makes change.

Career-Sustaining Marketing Occupations

Career-sustaining occupations often require more education, training, and experience than entry-level jobs and usually provide full-time employment. Jobs in this category require an understanding of marketing functions as well as knowledge of the products or services being marketed.

These jobs involve greater responsibility than entry-level jobs. They are held by individuals who have a commitment to a career. Successful performance at the career-sustaining level may lead to a higher level position and increased earning power. Examples of job titles in this category are full-time retail salesperson; hotel (motel) front desk manager; automobile salesperson, parts salesperson, or leasing agent; display person; waiter or waitress; cashier or checkout person; route salesperson; restaurant host or hostess; loan collection clerk; bank teller; door-to-door salesperson; and travel agent. Typical job descriptions for several career-sustaining occupational titles follow:

- *Hotel-motel front desk manager.* Performs a variety of duties for guests of hotel, motel, motor lodge, or condominium hotel. Registers and assigns rooms to guests. Dates, sorts, and racks incoming mail and messages. Transmits and receives telephone messages. Gives information about hotel services. Computes bill and collects payment from guests. Makes and confirms reservations. May supervise several other workers.
- *Travel agent.* Plans travel schedule and arranges accommodations for customers of travel agency. Gives the customer travel infor-

mation and makes suggestions and recommendations. Calculates cost of travel and accommodations using business machines, computer terminals, tariff books, and hotel rates books. Makes transportation and hotel reservations. Writes tickets and collects payment.

- *Retail salesperson.* Sells merchandise to customers and answers questions about products and prices. Accepts payment and makes change or writes up charge sales. May demonstrate products. Handles items and exchanges merchandise. Keeps work area neat and shelves adequately stocked. Responsibilities vary with the type of merchandise being sold and the type of retail business.
- *Display person.* Displays merchandise such as clothes, accessories, and furniture in windows, showcases, and on the sales floor of retail stores to attract attention of customers. Constructs or assembles displays and arranges mannequins, furniture, merchandise, and backdrop according to predetermined plan.

Specialized Marketing Occupations

Specialized occupations in marketing involve the performance of tasks that require extensive technical knowledge of the products or services. These positions require training and experience in specific marketing functions such as merchandising, advertising, marketing research, and sales promotion. These jobs often involve supervisory responsibilities, and persons employed in specialized marketing jobs usually are partially responsible for the success or profitability of the business. Examples of job titles in this area are manufacturer's representative, real estate agent, insurance sales agent, fashion coordinator, packaging specialist, mortgage loan counselor, retail buyer, media buyer, industrial purchasing agent, restaurant manager, advertising specialist, marketing researcher, public relations director, and securities sales agent. Typical job descriptions for several specialized marketing occupations follow:

- *Securities sales agent.* Buys and sells stocks and bonds for individuals and organizations as the representative of a stock brokerage firm. Uses knowledge of securities, market conditions, government regulations, and customers' needs to advise them about investments. Sends buy or sell order to securities exchange or dealer. Uses quoted price to calculate charge for service.
- *Retail buyer.* Buys merchandise for resale. Inspects merchandise and estimates resale value. Orders goods from manufacturers' representatives or directly from manufacturers. Arranges for transportation of goods. Authorizes payment of invoices or return of

merchandise. The buyer generally concentrates on a product area and develops a plan for proper styles, assortments, sizes, and amounts of the product. Analyzes suppliers on the basis of quality, style, availability, fit, flexibility, reliability, and price.

- *Insurance sales agent.* Sells insurance to new and present clients. Analyzes client's situation and recommends amount and type of insurance coverage. Explains policies to clients. Calculates and quotes premium rates. Finds and contacts prospective clients.
- *Marketing researcher.* Develops research methodology, evaluates the accuracy of different sample sizes, analyzes information (data), and assesses statistical errors in solving marketing problems. Conducts research following appropriate data collection techniques and draws conclusions and makes recommendations based on the findings of the research.

Supervisory Marketing Occupations

Supervisory occupations in marketing require decision making, communications, and supervisory skills. Supervisory personnel need to be skilled and experienced in such areas as delegating assignments to subordinates, giving directions, solving problems in the organization, and resolving conflicts. Supervisory positions usually require some type of post-high school or collegiate training and several years of work experience. Individuals functioning at this level will generally be responsible for the profitability of a portion, segment, or department of a marketing business. Examples of job titles in this area include supermarket department manager, small specialty store manager or assistant manager, chain store department manager and assistant manager, supermarket front end manager, supervisor of shipping and receiving, restaurant shift supervisor, and sales manager and supervisor. Sample job descriptions for several supervisory marketing occupations follow:

- *Sales manager or supervisor.* Manages or supervises sales activity of a business. Is usually responsible for recruiting, hiring, training, and evaluating sales personnel in a given sales territory. Coordinates sales activities by establishing sales territories, quotas, and goals. Advises dealers and distributors concerning sales and advertising techniques. Assigns sales territories to sales representatives. Analyzes and controls expenses. Reviews market conditions to determine customer needs, volume potential, price schedules, and discount rates.
- *Retail department manager or assistant manager.* Is responsible for the overall profitability of department or units within a retail

department store or retail discount store. Hires and schedules all employees who are assigned to work in that unit or department. Is responsible for the overall appearance of the department, including the stocking and maintenance of merchandise. Provides on-the-job sales training for sales personnel. Deals with customer complaints and works cooperatively with the buyer(s) for the particular department or unit.

- *Restaurant assistant or shift manager.* Supervises a small group (crew) of restaurant workers during a given shift of the day. Trains beginning workers and conducts an evaluation of the job performance for each of these workers. Has the major responsibility for scheduling part- and full-time workers to cover the total operations during a given time period.
- *Manager of specialty store.* Major responsibility includes recruiting, selecting, and training retail sales workers. Completes daily sales records required for the store and for the control of the dollar monies taken in during the day. May have some responsibility for local advertising and supervision of the store's visual merchandising efforts.

Illustration 3-3

A sales manager directs staffing, training, and performance evaluations to develop and control sales programs.

▰ Managerial/Entrepreneurial Marketing Occupations

Managerial/entrepreneurial marketing occupations involve the various dimensions of owning or managing a business and include the marketing functions of a large business. Usually persons in these jobs have extensive knowledge of the products or services they are marketing. Jobs in this category require continuous decision making and a thorough understanding of all marketing functions. Examples of job titles in this category are retail sales manager, hotel (motel) manager, industrial traffic manager, product (brand) manager, franchisee, independent business owner, advertising account executive, director of marketing research, wholesale manager, marketing manager (vice president of marketing), marketing channel manager, and financial institution manager. Some typical job descriptions for several managerial/entrepreneurial marketing occupations follow:

- *Advertising account executive.* Represents the communication link between the client (customer) and the advertising agency. Exhibits a thorough knowledge and understanding of marketing and its components. Explains clients' plans and objectives to the agency's creative teams and supervises the development of the total advertising plan for their accounts. Carries out major task of keeping the client satisfied with the advertising agency.
- *Hotel-motel manager.* Manages hotel or motel to insure efficient and profitable operations. Establishes standards of worker performance, service levels to customers, room rates, advertising, credit, and food selection and service. Plans dining room, bar, and banquet operations. Hires staff and assigns duties and responsibilities to department heads. Manages distribution of funds.
- *Marketing manager (vice president of marketing).* Plans, leads, and controls the entire marketing functions of a business. Oversees all marketing decisions and personnel. Supervises personnel in such areas as product development, advertising, sales promotion, market research, and marketing channel selection.
- *Financial institution manager.* Manages office of a financial institution such as a bank, finance company, mortgage-banking company, savings and loan association, or trust company. Directs supervisors who manage activities of financial institution employees. Directs procedures for custody and control of assets and records. Develops community relations and is responsible for the marketing of the financial business' services.
- *Small business manager.* Owns and operates own small retail or service business and represents one category of entrepreneurship.

Plans and oversees all business and marketing functions, from raising the required financial resources to operate the business through buying and selling merchandise to ultimate customers. Selects and hires all personnel, directs advertising efforts, conducts local marketing research, and keeps track of daily financial records. Is responsible for profit or loss in own business enterprise.

FINDING OUT MORE ABOUT MARKETING CAREER OPPORTUNITIES

There are several ways to find out more about careers in marketing. One way is to research various marketing career options. Another is to talk with people who have jobs that interest you. A third alternative is to actually find the type of job in which you are interested and try it out to see if you are suited for that kind of work.

Researching Marketing Careers

One source of information is the *Occupational Outlook Handbook*. This publication is compiled by the U.S. Department of Labor, Bureau of Labor Statistics. It usually is found in public libraries, school libraries, and school counselors' offices. This handbook presents an analysis of working conditions, salaries, employer requirements, and future employment needs for a number of different marketing occupations. To use this publication, simply look through the table of contents, find the marketing job title that you are interested in, and read the section covering that occupation. The handbook also contains a section that lists other sources that provide additional career information. Public libraries, local job service offices, and school career centers also have information about marketing careers. In addition, professional organizations, such as the American Marketing Association, can assist persons interested in marketing careers.

Talking with People in Marketing Occupations

Talking with individuals who are successful in the career area in which you are interested is an informative way of learning more about marketing. If possible, this conversation (or interview) should take place at the workplace of the person you wish to consult. If you use this approach, be sure to arrange an appointment and prepare a list of questions that you would like to ask. By asking the right questions, you can find out the kinds of skills and training that are necessary for the job, how the person got the current position, and also the individual's like and dislikes about the work. Here is a suggested list of questions you may want to consider.

1. What education and training are necessary to reach a position such as yours?
2. What personal qualities and technical information does an individual need to be successful in a similar position?
3. What other types of work experience did you have prior to your present position?
4. What led you to your present position?
5. What do you like most about your current marketing job? What do you like least?
6. What are your general recommendations as to how to be successful in a marketing career?

An interview such as this serves several purposes: you get out into the business world, you learn about an occupation in which you are interested, you gain experience at interviewing, and you meet people you can contact when you start looking for a job.

Working Part-Time in Marketing Occupations

A third way of finding out more about marketing careers is to work part-time or during summers in entry-level jobs. Practical work experience is a good way to learn about careers and to find out first-hand what marketing is all about. Even though the entry-level job you obtain may not be in the field you desire, the knowledge and experience you gain will often be useful in other marketing jobs. Many schools have cooperative work programs that allow students to work part-time in jobs that are actually entry-level marketing positions.

PLANNING FOR YOUR FUTURE MARKETING CAREER

Before you make a commitment to a particular area in marketing, you should take a careful look both at yourself and at the requirements of your chosen career. It is helpful to prepare a personal **career plan;** that is, a plan based on your career goal that includes information about your interests, personality, and abilities. A career plan will also include an analysis of the competencies (knowledges, attitudes, and skills) you will need in order to be successful and the education and training that are required to reach your goal.

After you have compiled this information and have identified the competencies for specific marketing jobs, you can be more objective in matching your personal qualities and abilities with the requirements for entry and future success in a marketing career.

◣ Examining Your Interests, Personality, and Abilities

In examining various marketing job opportunities, you should look closely at your interests, personality, and abilities. Interests are those activities that you enjoy. For example, if you like activities that involve leading, managing, and persuading others, you may be drawn to a career in marketing. On the other hand, if you like activities that involve only a few persons and playing games requiring mental exercise, you probably should seek employment in a structured setting where you will process information or work with numbers. In this case, a marketing career would not be attractive to you. Guidance counselors at your school should be able to help you determine your career interests. Most school counselors are trained to give vocational interest tests that will help you assess your potential career interests.

Personality is also important in your choice of a career. You personality is the sum of all your personal traits, attitudes, and habits that make you different from others. If you like to work with people and are aggressive and outgoing, you may be suited for a career in one of the marketing fields.

In order to successfully complete a task you must have the ability to perform the task. To have the ability to be successful at a job means that you have the knowledge and skill—you are competent—to accomplish the tasks required for the job. Ability can be natural, acquired (learned) through experience on the job, or gained through education and training. Different marketing positions require different levels of ability.

A simple entry-level job that involves performing routine duties, such as bagging groceries, requires minimum ability. What you must do in this type of job can be learned easily through work experience.

On the other hand, if you are attracted to a specialized position or a management position in marketing you will require additional education and training along with experience. Some positions have state licensing requirements for which formal education and training are necessary. For example, to sell real estate, insurance, or securities you must first pass a rigorous state examination in order to acquire a license.

To summarize, you should always be alert to any changes in your interests, personality, and abilities that can affect your career choice or alter your plans for higher education.

UNDERSTANDING THE COMPETENCIES REQUIRED FOR MARKETING CAREERS

To enter and advance successfully in a marketing career, you need to be aware of some of the competencies that marketing employees need to understand and be able to perform. **Competencies** are usually stated in terms of skills, knowledge, and attitudes that marketing employees must perform in order to be successful in their chosen career fields. Competencies in the marketing field generally fall into four major areas: (1) competencies in **basic marketing functions,** (2) competencies relating to understanding economic concepts impacted on by marketing **(economic foundations)**, (3) competencies in **human resource foundations,** and (4) competencies in **marketing and business foundations.** Examples of specific competencies in each of these areas are shown in Figure 3-4 on page 70–71. The level of the position you achieve in marketing will determine how much you must know and what knowledge, skills, and attitudes you must have in order to be successful. The more complex the job you have in marketing, the greater the level of competency required in each of these areas.

Once you determine the level of competency needed in your chosen career field, you can evaluate your level of skill and knowledge from the table in Figure 3-4. You will then be able to strengthen your preparation in those areas which need improvement. Prospective employers will be impressed if they see that you understand both the competencies required for the job and your personal abilities in relation to the knowledge and skills needed for successful performance. Figure 3-5 lists some requirements needed to be successful in marketing occupations, as viewed from the perspective of a marketing professional.

Figure 3-4   Competencies required for marketing careers.

COMPETENCIES	EXAMPLES OF KNOWLEDGE AND SKILLS REQUIRED
BASIC MARKETING FUNCTIONS	1. Product or service planning 2. Purchasing or buying 3. Physical distribution (transportation and storage) 4. Promoting and selling 5. Pricing 6. Financing 7. Obtaining and using marketing information 8. Risk management
HUMAN RESOURCE FOUNDATIONS	1. Human relations skills 2. Leadership skills 3. Self-image and self-concept 4. Attitudes 5. Problem-solving and decision-making skills 6. Personality development 7. Customer and co-worker relations 8. Communications skills (listening, written, oral) 9. Marketing math skills 10. Marketing and business ethics 11. Career development skills 12. Interpersonal communications skills
MARKETING AND BUSINESS FOUNDATIONS *(continued)*	1. Types of business ownership 2. Management and organizational structure 3. Marketing mix 4. Channels of distribution 5. Market segmentation and target marketing 6. Product or service life cycle 7. Uses and benefits of products or services 8. Special terminology or technical features of products or services 9. Guarantee and warranty information 10. Knowledge of competitors' products or services

COMPETENCIES	EXAMPLES OF KNOWLEDGE AND SKILLS REQUIRED
ECONOMIC FOUNDATIONS	1. Relationship of marketing to American economic system 2. Supply and demand 3. Job opportunities in marketing 4. Understanding the concept of product or service utility 5. Understanding the concepts of decision making, competition, profits, and risk in marketing 6. Federal, state, and local laws affecting marketing 7. Relationship of marketing to Gross National Product (GNP)

Source: Adapted from *National Curriculum Framework and Core Competencies,* Marketing Education Resource Center, Columbus, Ohio, 43212-0226, 1987.

Figure 3-5   Success in marketing requires many skills.

REQUIREMENTS FOR BEING SUCCESSFUL IN MARKETING

1. A thorough understanding of the marketing concept.
2. Obsession with customer satisfaction.
3. Entrepreneurial personality and willingness to take risks.
4. Understanding that marketing is a results-oriented business activity and that those involved will be held accountable for their performance.
5. Belief that the marketing activity in any organization is the cornerstone of the business enterprise.
6. Strong written and oral communication skills and ability to sell the marketing concept.
7. A vision of the future.
8. An understanding of basic business concepts such as ROI (return on investment), business planning, measuring profitability, and evaluating marketing risks.

Source: Adapted from a speech given by Don Woodbury, Director of Marketing for Logan Regional Hospital, to Utah State University American Marketing Association, October, 1989, Logan, Utah.

APPLYING MARKETING TERMS

Name _____

Match each term with the statement that best describes an application of that term. Write the letter in the space provided.

a. general merchandise retailing
b. production businesses
c. career-sustaining position
d. career plan
e. entrepreneur

f. hospitality and recreation marketing
g. supervisory position
h. service businesses
i. nonprofit organizations
j. marketing business

_____ 1. Hotels and resorts are examples of types of businesses found in this marketing occupational specialty area.

_____ 2. A supermarket in your local area would be an example of this type of business enterprise.

_____ 3. General Motors, Ford, and Chrysler Motors are examples of this type of business enterprise.

_____ 4. The job of a department manager in a department store at a local mall would be referred to as this level of marketing position.

_____ 5. A written plan that would estimate where you might be in a marketing career in 5 or 10 years, and what education and training are required to get there.

_____ 6. What you might be called if you were to start up and be successful in your own small business.

_____ 7. Discount department stores would be included in this marketing occupational specialty area.

_____ 8. Real estate and insurance companies are examples of this broad category of business enterprise.

_____ 9. A retail salesperson holds this level of marketing job, which involves greater responsibility than an entry-level position in marketing.

_____ 10. Organizations which do not have "making a profit" as their primary goal.

Answer each of the following questions in the space provided.

1. Explain what is meant by this statement: *Marketing affects each of us every day.*

2. How do a production business, a marketing business, and a service business differ?

3. Name five marketing occupations that are expected to offer increased employment opportunities in the near future.

4. Explain what is meant by this statement: *Marketing occupations can be classified by function or by type of institutional environment or setting.*

5. List the eight marketing functions.

6. List five occupational specialty areas found in marketing.

7. Explain the major difference between the following levels of occupations.
   a. Entry-level and career-sustaining marketing occupations

   b. Career-sustaining and specialized marketing occupations

   c. Specialized and supervisory marketing occupations

   d. Supervisory and managerial/entrepreneurial occupations

8. What are three different ways you can increase your information about careers in marketing?

DEVELOPING PEOPLE SKILLS

Read the following description of a human relations situation. Then complete your answers on a separate piece of paper.

The Deadline Draws Near!

Nancy Wong is a junior at Skyline High School. She has completed several business classes including typewriting, accounting, and business law. Her grades in these classes have been about average. This year Nancy enrolled in the first-year marketing class at school. She is not sure why she is taking this class, only that she needed a class offered at this hour, and marketing sounded like it might be interesting.

In this class, Nancy's marketing teacher has required that all students develop a written career plan which must be turned in by the end of the quarter. Part of this career planning project requires that Nancy work with three other students in a small group. Groups are to be made up of those who have interests in a similar marketing career field. Each group will then be asked to make a presentation to the class on the opportunities and requirements in this career field.

The quarter ends in two weeks. Nancy can't find a group to join because she doesn't know which marketing career field is really of interest to her. Although Nancy knew about this project requirement several weeks ago, she has yet to start working on it. Needless to say Nancy is very frustrated with this project and she is considering just bagging it and taking an F for the assignment.

1. What do you see as Nancy's major problem in this case?
2. What alternatives could Nancy consider in trying to solve her problem?
3. Is Nancy in a position different than many other high school students relative to knowing exactly what her career field in marketing might be?
4. What suggestions would you make to Nancy regarding how she could get started on this assignment?

 **MARKETING PROJECT 3**

Use you own paper to complete this project.

Developing a Career Plan in Marketing

Develop a career plan for a marketing position you are interested in. If available, use the *Occupational Outlook Handbook* to help construct your plan. Include the following information in your plan.

1. What is your career goal? Into which major specialized marketing area does your career goal fit?
2. Identify the specific duties and tasks involved in this position. Do you think that you would enjoy performing these tasks?
3. Outline the working conditions you will encounter in this type of position.
4. Describe your personal interests. If you have completed an interest inventory or test at your school, what did you learn about your interests that relate to your career choice? Are your interests compatible with the requirements of the position you plan to seek?
5. Discuss the local, state, and national employment opportunities for this kind of position.
6. If possible, interview a person working in this career field. What does this person see as the advantages and disadvantages of this career field?
7. What are the educational and training requirements for this position?
8. What is the salary range for a position such as this?
9. Where could you look for further information relating to this career?

MARKETING INSIGHT

Read the following description of real-life marketing practices. Then complete your answers on a separate piece of paper.

Executives Support Marketing Job Growth

Employment levels in sales, marketing, and advertising will grow during the next five years and outpace increases in other departments, according to a survey of corporate officers commissioned by Dunhill Personnel System, Inc.[2]

Nearly 75 percent of the 208 executives polled expected their firms' overall employment levels to rise. Respondents included chairpersons, CEOs, presidents, chief financial officers, COOs, and high-ranking vice presidents from *Fortune 500* and other companies.

"The optimistic viewpoints on employment growth over the next five years seem tied to a generally optimistic feeling on business growth," said Fred Henry, executive vice president of Dunhill, Carle Place, New York. "More than half of those surveyed felt their businesses and those of their competitors had improved compared to last year."

Service company executives were more positive about employment growth than were industrial corporation executives. "In recent years we have heard a great deal about the growth of the service sector. The greater hiring expectations in this sector reflect this," Henry said.

Asked to rank four typical divisions in their companies by employment growth opportunities in the future, 54 percent of the respondents ranked sales, marketing, and advertising first, followed by data processing and systems (23 percent), technical and engineering (18 percent), and administration (5 percent).

Sales-marketing-advertising also was perceived by 27 percent of the executives as the department that has received the most support from management for growth. Manufacturing came in next with 18 percent, followed closely by financial with 17 percent.

1. Why would service sector executives be more positive about employment growth in marketing than industrial corporation executives?
2. Why would sales-marketing-advertising receive the most support from management for growth?

---

[2]"Marketing Job Outlook Optimistic," *Collegiate Edition Marketing News* (Courtesy of American Marketing Association) (1 January 1988), p. 1.

UNIT 2
ANALYZING THE MARKETPLACE

4   **OBTAINING AND USING MARKETING INFORMATION**

5   **UNDERSTANDING THE PRODUCTS AND SERVICES YOU MARKET**

6   **CONSUMER BUYING BEHAVIOR**

7   **ORGANIZATIONAL BUYING BEHAVIOR**

8   **DIVIDING A MARKET INTO SEGMENTS**

CHAPTER 4
OBTAINING AND USING
MARKETING INFORMATION

After you read this chapter and complete the activities at the end, you will be able to:

1. **Define marketing information and discuss its importance in making marketing decisions.**
2. **Explain and give examples of primary and secondary marketing information.**
3. **Explain and give examples of internal and external marketing information.**
4. **Define marketing research and discuss its relationship to the process of obtaining marketing information.**
5. **Discuss how marketing research relates to the marketing mix.**
6. **Define test marketing and explain its three major purposes.**
7. **Identify and explain the six steps of the marketing research process.**
8. **Explain how computers are used to manage marketing information and what constitutes a marketing information system.**

Imagine that you would like to start your own small marketing business in the town or city where you live. Where would you start? What type of product or service would you choose to market? Where would you locate your marketing business? What would be your hours of operation? How would you advertise the products or services that you would be marketing? What prices would you charge for your products or services? What is the level and amount of competition for this or a similar type of marketing business in your community?

These and related questions need to be answered before you can open the doors of your business. Failure to answer such questions may lead to the failure of your business. Therefore, the first step in starting a new marketing business should be to collect and analyze the necessary marketing information surrounding the creation of the marketing business.

There are a number of methods that you could use to collect the marketing information necessary for your hypothetical marketing business. Asking your potential customers to fill out a questionnaire is one very popular method of collecting marketing information. Studying local census data is another good way of looking at the basic demographics of your market area. Personally visiting the businesses you would be competing with and examining their product line and pricing structure might give you some very useful information. Everyone involved in marketing is involved in collecting and analyzing marketing information so that more effective marketing decisions can be made.

MARKETING INFORMATION

As you learned in Chapter 1, the primary goal of most businesses in the American economy is to meet the needs and wants of customers at a profit. In order for a business, large or small, to reach this goal its managers must be up to date on all developments in their field. Business owners and managers need adequate and timely information on which to base important decisions. One type of information required by most businesses is called marketing information. **Marketing information** is any information that aids the transfer or movement of goods and services from producer to customer.

Obtaining and using marketing information is essential if a business is to operate according to the marketing concept. Finding out what customers want and then providing those items is a major component of the marketing concept. Marketing information is necessary in order to make such important marketing decisions.

Marketing personnel also need up-to-date information in order to make routine marketing decisions. Simple decisions such as how much of a particular product to reorder or how to schedule the working hours of sales personnel require marketing information. Marketing personnel must sometimes solve marketing problems that are nonrepetitive in nature. For example, if a company is planning to open a new video rental outlet, management must choose an appropriate location. Selecting the best location requires the collection and analysis of information. Some information the video outlet managers would need includes traffic patterns, previous rental history, and the number of square feet available and required.

◣ Primary and Secondary Marketing Information

Marketing information is gathered to aid marketers in the decision-making process. This information can be gathered with a specific marketing question or problem in mind. When this is the case the information collected is referred to as **primary marketing information.** For example, if a travel agency surveyed its customers specifically to determine their level of satisfaction with the quality of

Illustration 4-1   Merchandise records help marketing personnel make decisions concerning product reorders.

travel services offered, this information would be an example of primary marketing information.

Secondary marketing information, on the other hand, is information that has been collected for some other purpose, but which still may be of value to managers in the decision-making process. If the travel agency mentioned above were to find some useful demographic data in one of its travel trade magazines or from government census data, this information would be an example of secondary marketing information. Secondary marketing information may be the only type of information that is available for many small and new business organizations.

Internal and External Marketing Information

Both primary and secondary marketing information may be further divided into internal and external information. Information collected from the records of a business, such as sales or inventory data, is called **internal marketing information.** Data collected from other sources, such as government reports or professional publications, are called **external marketing information.** Figures 4-1 and 4-2 list examples of internal and external marketing information.

Figure 4-1   Some sources of internal marketing information.

INTERNAL MARKETING INFORMATION

1. Sales records (includes sales records of individual items as well as total sales)
2. Merchandise and stock control records (includes records of the amount of merchandise sold, the amount currently in inventory, and the amount that has been reordered)
3. Customer want slips (completed forms describing items that customers would like a business to sell)
4. Invoices and receiving records
5. Records of merchandise returned to manufacturers or suppliers
6. Customer complaint and adjustment records
7. Advertising records (records of the amount spent on advertising and the impact of advertising on sales)
8. Customer credit records
9. Operating statements (the financial statements of a business; i.e., income statements and balance sheets)
10. Records on price markdowns
11. Salespersons' reports

Figure 4-2   Some sources of external marketing information.

EXTERNAL MARKETING INFORMATION

1. Government agencies such as the Department of Labor (Bureau of Labor Statistics), the Department of Commerce, and the Congressional Information Service
2. Census data provided by the U.S. Department of Commerce, Bureau of the Census (includes population, retailing, and manufacturing statistics)
3. Trade association information
4. Voter registration data
5. Reports in current trade magazines such as *Advertising Age, Sales & Marketing Management, Business Week, Stores,* and *Marketing News*
6. Commercial subscriptions from Dun & Bradstreet, Inc.; A. C. Nielson Co.; Market Research Corporation of America; and Standard Rate and Data Service, Inc.
7. Reports in current daily periodicals such as *The Wall Street Journal, USA Today,* and local newspapers

MARKETING RESEARCH

In order to solve specific problems and make informed decisions, marketing personnel must collect, record, and analyze marketing information. This activity is called **marketing research.** Marketing research is essential for all businesses if they are to meet the needs of customers and remain competitive and profitable. Marketing research is an organized way of finding answers to questions or solutions to problems. It is an ongoing activity in any business enterprise that markets goods or services. Businesses of all sizes conduct marketing research in order to improve the quality of their marketing decisions. Decisions can range from the informal, simple, and routine to the complex and nonrepetitive.

Large businesses that operate at the national or regional level usually have a marketing research department to plan and carry out marketing research projects. These departments employ **marketing researchers** who are responsible for collecting and analyzing marketing information. Large businesses frequently employ specialized research consultants who conduct research on special problems. They also employ outside technical specialists who collect information through customer interviews and then tabulate the data. Small businesses do not usually have separate marketing research departments;

they rely on salespeople and marketing managers to conduct any necessary research.

Marketing employees at all levels are responsible for collecting marketing information. Sales personnel for textbook publishing companies are frequently asked to provide customer feedback to the central office regarding how teachers in their territory feel about the company's publications. The information collected through this feedback process is then provided to the authors for their use in the next edition of the textbook. A cashier in a retail store enters stock or classification numbers in the cash register when merchandise is sold or returned for credit. The sales records generated by the cash register provide management with information on what merchandise is selling and must be reordered. An insurance agent who is promoting a new insurance plan may be required to provide written reports to the insurance company's home office concerning the sales resistance or acceptance by customers. Thus, everyone who comes in contact with customers has the opportunity to become involved in the marketing research process.

Illustration 4-2

Large businesses employ technical specialists who collect information through interviews and then tabulate the data.

◣ MARKETING RESEARCH AND THE MARKETING MIX

Businesses rely on the people involved in marketing research to collect and analyze information systematically and objectively. This information may be primary or secondary, internal or external. The primary goal of marketing research is to obtain the information necessary to ensure the proper blending of the factors of the marketing mix.

As mentioned in Chapter 2, the **marketing mix** is a combination of product or service, promotion, place, and price decisions. For example, if an imported line of microcomputers that is introduced to the United States market costs less than similar domestic microcomputers, American producers will have to adjust the components of their marketing mixes. They may decide to lower their prices in order to remain competitive or to increase their promotion budgets in order to convince customers that the American-made microcomputers are worth the extra investment. American producers may try a combination of lower prices and increased promotion. Before making a final decision, however, marketing research employees will attempt to determine what effect either of these two strategies (lowering prices or increasing promotion) will have on sales of microcomputers produced in this country. If the impact of these adjustments is estimated to be positive, the decision will be to use either or both of these strategies. This example shows how changing market conditions (the introduction of foreign competition) can require American producers to devise new marketing mixes.

The information gathered through marketing research can relate to any of the factors of the marketing mix. The questions discussed in the next four sections reveal the kinds of information that may be required before final product or service, promotion, place, and price decisions can be made.

◣ Product or Service Decisions

These questions may help a manager make decisions relating to a product or service.

1. *Deciding what to produce.* What goods should be produced? What products should be purchased for resale to customers? What do customers want to buy? What is the proper product or service mix?

2. *Product or service features.* What styles and colors will sell best? What special features should the products or services have? What sizes should be produced or purchased?

3. *Packaging and labeling.* How should the product be packaged? How can the packaging be made both attractive and protective? What information should be included on the label?

4. *Quantity.* How much of each product should be produced? How much should be ordered for resale to customers?

5. *Services.* What services should be offered to support the product or service?

◤ Promotion Decisions

The following questions relate to promotion decisions.

1. *Advertising.* What is the best advertising strategy? Should national, regional, or local advertising be used? What advertising media will be most effective? Should cooperative advertising be used; that is, should we share the distributor's advertising costs? What advertising budget should be established? How much and what type of advertising is the competition using?

2. *Visual merchandising.* Does the product or service lend itself to any type of visual merchandising? How can it be properly displayed? Should there be point-of-purchase (at the register) displays? Where should the merchandise be displayed? Where on the shelves should specific items be located?

3. *Public relations and publicity.* Can news releases and special public relations activities help promote the product or service?

4. *Personal selling.* How can sales personnel be properly trained? What techniques (sales incentives) can be used to motivate sales personnel? How can we insure that sales personnel have adequate product or service knowledge? How can target market areas be divided into sales territories to insure proper coverage?

◤ Place Decisions

These questions will help a manager in considering transportation and location decisions.

1. *Transportation and storage.* What is the most efficient and effective method of transporting the goods? How important is the speed of delivery service? What is the most cost-effective means

of transportation? Should warehouses be set up at strategic locations to insure an adequate and prompt supply? What techniques should be used to insure that an adequate supply of goods and services is available at the right time and right place? Does the product need to be frozen or kept refrigerated?

2. *Channels of distribution.* What channels of distribution should be used? What intermediaries should be involved? Should the product be sold directly to the retailer or should a wholesaler be used?

3. *Business location.* What is the best location for the business? How and where should goods be stored? Where is the competition located? Where are our customers likely to shop?

Price Decisions

Answers to these questions will help a manager determine price in relation to certain factors.

1. *Pricing structure.* What should be the planned price for the product or service? Will the planned price permit an adequate sales volume and profit? Will the planned price convey the proper image? What effect will providing customer services have on the pricing structure? What price should wholesalers be charged?

2. *Supply and demand.* What effect will pricing have on supply and demand? Will a lower price insure a sales volume that will meet expenses and yield an adequate profit?

3. *Discounts.* Should discounts, based on the quantity purchased or speed of payment, be made available to retailers and wholesalers? What impact will trade discounts have on sales?

4. *Competition.* What prices are competitors charging for similar products or services? Is our price structure competitive?

TEST MARKETING

In order to provide higher quality answers to the above mentioned marketing mix questions, especially those dealing with product, promotion, and price, organizations will frequently become involved in what is referred to as test marketing. **Test marketing** occurs when an organization makes a product or service available to the market in a limited geographic area. Test marketing generally has three major purposes: (1) to estimate the sales volume when the product or service is made available to the entire market, (2) to test the effectiveness of the promotional campaign used in the test market, and (3) to determine what might represent an ideal or optimal selling price. Even though test marketing is very expensive to conduct, it can save an organization millions of dollars in the long run. Through the use of test marketing results, the organization can avoid the even greater expense of marketing unsuccessful products or services on a more extensive basis.

STEPS IN THE MARKETING RESEARCH PROCESS

Marketing research is used to solve specific problems. As an essential part of the decision-making process, marketing research should be conducted in an orderly manner that allows owners and managers to evaluate objectively the information that has been collected. Marketing research should be a continuous process that enables management to make effective, timely marketing decisions. Figure 4-3 shows the six steps that are usually included in the marketing research process.

Figure 4-3   Steps of the marketing research process.

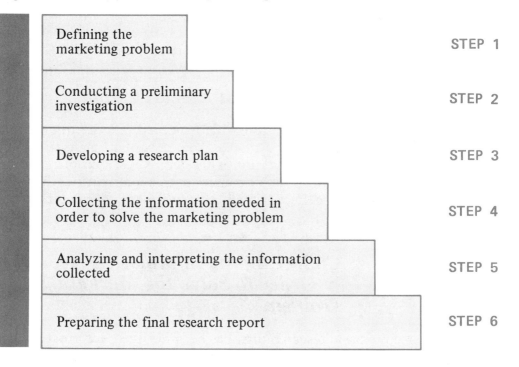

Defining the marketing problem	STEP 1
Conducting a preliminary investigation	STEP 2
Developing a research plan	STEP 3
Collecting the information needed in order to solve the marketing problem	STEP 4
Analyzing and interpreting the information collected	STEP 5
Preparing the final research report	STEP 6

Step 1: *Defining the Marketing Problem*

This step in the marketing research process is so obvious that it is often overlooked, yet it is *the* most important step. Before you can discover the source(s), you must determine the exact nature of the problem. You have to see beyond the symptoms to find the cause(s). To state a problem as "a decrease in sales volume" is not defining the problem; it is listing a symptom. In Step 1 of the marketing research process, the problem is clearly and accurately stated in order to determine what issues are involved, what questions must be asked, and what types of information must be collected. Defining the problem is a critical step that should not be hurried through in order to finish the research.

Step 2: *Conducting a Preliminary Investigation*

Once the problem has been formally defined, you should assess your ability to reach a solution. You may already have all the information you need to find the solution. It may have become obvious when the problem was defined. If, however, the solution is not clear or all the necessary information is not readily available, you may need to collect additional data. Perhaps all the required information may be obtained from internal business records or from the sales staff. Nevertheless, the total cost of acquiring any additional information should be weighed against its potential usefulness.

Step 3: *Developing a Research Plan*

You now know what information is needed in order to resolve a problem and what facts are available. You must make plans to collect whatever additional information is needed. A research plan should include a listing of the possible sources of this information, the techniques required to collect it, and tentative plans for analyzing the resulting data.

Step 4: *Collecting the Information Needed in Order to Solve the Marketing Problem*

Once the basic research plan has been outlined, information can be collected. The collection techniques used—mail, telephone, personal interviews—depend on the research plan established in Step 3 and the research budget.

Step 5: *Analyzing and Interpreting the Information Collected*

Facts alone do not always provide a sound solution to a marketing research problem. They must be analyzed and interpreted. Simple statistical techniques are often used to analyze the data collected.

Step 6: *Preparing the Final Research Report*

The final report contains a summary of the major research findings, conclusions, and recommendations based on the information collected. Sometimes the conclusions and recommendations become obvious when the facts are interpreted. In other cases, however, reaching a conclusion and making recommendations may not be easy because of information gaps or intangible factors that are difficult to evaluate or control. If information is adequate or if intangible factors are involved, it is important to state this when drawing conclusions and making recommendations. If several recommendations are made, an owner or manager must decide which recommendation to implement. As a follow-up, evaluation of the impact of this decision on the success of a business should be completed. This will help determine if the marketing research process is functioning properly or if changes need to be made in research procedures.

Marketing research is not an exact science. It deals with people and their constantly changing likes and dislikes, factors which are affected by hundreds of different influences that cannot be identified or measured. When properly directed, the marketing research process does help owners and managers gather facts in an orderly, objective way to determine what is happening in the marketplace so that their marketing decisions can be effective.

COMPUTERS AND MARKETING INFORMATION

Computers, especially the newest generation of microcomputers, have had a tremendous impact on the collection, storage, and analysis of all types of marketing information. Computers have become very useful in new product development and testing, distribution management, and marketing research. It is now possible to use the computer to simulate the introduction of a new product into a particular market and to project how well this new product will do under certain types of situations. Physical distribution can be aided by computers in that the marketing manager can now keep track of where an oversupply of a particular product is located. In marketing research, many statistical analyses formerly required the use of a very powerful computer. Today, these same statistical analyses can easily be performed by a microcomputer, which makes the recorded information contained in surveys and other research easy to analyze and report. Figure 4-4 shows many of the different applications of computers for obtaining and using marketing information.

Data Bases and Networking

When marketing information is stored in computer format it is usually stored in what is referred to as a **data base.** A data base is used to store, organize, and help manage similar types of marketing information. For example, all of the United States Census Bureau's information is considered a data base. It is now possible to purchase selected portions of the Census Bureau's data base. This information can then be accessed by the marketing manager via a desktop microcomputer.

Microcomputers can be linked via telephone lines to mainframe computers, minicomputers, and other microcomputers, even when they are located in different geographic locations. When computers are linked together, this is known as a **computer network** or **networking.** Networking makes it possible for a marketing research firm in Florida to gain access to a data base sold by a marketing research firm in New York City.

Organizations can develop their own data bases of information to help the marketing manager make better marketing decisions. For example, if you filled out a warranty card for a product you recently purchased, the information you provided will become part of the marketing data base for the organization that sold you the product. A data base can also be as simple as a listing of customers, with their addresses and telephone numbers.

Developing a Marketing Information System

With the advances in computer technology it is now possible for an organization to develop and utilize what is referred to as a **marketing information system.** A marketing information system allows marketing personnel to collect, analyze, and organize their market-

Figure 4-4   Uses of computers in marketing.

COMPUTER APPLICATIONS IN MARKETING GROW

FUNCTION	1988: Performed	
	Computer	Manually
Mail lists: preparation & maintenance	91%	9%
Order processing: follow-up, backlog control	86	11
Sales performance: product mix analysis	76	14
Inventory/distribution: control, record, report	75	6
Customer analysis: volume, product trends	72	19
Inquiry handling: analysis, processing	71	29
Marketing budget: control, status, report	68	32
Sales performance: analyses of staff, reps, distributors	68	23
Marketing information systems: storage & retrieval	66	20
Pricing analysis	65	28
Profit analysis: gross by line & territory	63	18
Territorial analysis: quotas, sales, achievements	59	32
Sales forecasting	49	46
Advertising research	37	35
New market/customer analysis: potential	26	60
Telemarketing	26	32
Market research: surveys	22	51
Lost sales/lost accounts analysis	19	59
Econometric models: input/output	9	14

Note: Details won't add to 100% because percent of "not performed" responses not shown.
Source: Reprinted with permission of MAINLY MARKETING, Copyright 1988, Schoonmakers Associates, P.O. Box 972, Corham, N.Y. 11727.

ing information. A marketing information system can help to integrate all of the different types of marketing information discussed in this chapter and to make this information available in an organized data base format to the marketing manager. Internal marketing information, such as sales records and inventory reports; external marketing information, such as trade reports; and information collected through the marketing research process can all be combined. This marketing information system can then be utilized when making marketing decisions. Figure 4-5 shows the relationship of different sources of information to a marketing information system.

Figure 4-5   A marketing information system can lead to quality marketing decisions.

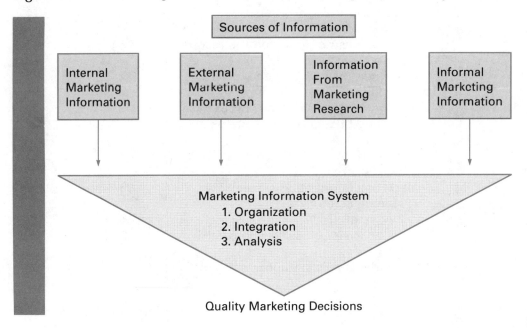

APPLYING MARKETING TERMS

Name _____

Match each term with the statement that best describes an application of that term. Write the letter in the space provided.

a. marketing data base
b. external marketing information
c. test marketing
d. marketing research
e. marketing information system

f. internal marketing information
g. primary marketing information
h. marketing information
i. secondary marketing information
j. marketing researcher

_____ 1. Information that is collected directly from consumers for use in making marketing decisions.

_____ 2. Information taken from marketing records of the business such as sales records.

_____ 3. Marketing information which has been collected for another purpose but which is still valuable to the marketer.

_____ 4. This computer format stores, organizes, and helps to manage marketing information.

_____ 5. Marketing information that is derived from such sources as the U.S. Census Bureau.

_____ 6. Conducting a telephone survey of potential customers is known as this type of research.

_____ 7. A person who is employed to collect and analyze marketing information.

_____ 8. A soap manufacturer sells a new laundry detergent in a small market to determine customer acceptance.

_____ 9. Information which is collected and analyzed for the purpose of improving the quality of marketing decisions.

_____ 10. A system that integrates, organizes, and analyzes all of the different marketing information and makes it available to decision makers.

MASTERING KEY CONCEPTS

Name _____

Answer each of the following questions in the space provided.

1. What role does timely and accurate marketing information play in the decision-making process?

2. How are marketing information and the marketing concept related?

3. What is the difference between primary and secondary marketing information?

4. Give three examples of internal marketing information.

5. Give three examples of external marketing information.

6. What is marketing research and what role does it play in maintaining the proper combination of the factors of the marketing mix?

7. Give an example of a typical marketing research question related to each of the four factors of the marketing mix.

   Product or service decisions:

   Promotion decisions:

   Place decisions:

   Price decisions:

8. What impact has computer technology had on the collection, storage, and analysis of marketing information?

9. List and explain the six steps of the marketing research process.

DEVELOPING PEOPLE SKILLS

Read the following description of a human relations situation. Then complete your answers on a separate piece of paper.

The Coupon Caper

Sally Anderson was recently hired as a customer service person at King's Supermarket. At King's, she is responsible for packaging and carrying out customer purchases, stocking shelves, and ordering for the candy section in the front of the store. King's is a medium-sized supermarket located in a small midwestern city.

Every Thursday evening the store owner places a full-page advertisement in the local newspaper. The ad identifies the special items that will be on sale starting the following Friday morning. Every other week the store manager places two coupons in the ad for popular items such as ice cream, soda pop, chips, snacks, or some other similar type of product. Coupons are used to stimulate sales, but they also help to give the store manager a good idea concerning how well the newspaper advertisements are working. By counting coupon redemptions the manager can estimate the number of people who are reading the store's advertisements. When the customer buys the merchandise with a coupon the cashier puts the coupon in a box near the cash register. At the end of the day or when the shift changes, the coupons are counted and recorded in the Coupon Sales Record.

Recently while Sally was bagging a customer's purchases she noticed that the cashier was simply discarding the coupons in the nearby wastebasket. When Sally asked the cashier why he was doing this, his response was, "I've been here for 10 years and these coupons are a real pain. The boss never does anything different even after he has counted the redemptions. I figure that I can speed up customer service and create less hassle for myself if I just throw them away."

After watching this happen for several weeks Sally decided that she needed to be honest and tell the manager what she saw happening. Before she did this she checked with one of the other customer service workers who had worked at King's for a longer period of time than Sally. When Sally told this person what she planned on doing, the response was, "I really wouldn't do that if I were you. George, the cashier, is the owner's nephew. If you tell the manager, you might get fired."

1. What is the major problem in this case?
2. If you were Sally, what would you do when you saw the cashier throwing out coupons at the register?
3. What are some of the ethical considerations that this case raises?

MARKETING PROJECT 4

Use your own paper to complete this project.

Conducting a Marketing Research Study

Conduct the following marketing research project at your school. Develop a questionnaire that will solicit answers to the following marketing research question: What are the buying habits of teenagers at (name of school) High School? Be sure to follow the six steps of the marketing research process as outlined in this chapter. Prepare a final report and submit it to your teacher. Examples of questions that you may want to consider as you conduct this project include the following:

1. How old are the students?
2. What kinds of family backgrounds do the students have?
3. On the average, how much money do they spend each week?
4. What are their sources of income?
5. How do they spend their money? For example, how much is spent on food, clothing, entertainment, transportation, or personal care products?
6. Did grade level have an effect on the spending patterns of students involved in this study?
7. What conclusions can you draw from the information you have collected? What recommendations can you make to businesses in your area that sell products and services to the teenage market?
8. If you were starting your own small business, what decisions would you make based on the information you collected in this research study?

MARKETING INSIGHT

Read the following description of real-life marketing practices. Then complete your answers on a separate piece of paper.

Follow-Up Surveys

Customer satisfaction will be one of the most crucial issues facing U.S. businesses in the next decade, affecting both repeat business and positive referrals. Current industry statistics show it costs five times more to acquire a new customer than to keep an existing one.

In recent years customer satisfaction follow-up and feedback programs using surveys have proliferated. Their purpose has been to gather customer perceptions of products and services. Follow-up surveys can assess customer perceptions in the treatment of customer at the time of product or service delivery, the product or service versus competitive offerings, warranty service, and product quality and performance after some period of ownership.

The ultimate goal is to assess the customers' total buying and service experience. The survey results can be both enlightening and alarming. At the start, few companies realize the responsibility that comes with asking their customers the simple question: What do you think?

Chances are great that a response will be required by the company. Complaints, problems, and disagreements about the product, service, manufacturer, distributor, or retailer are the most common customer comments. There are cases, however, where positive comments are also deserving of a response by the company.

Developing an effective and manageable customer satisfaction program requires a review of the process from beginning to end. Companies that are successful pay special attention to using appropriate survey sampling techniques, designing effective questionnaires, and establishing a procedure for handling the results generated with the survey.[1]

1. Why do you think that it is important for companies to measure customers' satisfaction with their products or services?
2. Why do you think that measuring customer satisfaction is part of the marketing research process?
3. How would a company utilize the information that is provided through customer satisfaction?

[1]Frank Uller, "Follow-up Surveys Assess Customer Satisfaction," *Marketing News* (2 January 1989) (Courtesy of American Marketing Association).

CHAPTER 5
UNDERSTANDING THE PRODUCTS AND SERVICES YOU MARKET

After you read this chapter and complete the activities at the end, you will be able to:

1. Describe the four stages in the product life cycle.
2. Explain the difference between consumer products and industrial products.
3. Explain the different types of brands and the major purposes of branding.
4. Explain the four major purposes of packaging.
5. Understand the importance of product and service information.
6. Identify and discuss the four types of product-service mixes.
7. Explain what employees should know about the products and services marketed by their business.
8. Identify the different sources of product and service information.
9. Explain how a salesperson can use product and service information successfully.

The central focus of marketing activities in an organization is deciding what to produce and how to get this proposed product, service, or idea to the marketplace. Imagine trying to create a business that would *not* be involved in trying to market something—either a product, service, or idea. If you had an opportunity to start any type of business, what would it be? What would be the first question that you would ask yourself? Would it be possible for you to begin your imaginary business without offering some type of product or service? Understanding the products, services, or ideas that you plan to market is very important to you as well as to your proposed business. Without knowledge of what you are going to market you would have difficulty being successful in your business enterprise.

◢ THE PRODUCT LIFE CYCLE

Every product goes through what is referred to in marketing as the product life cycle. The **product life cycle** has four distinctly recognizable stages: introduction, growth, maturity, and decline. Novelty products, such as pet rocks, and stylish clothing go through the cycle with great speed. Other products such as lawn mowers, automobiles, and household appliances have a much longer product life cycle.

The **introduction stage** in the product life cycle is when a product has just been developed and introduced to the marketplace. When sales for the product begin to increase at a rapid rate the product has entered the **growth stage.** When sales for the product slow and perhaps level off the product is in the **maturity stage.** The **decline stage** occurs when sales begin to drop off and substitute products become available. Figure 5-1 shows a graphic view of the product life cycle.

Figure 5-1   Graphic view of the product life cycle.

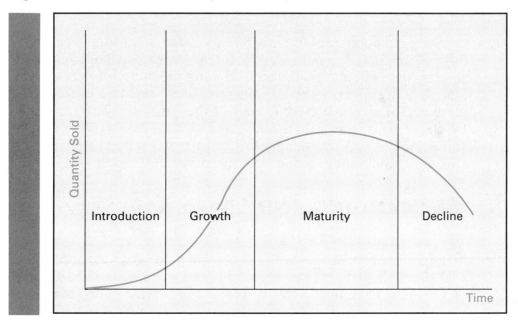

Where the product is positioned in the product life cycle and the speed at which it is moving through the various stages both have strong implications for marketing efforts. For example, a product in the introductory stage will require extensive promotion and advertising. A product in the growth stage will require timely distribution throughout the marketing channels to assure an adequate supply to vendors. Products in the decline stage may need some price adjustments in order to be competitive with less expensive substitute products.

CLASSIFYING PRODUCTS

Classifying products into different categories can be helpful to the marketer. Different categories of products require different marketing approaches and strategies. Products can be classified into two distinct categories: consumer products and industrial products. **Consumer products** are those products purchased by individuals for their personal use. Clothing, home appliances, food items, personal travel, and life insurance are examples of consumer products. **Industrial products** are those purchased by extractors, manufacturers, service firms, and nonprofit organizations for use in running their businesses. Computer equipment, business insurance, office supplies, telephone service, and machinery are all examples of industrial products.

Some products can be classified as either a consumer or an industrial product, depending on the intended usage. A house cleaning service, for example, might buy cleaning products for use in their business. In this case the cleaning products would be classified as industrial products. If these same cleaning products were purchased by a family for use in their home, they would be classified as consumer products. Consumer products are discussed in greater detail in Chapter 6. Industrial products are discussed in Chapter 7.

BRANDING AND TRADEMARKS

The majority of products are identified by a brand of some type. A **brand** can be defined as a name, sign, symbol, design, or combination of these elements which identifies a product or service. The purpose of a brand is to differentiate the product or service of one manufacturer or seller from those of competitors. In the most simple terms a brand is a way a business identifies its products or services to its customers.

A **trademark** is a brand or part of a brand which has been granted legal protection by the U.S. Patent Office. When a ™ follows the brand this means that the business or organization has applied for registration of its brand with the U.S. Patent Office. Once a brand has been officially approved, the business or organization is given a registered trademark and an ® is placed behind the brand. Both a ™ and an ® protect the brand name, sign, symbol, or design from being used by any other business or organization. Illustration 5-1 shows a Levi Strauss and Company Levi's® 501® jean brand label. Two parts of the label are identified for protection by registration with the U.S. Patent Office: Levi's® and 501®.

Illustration 5-1 Levi's® brand label depicts the use of trademark registration.

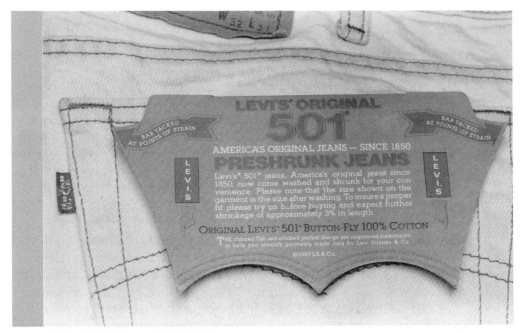

LEVI STRAUSS & COMPANY

Classification of Brands

Brands can be classified as either national or private. A **national brand** is a manufacturer's branded product sold on a nationwide basis. Manhattan shirts, Levi jeans, Sunkist oranges, White Westinghouse appliances, and Del Monte vegetables are examples of nationally branded products. A **private brand** is a product sold under a brand name created by individual retailers. Craftsman tools sold by Sears, Janet Lee food products marketed by Albertson's supermarkets, and Scotch Boy products sold at Safeway stores are all examples of privately branded products.

Brands can also be classified as family brands and individual brands. A **family brand** means that the seller will use the same brand on its entire product line. Heinz 57 Variety, General Electric, and Campbell Soups are examples of family brands. An **individual brand** means that the product is known by its own name rather than the name of the company producing the product. General Motors utilizes an individual branding policy with such brand names as Buick, Oldsmobile, Chevrolet, and Cadillac. Procter and Gamble produces ten different laundry detergents, each of which is marketed under its own brand name.

Purposes of Branding

Businesses and organizations use branding for two primary reasons. The first and most important of these is to identify the manufacturer or seller. Organizations spend millions of dollars annually in advertising and packaging to insure that customers can recognize the products or services that they market by their brand names. For example, the Texaco Corporation identifies its retail service station outlets with a large red Texaco Star. To many customers, this star stands for a uniform quality petroleum product which has a strong national reputation.

The second reason for branding relates to the ease with which a manufacturer or seller can introduce a new product or service to the marketplace. When an organization uses an existing brand name to facilitate or help with new product introductions, it is referred to as **brand extension.** In this manner an organization can use the reputation of its older established brand to help establish and promote the quality of new products it is introducing. The Levi Strauss Company provides a good example of this use of branding. When Levi introduces a new clothing item or line that carries the Levi brand, they are attempting to use or ride on the reputation of their previously successful products.

PRODUCT PACKAGING

When you think of merchandise sitting on the shelf of a supermarket you usually visualize the package the product comes in rather than the actual product itself. For example, when you think of the toothpaste you use, what do you see? Chances are good that you see a familiar brand name such as Crest or Colgate on the package and tube and not the actual toothpaste.

Without packaging it would be very difficult to market many of the products that we enjoy on an everyday basis. Packaging is so important that it has led some to refer to this activity as the fifth "P" of marketing. U.S. manufacturers spend billions of dollars annually on packaging. The costs of some sophisticated product packages may actually exceed the value of the enclosed product itself. Self-service retailing in combination with new packaging materials and techniques have been the primary forces behind the growth and importance of packaging.

There are four primary functions of packaging. First, the package provides physical protection to the product from the time it is manufactured until it is consumed. Second, product packaging provides important product information for consumers. In a self-service retail environment, the information contained on the package becomes critical in helping to sell products to customers. In Illustration 5-2 notice the different types of product information that are included as part of the product packages.

Illustration 5-2   The product's package often contains important product information for the consumer.

The third function of packaging is to help provide product differentiation at the point of the sale to the ultimate consumer. The product's package must catch the customer's eye and stimulate interest and desire for purchasing the product. When a customer walks through a supermarket which carries thousands of different products, packaging becomes critically important. The fourth function of packaging is to establish an image for the product. Expensive jewelry may be packaged in a leather case, not because the leather case provides better protection, but because the leather case sends the message that the product is of high quality.

▲ THE IMPORTANCE OF PRODUCT OR SERVICE INFORMATION

Many of the marketing careers mentioned in Chapter 3 involve direct contact with potential customers. Sales personnel have frequent, direct contact with customers. Thus, they should be familiar with the facts or features of the products or services they are selling. This knowledge alone is not enough. Sales personnel must also be able to convert information into benefits customers will receive when they purchase a product or service. A **customer benefit** is what a product or service will or may do for a customer. Customers are not interested in buying facts or features only; they are interested in buying advantages and satisfaction.

Generally the more complex or complicated a product or service is the more information customers require. Hence, a salesperson must have the appropriate level of knowledge of the product or service. Compare, for example, the level and amount of product knowledge required to sell a microcomputer with that required to sell a simple calculator. Customers today are sophisticated; they are capable of making informed buying decisions and expect sales personnel to provide the necessary information. Thus, customers demand expertise from salespeople.

A successful marketing effort requires meeting customer needs and wants. Sales personnel attempt to match these needs and wants with the characteristics and uses of available products or services. The first task of a salesperson, then, is to determine the needs and wants of the customer. The second task is to supply the appropriate product or service information required to satisfy these needs and wants.

Knowledge of the products or services available is important for the following reasons.

1. A well-planned sales presentation is based on a thorough knowledge of the product or service.
2. Most marketing activities occur within a competitive environment. Marketing businesses that employ knowledgeable salespeople often have a competitive edge over other businesses.
3. Product or service knowledge helps salespeople answer questions intelligently and overcome customer objections.
4. Buyer confidence and satisfaction are increased if products or services are purchased from marketing businesses that employ knowledgeable salespeople.
5. Product or service knowledge helps the salesperson develop self-confidence. As a result, sales productivity is likely to increase.
6. Knowledgeable salespeople sell larger quantities of products and services, thus increasing sales productivity.

THE PRODUCT-SERVICE MIX

In previous chapters references have been made to businesses which market either products or services. Actually the product-service mix offered by most marketing businesses is more complex. A **product** is a tangible item; it can be seen, handled, or consumed. It is produced, grown, or extracted. A **service** is intangible and is performed rather than produced. A **product-service mix** is the sum of all the products and/or services offered by a business.

Some marketing businesses offer only products. Self-service convenience stores, for example, generally sell products that do not require any accompanying services. Other marketing businesses, such as insurance and real estate companies, market only services. Most services, however, do require supporting goods. A house painter's skill is of little value if the painter does not have access to paints and equipment.

On the other hand, most products also require supporting services. For example, a submarine sandwich has value because of the accompanying services offered by the delicatessen where it is sold. Someone has to make the sandwich, serve it, and provide eating utensils before it can be useful to a customer.

Thus, there are four types of product-service mixes: completely product, product with supporting services, service with supporting products, and completely service. The following sections will describe each of these mixes.

Completely Product

Businesses that have this type of product-service mix market products that do not require any supporting services. There are thousands of products without additional services attached that are useful to customers. These are generally sold in self-service outlets, by direct mail, and through catalogs. They can be utilized by customers without special directions and purchased without the help of salespeople. Examples of a few products in this category are grocery store items, simple clothing items, toiletries, books and magazines, automobile cleaning products, and small appliances.

Product with Supporting Services

Marketing businesses with this type of product-service mix offer goods that may require supporting services to make them valuable to consumers. These goods are usually complex and generally are purchased with the assistance of sales personnel. Examples of products in this category are men's and women's expensive clothing which

Illustration 5-3

Some products require supporting services to make them valuable to consumers.

may require color coordination and alteration, camping equipment, cameras, automobiles and trucks, recreational vehicles and boats, major appliances, office equipment, stereo equipment, and computer equipment. Many of the products in this category are covered by product warranties, require installation, offer alteration services, and provide extensive assistance including product demonstrations by sales personnel. The related services that are provided with these products often govern customer decisions to deal with a particular company instead of a competitor.

Service with Supporting Products

Companies that market services requiring supporting products have this type of product-service mix. Many services need accompanying products in order to have value. If you employ an interior decorator to help you plan your home furnishings, you may be im-

Illustration 5-4

Automobile technicians combine their skills with parts and equipment to provide a service to customers.

pressed by the knowledge and skill of the person marketing this service. However, you also have to be satisfied with the products recommended by the interior decorator. Other examples of businesses that market services requiring supporting products are hospitals, hair styling salons, house painters, automobile service stations and repair shops, auto body shops, and recreation and tourism agencies.

▲ Completely Service

Companies that offer services that do not need supporting products have this type of product-service mix. When you buy an insurance policy, you buy protection. The only tangible item is the insurance policy itself. If you use an investment broker to invest your money, you are buying the broker's services. Examples of completely service-oriented businesses are insurance companies, brokerage firms, banks and savings and loans, and in-home childcare workers.

▲ WHAT SALES PERSONNEL SHOULD KNOW ABOUT PRODUCTS OR SERVICES

There are many things salespeople need to know about the products or services marketed by their employers. This information helps them make successful sales presentations including effectively responding to customer questions and objections. Although customer questions and objections are usually specific, they most often fall into one of the general categories identified in Figure 5-2.

▲ SOURCES OF INFORMATION ABOUT PRODUCTS OR SERVICES

Keeping informed about products or services is a continuous activity. A number of sources of product or service information are available to salespeople. Some marketing businesses conduct specialized training programs or seminars that are designed specifically to supply current information on products and services to sales personnel. Other businesses expect supervisors, buyers, or more experienced sales personnel to work with salespeople on an individual basis to help them acquire the latest information.

Figure 5-2   Categories of questions and objections consumers might raise during
a sales presentation.

CATEGORIES OF QUESTIONS AND OBJECTIONS

PRODUCTS	SERVICES
How will this product meet my needs?	How will this service meet my needs?
How is it constructed?	What are the advantages and disadvantages of buying this service?
How do I take care of this product?	What are the risks if I buy this service?
What is the warranty?	What is the scope and duration of the service?
How do I use this product?	How do I use this service?
How does it work?	How does it work?
How much does this product cost and is it economical?	How much does this service cost and is it economical?
How does this product compare to those offered by the competition?	How does this service compare to those offered by the competition?
What is the reputation of the manufacturer?	What is the reputation of the supplier?
What services usually accompany this product?	What products usually accompany this service?

Companies that manufacture complex products or provide complicated services—home computers, heavy industrial equipment, financial investment services—usually conduct periodic training seminars and also provide loose-leaf manuals that are kept current by means of periodic supplements containing the latest technical information.

Sales personnel can also learn a great deal about products or services on their own. **Trade publications** are specialized magazines for specific industries. They often contain technical articles on new products or services that are being introduced to the market. Information can also be gained by reading popular magazines such as *Consumer Reports* or *Better Homes and Gardens.*

Examination of the products is another valuable source of information. Sales personnel should practice using any product that will be demonstrated for customers. They should read the labels on products or packages and the descriptive literature that is usually included in packages.

Illustration 5-5

Specialized training programs or seminars supply current product or service information to sales personnel.

The product label for a Samsonite® Silhouette® 4 suitcase is shown in Illustration 5-6. This label contains a variety of information which could be useful in making a sales presentation and answering customers' questions. In only a few moments a conscientious salesperson could read the label and translate the information given into customer benefits. The following information appears on the label:

1. Brand Name:
   Samsonite® Silhouette® 4
2. Product Characteristics:
   Durable Absolite® shell
   Retractable pull strap
   Removable plastic-lined pocket
   Shock absorbing bumpers
   Covered exterior compartment
   Four sturdy wheels
   Divider pad, tie tapes, and packing bar
3. Size:
   26″ Valet
4. Product Construction:
   Laboratory tested exterior
   Heavy duty hardware
   Recessed latches and wheels
   Puncture and tear resistant materials
5. Warranty:
   Full three-year warranty

Illustration 5-6   A variety of useful sales information is often contained on a product
label.

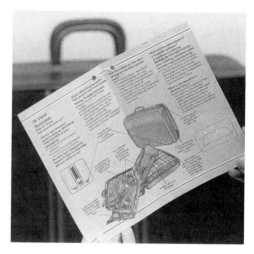

Samsonite Corporation

Information can also be gained by observing what competitors are
offering and by listening to customer comments. A salesperson's own
experience as a consumer can also be a valuable source of product or
service information.

USING PRODUCT OR SERVICE INFORMATION SUCCESSFULLY

Product or service knowledge alone will not guarantee success in
selling. Knowledge is essential, but skillful use of knowledge can
make the difference between an average and a superior salesperson.
Thus, when dealing directly with customers, there are three things to
keep in mind.

Learn as Much as You Can

First, learn as much as you can about the products or services you
are marketing. It is not necessary to memorize volumes of facts;
rather, significant facts that probably will be of interest to the buyer
should be gathered and studied. This set of facts or features should be
organized so that it will be available for use during the sales presentation. You may not need to use all the facts you have gathered for
every customer. As a guide, ask yourself the following questions: Is

this buyer interested in this product or service information? Will the information affect the customer's purchasing decision?

▲ Determine What the Customer Already Knows About the Product or Service

Second, before using the information you have collected in a sales presentation, attempt to determine how much the customer already knows about the particular product or service. Some customers will know nothing about the product or service; others may have previously purchased and used similar products or services. The best way to find out what information you will need to present is to question the customer regarding his or her familiarity with the product or service. You can then determine which facts to include in your sales presentation.

▲ Turn Product or Service Facts into Customer Benefits

Finally, keep in mind that customers are not interested in product or service facts or features only. As a salesperson, you not only provide information for customers, you convert it into benefits that buyers will receive when they purchase the product or service. In order to accomplish this, you should complete a fact-feature benefit analysis form for each major product or service you are responsible for selling.

Preparing a **fact-feature benefit analysis** for a specific product or service is not a difficult task and requires only two steps. First, take a sheet of paper and list the significant facts or features of the product or service on the left. Second, for each fact or feature you have listed, identify a customer benefit on the right. For example, if you are selling a digital clock radio, its battery backup system is a fact or feature of importance to potential customers. The benefit is that customers do not have to worry about power failures that will cause the clock to stop and lose time. Thus, this feature provides peace of mind. Customers benefit because they know that the clock radio will function even when there is a power failure. Figure 5-3 provides an example of a fact-feature benefit analysis of a product, a telephone answering machine. Figure 5-4 provides a similar example for a service, a package delivery firm.

Keep completed fact-feature benefit analysis forms in a notebook or file folder for future reference. When business is slow, review these forms to learn more about the products or services you are selling.

Add fact-feature benefit analysis forms to your notebook or folder for new and different products or services.

Preparing the fact-feature benefit analysis forces salespeople to translate product or service information into corresponding customer benefits. Thus, it helps them prepare for sales presentations and develop self-confidence. Customers have more faith in knowledgeable and confident sales personnel.

Figure 5-3   A fact-feature benefit analysis for a telephone answering machine.

PRODUCT: TELEPHONE ANSWERING MACHINE
COST: $69.95

FACT OR FEATURE	CUSTOMER BENEFIT
1. One-touch control	1. You will find it simple to operate.
2. Remote turn-on	2. You can check to see if you have messages from any location by simply dialing your own telephone number from a touch tone telephone.
3. Message counter	3. You can easily tell the number of messages you have received.
4. Personalized greeting	4. You can personalize your greeting and change it as often as you like.
5. Voice activation	5. Your callers can leave a message up to 5 minutes in length.
6. Call screening	6. When you are at home this feature allows you to hear the messages and answer only if you choose.
7. Inexpensive	7. You will spend less than if you purchased a comparable machine with similar features.
8. Compact and attractive case	8. It will look good in any location in your home.
9. One-year warranty	9. If you have any problems with the answering machine within one year, it can be returned to the dealer, who will exchange it for a new machine.

Figure 5-4   A fact-feature benefit analysis for a package delivery service.

SERVICE: PACKAGE DELIVERY SERVICE
COST: VARIABLE DEPENDING ON THE SIZE OF THE PACKAGE SHIPPED AND THE METHOD OF SHIPMENT CHOSEN.

FACT OR FEATURE	CUSTOMER BENEFIT
1. All sizes of boxes available for shipment of packages.	1. You will no longer need to spend time searching for boxes.
2. Packaging materials available including tape, packing materials, and shipping labels.	2. You are confident that packages will be securely held together and will not break apart during transit.
3. Professional assistance in packaging shipments.	3. You eliminate the hassle of having to prepare your own packages for shipment. Also assures that packages will meet any shipping regulations.
4. Adequate free vehicle parking near office.	4. It is easy to carry your packages to our office for shipment from nearby parking spaces.
5. Variety of shipping methods.	5. Different shipping time requirements can easily be met by choosing different shipping methods. You don't have to worry about missing deadlines.
6. Located near major shopping center; within 20 minutes of 90% of the homes in the region.	6. You won't need to drive very far.
7. Moving dolly available for heavy packages.	7. You will avoid injury when moving heavy or clumsy packages.
8. Low service charges.	8. You pay only a small charge in exchange for eliminating the trouble of having to pack your own packages.
9. Automatic insurance coverage.	9. The free $200 insurance coverage for each parcel shipped reduces your worry.

APPLYING MARKETING TERMS

Name _____

Match each term with the statement that best describes an application of that term. Write the letter in the space provided.

a. product life cycle
b. private brand
c. industrial product
d. brand
e. product-service mix
f. national brand

g. fact-feature benefit analysis
h. trademark
i. consumer product
j. service
k. family brand
l. individual brand

_____ 1. Dial soap, marketed at retailers across the U.S., is an example of this type of a brand.

_____ 2. Homeowners purchase this intangible when they contract with a real estate agency to sell their home.

_____ 3. A product branding system where an entire product line carries the same brand name, such as Campbell Soups.

_____ 4. A term used to describe the sum of all of the products and/or services offered by an organization.

_____ 5. A product branding system where a product is known by its own name, such as Tide laundry detergent.

_____ 6. A tool that can be used by sales personnel to better understand the products or services they are selling.

_____ 7. A parent who goes to the supermarket to get milk and bread for dinner is buying this type of product.

_____ 8. A clerk who orders paper for the copy machines is purchasing this type of product.

_____ 9. Consumer product manufacturers often use this identifying name, symbol, or sign to differentiate their products from competitors.

_____ 10. A designation given to a brand when its registration has been requested from the U.S. Patent Office.

_____ 11. A retailer might choose to have some products branded in this fashion to increase store loyalty.

_____ 12. A cycle that all products or services go through, beginning when they are introduced and ending with their actual decline.

MASTERING KEY CONCEPTS

Name _____

Answer each of the following questions in the space provided.

1. Explain each of the four stages of the product life cycle.

2. Explain the differences between an industrial product and a consumer product.

3. Explain the difference between the designations ™ and ® in product branding.

4. Explain the differences between a national brand, a private brand, an individual brand, and a family brand.

5. Identify the two major purposes of branding.

6. List and explain the four major purposes of product packaging.

7. Explain the following statement: *Customers are not interested in buying facts or features only; they are interested in buying advantages and satisfaction.*

8. List three reasons why a salesperson's knowledge of products or services is important.

9. Identify the four types of product-service mixes.

10. Give examples of information that salespeople should know about their products or services in order to respond to customer questions.

11. Explain how sales personnel can gain product and service information on their own.

12. List three things to keep in mind when using product or service information to assure an effective sales presentation.

DEVELOPING PEOPLE SKILLS

Read the following description of a human relations situation. Then complete your answers on a separate piece of paper.

The Compact Car Crisis

Economy Car Rentals is known for its discount rates. Michelle Healey is the manager of a branch office of Economy Car Rentals. Economy maintains three classes of cars—full size, intermediate, and compact—that rent for different rates. The branch office, however, has more full- and intermediate-size cars available than it does compact cars. Since the compact cars have the lowest rental rates the office usually rents all these by noon each day. The company's policy is to upgrade customers to the next class of car, with the customer being responsible for the additional rental charge.

On a recent afternoon, a customer appeared at the rental counter and asked to rent a compact car. The rental agent on duty, Mark Sanchez, politely informed the customer that there were no compact cars remaining that day but he would be happy to rent him an intermediate-size car for an additional $12 a day. The customer insisted that he should be able to substitute an intermediate-size car at no extra charge. Mark Sanchez explained that this was not company policy. He repeated that he would be pleased to rent him an intermediate-size car for the slightly higher rate. The customer then asked to speak with the manager.

Ms. Healey introduced herself and asked what she could do to help. He responded, "Simply rent me the intermediate-size car at the compact rate and there won't be a problem." Ms. Healey replied gruffly, "You evidently didn't understand our company policy regarding upgrading to more expensive cars. I thought that Mr. Sanchez had explained that to you. I'm afraid we don't have a choice." At this point the customer commented that he would no longer do business with Economy Car Rentals and left the agency in a huff.

1. What is the main problem in this case?
2. In serving this customer, were there alternative courses of action available to Ms. Healey or Mr. Sanchez? If so, how could this problem have been handled differently?
3. How was the problem handled by Mark Sanchez?
4. How was the problem handled by Michelle Healey?
5. Would Mark Sanchez have been more successful with this customer if he had presented the advantages of renting an intermediate-size car? Why?

MARKETING PROJECT 5

Use the blank form below and your own paper to complete this project.

Preparing and Using a Fact-Feature Benefit Analysis

Step 1. Using a product or service of your choice or one provided by your teacher, complete the fact-feature benefit analysis form below. List at least five facts or features and their corresponding customer benefits.

Step 2. On a separate sheet of paper, explain how you could use the information in your fact-feature benefit analysis to convince customers that the product or service will meet their needs.

PRODUCT OR SERVICE:
COST:

FACT OR FEATURE	CUSTOMER BENEFIT

MARKETING INSIGHT

Read the following description of real-life marketing practices. Then complete your answers on a separate piece of paper.

Convenience vs. Environment

The Colgate-Palmolive Co. (Colgate) has introduced Palmolive dishwashing detergent in soft plastic pouches. The flexible Palmolive pouches are designed to be used with refillable containers, and each will come emblazoned with a "Protect Our Planet" logo. Procter & Gamble (P&G) is also readying a similar package for one of its detergent brands. For U.S. consumers, the containers will look and perform differently than anything they've ever seen. The adoption of refillable packaging by major marketers signals an entirely new era of detergent marketing.

The environmental issue has moved to the forefront of consumer consciousness. Prodded by calls for legislation that would ban plastic containers, marketers are scrambling to import overseas technologies acceptable to U.S. shoppers. And the packaging changes in detergents are only the beginning. The containers are all designed as refills for plastic bottles, which consumers will no longer toss in the trash.

But Colgate and P&G must first overcome consumer resistance. Many consumers will find the new packaging hard to handle. For all their environmental concern, American shoppers are notoriously resistant to packaging overhauls and the bells-and-whistles of fancy containers. "We've got to study consumer reaction," says Robert Murray, Colgate's corporate communications director. "In the U.S., people have been so oriented to convenience that there's some question whether they'll do something less convenient for the sake of the environment."[1]

1. What impact do you think the new refillable containers will have on product sales? Why?
2. Why would a company such as Colgate be concerned with the effect their packaging has on the environment?
3. Why is test marketing important to the organizations introducing refillable packages?

---

[1]Dan Koeppel, "Colgate Goes 'Green' With Palmolive in a Bag," *Adweek's Marketing News* (23 October 1989), p. 3.

CHAPTER 6
CONSUMER BUYING BEHAVIOR

After you read this chapter and complete the activities at the end, you will be able to:

1. **Describe the steps in the consumer decision process.**
2. **Discuss factors that influence consumer buying behavior.**
3. **Describe the three classifications of consumer products.**

Did you ever think about all the steps you go through before deciding which product or service to buy? Heidi realized she had a problem when the hand-me-down stereo system her older brother gave her stopped working. She decided she needed a new system because she was used to going into her room, closing the door, and listening to her favorite music. She had some savings she could use to pay for the stereo. The problem was that Heidi didn't know what to buy.

She needed some information to help her decide exactly what she wanted in a sound system. Heidi also started making a list of the brands she wanted to consider. She talked to friends who had recently bought new sound systems. She even consulted publications and reports that compare the quality, price, and options on various sound systems. She obtained additional information from newspaper advertisements and by talking to salespeople knowledgeable about the product. When Heidi had collected all this information, she thought she knew what to look for when she went shopping for a new sound system.

Heidi started shopping and comparing several different brands and models. She decided she would consider only those systems that were within a certain price range. She couldn't afford the most expensive model. At the same time, she didn't want to buy the least expensive one because she did not believe her friends would do that, and she did not want to do anything her friends wouldn't do. Heidi was also interested in a model that had a good reputation, was small enough to fit on the bookcase in her room, and had some of the features her friends recommended. She went to various types of stores including electronics stores, discount stores, and department stores.

When she felt she had done enough shopping, Heidi decided that she was ready to buy. She made the purchase at a store in town that people regarded as a good place to do business. The unit she bought included an AM/FM stereo tuner, a compact disc player, and a dual cassette deck. It was also within her price range.

Heidi took the sound system home and set it up in her room. She put on a tape and listened to the music. She wanted to make sure the system sounded as good at home as it did in the store's sound room. She wanted to make sure she had made the right purchase decision. As it turned out, she liked the sound system she bought and she told her relatives and friends how satisfied she was.

THE CONSUMER DECISION PROCESS

When people make a decision about what goods and services to buy, they go through a series of steps called the **consumer decision process.** Heidi went through this process when deciding which sound system to buy.

The steps in the consumer decision process are:

1. Problem recognition.
2. Information search.
3. Evaluation of alternatives.
4. Purchase.
5. Postpurchase evaluation.

The five steps of the consumer decision process are explained in more detail in the following sections.

Problem Recognition

Problem recognition occurs when consumers realize there is a discrepancy between the existing state of affairs (the way things are) and the desired state of affairs (the way they would like things to be). Once consumers recognize the problem, they are motivated to achieve the desired state. This often means buying the product or service that will fill the need.

Problem recognition may occur over a period of time, or it may happen quickly, such as when a driver gets in the car and notices that the fuel gauge is pointing to empty. Heidi recognized a problem when her old sound system stopped working and she wanted to continue listening to music in the privacy of her room. For a product like shampoo, problem recognition may occur when you realize that the current bottle is empty.

Advertisements or personal selling may trigger problem recognition. For example, a company's television commercials may try to convince consumers they have a particular need and then offer a product or service to fill that need. Also, the problem recognition step to buy a new car could start when a friend or relative buys a new one.

Information Search

After a person recognizes a problem or need, the next step is **information search,** or the gathering of information related to the problem or need. In many cases, the search for information will yield an **evoked set,** which is a group of brands that a consumer actually considers and gathers information about.

Heidi knew she needed a new sound system, but she didn't know which system to buy. She gathered information by talking to friends and salespeople and by reading comparison studies and advertisements. She started shopping when she felt she had sufficient information and knew which brands she wanted to look at in the stores.

Evaluation of Alternatives

The third step in the consumer decision process involves the evaluation of the alternatives identified during the search for information. The outcome of this step is the choice of the product or service to buy. Therefore, it is important to identify the **choice criteria,** which are the product or service characteristics used in evaluating the various alternatives. Some commonly used choice criteria are the reputation of the brand, price, size, and features available.

Regarding choice criteria, Heidi considered only those systems that were in a certain price range, had a good reputation, were small enough to fit on the bookcase in her room, and had some of the features her friends recommended. She went to various types of stores, including electronics stores, discount stores, and department stores, shopping for the unit that met her criteria.

Purchase

As a result of searching for information and evaluating alternatives, the consumer decides what to buy by narrowing the alternatives down to one. In some cases, the consumer may have to be prepared to buy the second-ranked choice because the first choice is not available.

Once you have decided to purchase a particular product or service, you must decide where you will buy it. The factors that influence this choice about where you will buy are called **patronage motives.** Some common patronage motives are (1) reputation of the seller, (2) past experience, (3) store personnel, (4) price, (5) service, (6) location, and (7) the merchandise carried.

- *Reputation of the seller.* Is the seller respected in the community? What do your friends and family say about the store? Do they regard it as a good place to shop?
- *Past experience.* How do you describe your experience(s) with the business? Do you think your patronage was appreciated?
- *Store personnel.* Are the employees knowledgeable about the products or services? Are they friendly and helpful?
- *Prices.* How do prices compare with those charged by similar stores? If prices are higher, do you believe that you get more value for your money?
- *Services.* Are services such as free assembly or free repair provided within a reasonable time? Does the store offer other supporting services such as delivery, check-cashing privileges, or charge accounts?
- *Location.* Is the business easy to reach? Is parking space available?
- *Merchandise carried.* Does the store carry a wide assortment of merchandise in various colors or styles? Are you able to compare several models or prices? Does the store carry the brand you prefer?

Heidi took patronage motives into consideration when she decided to buy her sound system from a store that people in town recommended as a good place to do business.

▲ Postpurchase Evaluation

Consumer decision making does not end with the purchase of the product or service. The final step in the process involves an evaluation of the purchase decision. In this step, called **postpurchase evaluation,** consumers consider how satisfied or dissatisfied they are with the product or service.

As noted earlier, problem recognition occurs when consumers realize there is a discrepancy between the existing state of affairs and the desired state of affairs. They are then motivated to achieve the desired state. This usually means buying a product or service that will fill the need.

During the postpurchase evaluation, consumers may ask themselves: Does the product fill the need as expected? Satisfied customers may buy the product or service again and also tell others of their satisfaction. Dissatisfied customers may switch to another brand or company and are likely to tell others of their dissatisfaction.

Heidi wanted to make sure she made the right purchase decision when she bought her sound system. She listened to it when she took it home and decided that she liked it. She also told her relatives and friends how satisfied she was.

After making a purchase, some consumers have second thoughts. They may regret making the purchase or wish they had chosen another alternative. Marketers who are aware of this can reassure consumers by providing product guarantees, advertisements showing satisfied customers, or toll-free telephone numbers customers may use to obtain answers to product or service questions.

In some cases, all five steps in the consumer decision process are used, while in others only a few steps are needed. For example, the purchase of a sound system requires more in the way of decision making than the purchase of a box of breakfast cereal.

The five-step consumer decision process assumes that the end result is the purchase of a product or service by the consumer. At any point in the process, however, a potential consumer may decide not to buy. The product or service may turn out to be unnecessary, unsatisfactory, or too expensive.

◣ INFLUENCES ON CONSUMER BUYING BEHAVIOR

Consumers direct their buying behavior toward meeting their needs and wants. **Needs** are those things considered essential to human existence. **Wants** are felt needs that are shaped by a person's knowledge, culture, and personality. For example, all people need food, but a person's culture largely determines what he or she will want to eat to satisfy that need. You probably realize that it is easy to confuse the definitions of needs and wants. Even the experts do not agree on the exact meanings of the two words. In this text we will use the two terms interchangeably.

Consumer buying behavior consists of the decisions people make in buying products and services. Marketers have identified the following factors that influence consumer buying behavior: (1) motivation, (2) lifestyle, (3) family, (4) reference groups, (5) social class, and (6) culture.

Motivation

Motivation is an internal force that causes a person to take the action necessary to satisfy a need. A **buying motive** is anything that prompts a consumer to make a purchase. Using various research methods, marketers try to find out the "whys" or motives of consumer buying behavior. If they can identify these motives and develop appropriate marketing mixes, they can generate consumer motivation to buy.

Maslow's Hierarchy of Needs. Abraham Maslow, a psychologist, grouped needs into five categories: physical needs, safety needs, social needs, esteem needs, and self-actualization needs.[1] Each category is a cluster of specific needs. As shown in Figure 6-1, Maslow arranged these five categories into a **hierarchy of needs** in which needs are ranked from bottom to top in the order they must be satisfied. According to Maslow, people always have needs and when a lower-level need has been satisfied (and is no longer a strong source of motivation), a person will be motivated to satisfy the next highest need.

Physical needs are the primary needs for food, shelter, and clothing. They are basic to survival and must be satisfied first. A restaurant's advertisement for a juicy steak appeals to the need for food.

Figure 6-1.   Maslow's hierarchy of needs.

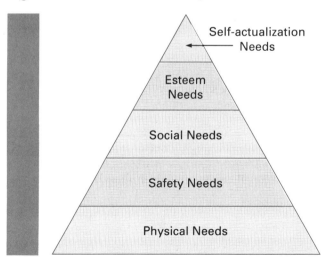

---

[1]Based on A. H. Maslow, *Motivation and Personality,* 2d ed. (New York: Harper & Row, 1970).

Once these physical needs have been met, the next highest need can be considered.

Safety needs include protection against danger, insecurity, illness, and pain. Smoke detector and burglar alarm manufacturers focus on these needs, as do insurance companies and providers of travelers checks.

Social needs are concerned with love, belonging, and friendship. In other words, it is the desire to be accepted by members of the family and other people and groups. In an effort to meet this need and be accepted by a particular group, a person may decide to wear only those clothes that conform to that group's standard of dress. Social needs may also influence the choice of hair style and prompt consumers to buy toothpaste and perfume.

Esteem needs are the needs for recognition, achievement, and accomplishment. The person desires to stand out from the crowd in some way. This desire to be different from others often influences purchasing decisions. In a neighborhood where one house looks like all the others, a homeowner might landscape the front yard in a distinctive way. Sometimes people buy stylish, unique, or expensive items as a way of gaining recognition from family members, friends, or co-workers. You may know people who buy their clothes at exclusive shops that have a reputation for carrying the latest fashions. Others display their individuality by listening to music that does not conform to the tastes of other members of their families.

Self-actualization needs involve personal fulfillment. This category can be thought of as the top of the pyramid of human needs because it relates to the maximum use of one's skills, abilities, and creativity.

Education, certain types of vacations, competitive sports, and the U.S. Army's slogan, "Be all that you can be" appeal to the need for self-actualization.

The need for creative self-expression has inspired many people to refinish old pieces of furniture, take piano lessons, assemble clocks from kits, or hook rugs. Countless others have purchased do-it-yourself books to teach themselves various crafts. The need for creativity motivates people to enroll in art or photography courses.

Emotional Buying Motives. Social, esteem, and self-actualization needs become **emotional buying motives** when they influence consumers to make purchases to satisfy emotional needs. You could say that these motives stem more from the heart than from the head. The decisions are often made with little or no conscious reasoning or thought involved.

Rational Buying Motives. Rational buying motives influence consumer behavior when purchasing decisions involve conscious thought and deliberation. A buyer identifies and weighs the arguments for and against a purchase. A number of rational buying motives may be involved in a purchasing decision, including (1) dependability, (2) convenience, (3) low purchase price, and (4) economy of operation.

Dependability. A dependable product or service provides reliable and consistent performance. For example, a consumer may want to buy a specific type of automobile battery because it is known for its dependability; it operates effectively in cold as well as hot weather. Many people may decide to use a bus service as their method of transportation to and from work because it consistently runs on schedule.

Convenience. How convenient a product or service is depends on how well it meets a particular customer's needs. A remote control garage door opener is often convenient, especially on rainy days. Foods that require only a few minutes in the microwave oven are convenient for those unable to spend more time preparing meals.

Low Purchase Price. The most common rational buying motive is low or bargain purchase prices. Consumers interested in buying at reduced prices are motivated to shop for clothing and other items at clearance sales. Price conscious consumers often plan new car purchases for late in the model year. Prior to the introduction of new models, car dealers often lower their prices in order to clear their showrooms and lots and make room for the new cars.

Economy of Operation. Economy of operation refers to the low cost of using and maintaining equipment. Cost conscious consumers pay close attention to gas mileage estimates when buying a car. The initial cost of buying and installing a solar heating system in a home is greater than the initial cost of natural gas or electric heating systems. Homeowners with solar heating systems, however, realize substantial savings on their monthly utility bills. The solar heating system is more economical to use than either natural gas or electric heating systems.

◣ Lifestyles

Lifestyles are the patterns that people follow in their lives. Your lifestyle is determined not only by your activities and interests but also by the opinions you have of yourself and the world around you. Because your lifestyle is how you spend your time and your money, it is easy to see that it can affect your behavior as a consumer.

Some of the recent trends in the United States include a shift toward a healthy, natural lifestyle and toward individualism. Marketers have responded to these trends in several ways.

Companies selling camping equipment and sporting goods have a ready market in the many people who enjoy the outdoor lifestyle. Many healthy and all-natural food products have been introduced over the last several years. Familiar examples are foods that are low in calories, fat, cholesterol, and salt. At the same time, makers of existing food items began emphasizing their products' nutritional benefits. Restaurants, including some fast food establishments, have advertised the nutritional values of their various menu items. Companies may be able to appeal to the individualism and personal independence of consumers by using celebrities in their advertisements who are known as individualists.

▲ Family

The **family life cycle** describes the series of life stages through which many people pass. These life stages are childhood, marriage, childrearing, and the dissolving of the marriage through death or divorce. Certain products and services are more likely to be used during certain life cycle stages than others. For example, baby food, tricycles, and music lessons are purchased for those in childhood. When people marry and form a household, they may buy furniture, major appliances, and life and health insurance. If they have children, they will become the purchasers of various childhood items. Later in life, when the children have left home to set up their own households, they may move into a smaller home or a retirement community and spend more money on vacations.

Marketers must also consider the **singles market,** made up of people who have never married, separated couples, surviving spouses, and divorced people. Specific purchasing needs of singles will depend on such factors as age and whether children reside in the household.

Because both husband and wife are likely to be working outside the home, either or both may be found shopping for the family. In addition, teenagers are doing more and more of the family shopping. Those responsible for cooking and cleaning may even decide which foods and cleaning products to buy.

Reference Groups

Your behavior, including your buying behavior, is probably influenced by one or more reference groups. A **reference group** is any group of people that influences a person's attitudes or behavior. People identify with or aspire to become members of this group. Groups, such as those at school or at work, are used by people as reference points in determining their own beliefs, attitudes, values, and behavior.

The importance of reference groups in consumer buying behavior often depends on the type of product. In general, the more conspicuous or visible a product is, the more important the influence of the reference group will be. This is particularly true when possession of the item carries with it a certain amount of status. For example, high school students attain status through owning a car. This is because the reference group, which consists of other students with whom they associate, value possession of a car. Also, some cars carry more status in the group than others.

By identifying the reference groups that affect consumers, marketers can adapt their marketing mixes for those consumers. For example, television advertisements that show products and services being used by college students, successful professionals, or physically-fit people often ask viewers to join the group and make a similar purchase.

Social Class

Social class is the group people belong to according to their prestige and power in society. A person's occupation, source of income, education, and family background determine his or her social class. Social classes are commonly categorized as upper, upper-middle, lower-middle, working, and lower.

The social class the consumer belongs to influences what is purchased. People in the upper and upper-middle classes are often the best customers for financial investments, original art, expensive cars, and luxury vacations. In comparison, lower-middle class people are the main customers of home improvement centers and auto parts stores. While people in the upper classes tend to read literary, travel, and news magazines, lower and working class people generally prefer sports and romance magazines.

Culture

As described in Chapter 2, culture is the sum of all ideas and structures, including social norms, customary beliefs, and values, that a society develops in order to cope with its environment and provide for the control of members' behavior.

Culture is handed down from one generation to another and gives society its unique values. What we eat and how we eat it are just two examples of how culture affects our lives. For example, cereal is the traditional breakfast food for American children, but not for children in many other countries of the world. The tradition may date back to the days when a hearty breakfast prepared pioneers for a long work day.

Values, which were also discussed in Chapter 2, are the ideas and principles that we consider correct, desirable, or important. Some American cultural values are individualism, freedom, youthfulness, activity, and humanitarianism. Each of these values influences consumer behavior. The value of activity, for example, is the idea that keeping busy is natural and healthy. This value stimulates consumers' interest in time-saving products and services that enhance leisure time activities.

The value of youthfulness may stimulate consumers to buy products and services related to maintaining youth. Advertisements for cosmetics typically show young models, even though the products are directed to adults in other age groups. Consumer spending on exercise equipment for the home, running shoes, and low-calorie foods are probably related, at least in part, to the value of youthfulness.

Marketers have found that consumers often buy products and services that are extensions of their values and self-image. When you are motivated by the value of individualism, you may search for distinctive clothing, jewelry, or hair styles that reflect your personality.

CLASSIFICATION OF CONSUMER PRODUCTS

As shown in Figure 6-2, consumer products may be classified as convenience goods, shopping goods, or specialty goods. These categories are based on consumer buying patterns.

Convenience Goods

Products that are purchased frequently with minimum shopping effort are called **convenience goods.** They are usually low-priced items that are sold by brand name. Bread, milk, chewing gum, soft drinks, candy bars, and eggs are examples of convenience goods. Con-

Figure 6-2.   Classification of consumer products.

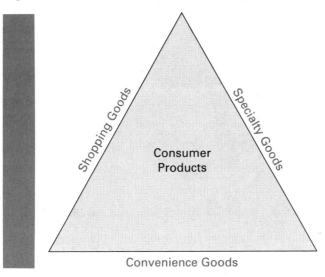

sumers are not willing to spend a lot of time and energy shopping for any of these items. The amount of satisfaction gained by going from store to store comparing brands of chewing gum, for example, is slight.

Most convenience goods are staple items. **Staple items** are basic products—bread, milk, soap, light bulbs—that households try to keep on hand. Like most convenience goods, they are purchased frequently.

Some convenience goods are impulse items. **Impulse items** are spur-of-the-moment purchases. They are usually displayed near store exits or in major traffic areas. Customers often add candy, packs of chewing gum, and magazines to their purchases as they go through check-out lines in supermarkets and drugstores.

When the parents of small children run out of milk or their supply is low, they need to buy more quickly with minimum effort. Because most of us want to buy milk and other convenience items without going too far from home, marketers must make these products as widely available as possible. This explains the large number of 24-hour convenience stores in many communities.

Shopping Goods

Shopping goods are items that are purchased after consumers have compared prices, qualities, styles, and colors at several stores. Customers usually seek information and advice about these products

Illustration 6-1   Bread is a staple item; it is a basic product that is purchased frequently.

from the salespeople at each store before making purchasing decisions. The satisfaction gained from the selected item makes comparison shopping worthwhile.

Shopping goods are usually more expensive than convenience goods and are purchased less often. Examples include clothing, home appliances, furniture, jewelry, and shoes. Shopping goods are sold in fewer stores than convenience goods. Most of the stores that sell shopping goods are large or specialized retail businesses such as department stores, carpet stores, paint and wallpaper stores, and so on.

Illustration 6-2

Fine china,
crystal, and
silverware are
examples of
shopping goods.

Shopping goods are usually sold by competing stores located near each other. You have probably noticed the relatively large number of shoe stores in shopping malls. This allows shoppers to compare the items offered by several shoe stores with ease. You might say that stores that sell shopping goods are located near competing stores because consumers want it that way.

Specialty Goods

Specialty goods are items with special features for which consumers are willing to make a major buying effort. Consumers know exactly what brand, style, or type of specialty good they want to buy and will not accept substitutes. Even though they are not conveniently located, a consumer will often visit several stores in order to find and purchase a specific item. A consumer may delay a purchase until a trip can be made to a store known to carry the exact item desired.

Specialty goods usually are high-priced items purchased infrequently. Examples include some items of clothing, home sound systems, and automobiles. Consumers who insist on purchasing specific brands must be willing to suffer inconvenience because the merchandise they want may be sold by only a few stores in large cities. Some merchandise may not even be available in small- and medium-sized cities.

Consumer goods can be classified as convenience, shopping, or specialty goods. These categories are based on consumer buying patterns. Marketing managers must understand these patterns in order to assure that products are available to shoppers at the appropriate locations.

APPLYING MARKETING TERMS

Name _____

Match each term with the statement that best describes an application of that term. Write the letter in the space provided.

a. information search
b. self-actualization needs
c. specialty goods
d. emotional buying motives
e. convenience goods

f. patronage buying motives
g. shopping goods
h. postpurchase evaluation
i. impulse items
j. reference groups

_____ 1. Consumer is willing to go to great lengths to get the item.

_____ 2. Purchased frequently.

_____ 3. Reading advertisements to learn more about a product.

_____ 4. Comparison shopping is worth the effort.

_____ 5. "I'm trying to decide if I'm happy with the car I just bought."

_____ 6. Deciding to take an art class.

_____ 7. You like the store because of its helpful employees.

_____ 8. Purchased on the spur of the moment.

_____ 9. You buy sunglasses like the ones your friends have.

_____ 10. They come more from the heart than the head.

MASTERING KEY CONCEPTS

Name _____

Answer each of the following questions in the space provided.

1. Identify the five steps in the consumer decision process.

2. What role does advertising play in problem recognition?

3. What are three choice criteria you might use when deciding to buy paint for your room?

4. Which three patronage motives are most important to you when shopping for clothes? Why?

5. Briefly explain the hierarchy of needs.

6. Which social class (upper, upper-middle, lower-middle, working, or lower) do you believe represents the largest consumer market in the United States? Explain your answer.

7. Place a check mark in the appropriate column to show whether each statement appeals to an emotional or a rational buying motive.

	Emotional Motive	Rational Motive
a. The breakfast of champions.		
b. The price marked is 40 cents off the regular price.		
c. It never needs ironing.		
d. Diamonds are forever.		
e. Ninety-day warranty.		
f. It's all the rage—brightly colored actionwear with definite style.		

8. Compare the three categories of consumer goods by placing check marks in the appropriate columns.

	Convenience Goods	Shopping Goods	Specialty Goods
a. Staple items.			
b. Sold by competing stores located near each other.			
c. Salesperson's advice is sought.			
d. Purchased infrequently.			
e. Widely available.			
f. Often found in inconveniently located stores.			

DEVELOPING PEOPLE SKILLS

Read the following description of a human relations situation. Then complete your answers on a separate piece of paper.

Longtime Friends

Ann and Heather had known each other since they were in the third grade. The two friends spent a lot of time together over the years. After school they could be found at either Ann's or Heather's house. When they went to summer camp, they shared the same cabin.

Ann and Heather are now in high school. They have some classes together and they are both on the volleyball team. They still see each other every day, but things are not the way they used to be; at least Ann doesn't think so. They are not spending as much time at each other's houses.

Recently, Heather has been spending most of her money on clothes and doesn't have any left to go ice skating or to a movie. Ann told Jill, her sister, "Heather has always had nice clothes. You know that. But now, for some reason, she's buying more clothes than she needs. We used to go shopping together. It was fun because we both liked the same kinds of clothes. Now she's buying styles she would not have tried on six months ago."

When Jill asked Ann if she and Heather were still close friends, Ann answered, "I don't think we are. We're drifting apart and that bothers me. Heather is trying to make friends with some people at school that I barely know. Heather is changing and I don't like it. I don't even understand it. Do you?"

Jill thought about Ann's comments and then answered, "You said that Heather has more clothes than she needs, but maybe buying new styles helps her satisfy what, to her, are real needs. It may be that Heather wants to win the acceptance of a certain group at school. Or, she may be trying to gain recognition as an individual."

1. Which of the needs in Maslow's hierarchy do you believe are affecting Heather's behavior? Explain your answer.
2. Explain how Heather's buying behavior may be influenced by a reference group.
3. What would you recommend if Ann asked your advice about maintaining her friendship with Heather?

MARKETING PROJECT 6

Use your own paper to complete this project. Select an advertisement from each of the following: the Yellow Pages of your telephone directory, a magazine, and a newspaper. Answer the following questions about each advertisement.

Appealing Advertisements

Yellow Pages

What product or service is featured in the advertisement?
What buying motive(s) is the seller of the product or service appealing to in the advertisement? Explain.

Magazine

What product or service is featured in the advertisement?
What buying motive(s) is the seller of the product or service appealing to in the advertisement? Explain.

Newspaper

What product or service is featured in the advertisement?
What buying motive(s) is the seller of the product or service appealing to in the advertisement? Explain.

Read the following description of real-life marketing practices. Then complete your answers on a separate piece of paper.

Renewed Interest in Customer Service

"May I help you?" If you've been shopping lately, and you didn't hear those words, you're not alone. Consumers have said that if retail salespeople talk to you at all, it is not uncommon to hear "This is not my department" or "If you don't see it on the shelf, we don't have it." Consumers have also had trouble getting good service from banks, insurance companies, airlines, and auto repair shops.

Customer service has slipped in many businesses. Why? Possible reasons include a declining work ethic, the growth of self-service discount stores, a trend toward the use of bank credit cards and away from store credit cards that often tie customers to particular merchants, and poorly trained employees.

Having reached bottom experts say that, " 'customer service' has become the new buzz phrase of the '90s."[2] According to an article in *The Wall Street Journal*, "The reason for the new emphasis is simple: Companies increasingly are finding that bad service costs customers. Seven of 10 customers who switch from one company to a competitor cite poor service—not price or quality—as the reason."[3]

Wanting to provide better customer service, or just talking about it, isn't enough. Corporate managers must take action. In television commercials promoting his chicken, Frank Perdue of Perdue Farms, Inc., asks customers to tell him what he's doing wrong. "Don't just sit there," he says, "Come on—let me have it. I can take it."

1. Do you agree or disagree with this statement: *If the price of the product is right, people don't care about customer service?* Explain your answer.
2. Describe an instance where you were given poor customer service. What could the employee or company have done to turn that negative experience into a positive one for you?
3. Describe an instance where you were given good customer service.
4. Some possible reasons for the decline of customer service were mentioned above. What other reasons can you add to the list?

[2]Marshall Hood, "Good, Old-Fashioned Service: It's Getting a New Emphasis," *The Columbus Dispatch* (16 July 1989), p. 1E.
[3]Amanda Bennett and Carol Hymowitz, "For Customers, More Than Lip Service," *The Wall Street Journal* (6 October 1989), p. B1.

Chapter 7
Organizational Buying Behavior

After you read this chapter and complete the activities at the end, you will be able to:

1. **Discuss the meaning of organizational buying.**
2. **Discuss the scope of organizational markets, including the industries involved.**
3. **Identify the different types of industrial products.**
4. **Discuss several differences between industrial and consumer markets.**
5. **Discuss different characteristics of organizational buying behavior.**

Did you realize that thousands of marketing activities are required to produce a new car? Iron ore is mined and transported to a plant where it is made into steel. The steel is delivered to an auto manufacturer and formed into the chassis and body of a car.

In order to construct a car requiring 12,000 different parts, the manufacturer will produce about 6,000 parts and buy the remaining 6,000 parts from other companies. Many of these companies make and supply only one type of part. Therefore, the automaker will have to deal with thousands of companies. Each of the following parts, for example, is manufactured by a different company: cast-aluminum wheels, door hinges, door locks, drive belts, electronic engine controls, front disk brake calipers, manual transaxles, outside mirrors, power-steering pumps, rear brake drums, seat belts, tires, and window glass.

The companies supplying these parts to the automaker, in turn, must buy raw materials and parts from their suppliers. Organizations, like consumers, are buyers of products and services. Just as marketers must understand consumer buying behavior, they must also understand organizational buying behavior.

◤ THE MEANING OF ORGANIZATIONAL BUYING

Buyers can be divided into two large groups: consumers and organizational buyers. Consumers are persons or households who purchase products or services to satisfy personal needs and wants. Their buying behavior was discussed in Chapter 6. **Organizational buyers** are businesses or institutions that buy products and services and resell them, with or without reprocessing, to other organizations or consumers. The nation's organizational buyers make up the **organizational market.** The products and services bought by organizations can be classified into three categories.

1. Products and services used to produce other products and services
2. Products and services used to carry on operations
3. Products bought for resale

The marketing of products and services to organizational buyers is often called **organizational marketing.**

Manufacturers, hospitals, banks, and supermarkets are all examples of organizational buyers. Manufacturers buy materials and parts to use in making other products. Hospitals buy beds and thermometers to provide service to their patients. Banks buy computer paper to use in keeping track of their customers' accounts. Supermarkets buy canned vegetables to be resold.

Many marketers sell in both the consumer market and the organizational market. IBM, for example, sells personal computers to be used by individual consumers. IBM also sells personal computers to banks, which are organizational buyers.

THE SCOPE OF ORGANIZATIONAL MARKETS

All buyers other than consumers are organizational buyers. More than 16.5 million organizational buyers in the United States make up the organizational market.[1] As shown in Figure 7-1 on page 152, the three major types of organizational markets are (1) the industrial market, (2) the reseller market, and (3) the government market.

The Industrial Market

The **industrial market** consists of firms that buy goods and services to be used, directly or indirectly, to produce other goods and

---

[1]U.S. Bureau of the Census, *Statistical Abstract of the United States: 1989,* 109th ed. (Washington, D.C.: U.S. Government Printing Office, 1988), pp. 284 and 517.

Figure 7-1   Types of organizational markets.

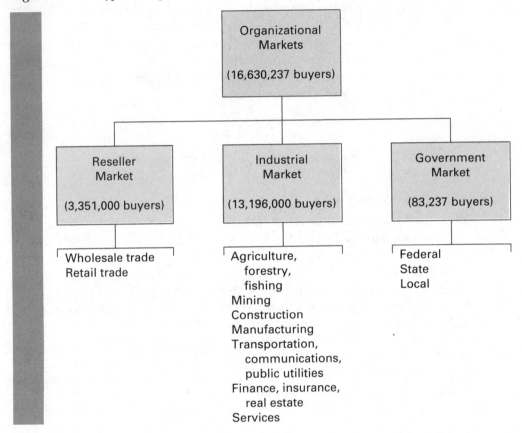

Source: Adapted from U.S. Bureau of the Census, *Statistical Abstract of the United States: 1989,* pp. 284 and 517.

services. The industrial market is the largest and the most diverse of the three types of organizational markets. With more than thirteen million firms, it accounts for 79 percent of the total number of organizational buyers.[2] In fact, the industrial market consists of all organizational buyers except the government and those in wholesale and retail trade.

Industrial products and services are bought and sold by organizations operating in many fields. Because they do not have direct contact with the industrial market, many people are not aware of its significance. It is estimated that about one-half of all manufactured

[2]U.S. Bureau of the Census, *Statistical Abstract of the United States: 1989,* pp. 284 and 517.

products are sold to organizational buyers. In addition, more than three-fourths of all farm products and nearly all products from the sea, mines, and forests are processed and eventually used by business and industry.

Most organizations in the industrial market fit into one of the following industry groups[3]:

1. Agriculture, forestry, and fishing
2. Mining
3. Construction
4. Manufacturing
5. Transportation, communications, and public utilities
6. Finance, insurance, and real estate
7. Services

Agriculture, Forestry, and Fishing. Agricultural enterprises include farms, ranches, dairies, greenhouses, nurseries, orchards, and poultry hatcheries. Other businesses offer landscaping or veterinary services or provide bulbs and flower or vegetable seeds. The fishing category includes commercial fishing companies and fish hatcheries.

Mining. The mining group includes enterprises that extract minerals such as coal, various ores, crude petroleum, and natural gas from the earth. Quarrying, crushing, and washing of stone and gravel are also considered a form of mining.

Construction. General building contractors construct homes, apartment and office buildings, factories, and stores. Heavy construction contractors build bridges, tunnels, highways, streets, water treatment plants, docks, and piers. Special trade contractors do plumbing, painting, carpentry, and electrical work.

Manufacturing. The manufacturing group includes companies that produce food products, textiles, apparel, furniture, paper, and various types of machinery. Manufacturers use raw materials and parts in the production of goods. These goods may be finished products or parts that will be used in the manufacture of other products. Manufacturers obtain raw materials and parts from agricultural, forestry, fishing, wholesaling, and mining concerns as well as from other manufactur-

---

[3]Adapted from Executive Office of the President, Office of Management and Budget, U.S. Department of Commerce, Office of Federal Statistical Policy and Standards, *Standard Industrial Classification Manual* (Washington, D.C.: U.S. Government Printing Office, 1972), pp. 5–7.

ers. Manufacturers also use the services of transportation, communication, public utility, finance, and insurance firms.

Transportation, Communications, and Public Utilities. A number of companies—bus lines, railroads, trucking firms, airlines—provide passenger or freight transportation for consumers and industrial users. Local and long-distance telephone services are provided by communications firms. Companies that provide electricity, natural gas, and water for homes and businesses are classified as public utilities.

Illustration 7-1   Airlines provide freight transportation services.

Photo compliments of Delta Air Lines, Inc.

Finance, Insurance, and Real Estate. The finance category includes banks and trust companies, credit agencies, investment companies, and stockbrokers and security dealers. The insurance group contains companies that offer insurance policies of all types as well as the agents who sell them. Real estate owners, agents, and developers comprise the real estate group.

Services. Thousands of businesses, aside from those services already described, provide a wide variety of services for consumers, business firms, government agencies, and various organizations. There are personal service providers such as travel agencies, photography studios, and household appliance or lawn mower repair shops. Companies such as advertising agencies and building security firms provide services for other businesses. Movie theaters, miniature golf courses, and hotels and motels are included in the services category. One of the fastest growing service areas is health care.

The Reseller Market

The **reseller market** consists of firms engaged in wholesale and retail trade. There are more than three million resellers doing business in the United States today.[4]

Wholesale Trade. Businesses in this category sell products to retailers, other wholesalers, and other industrial, institutional, agricultural, or professional users. The two principal types of wholesalers are merchant wholesalers, who take title to the goods they sell, and agents, who assist in the exchange of products without owning them.

Retail Trade. Businesses engaged in retailing buy merchandise and resell it to consumers for personal or household use. Some common types of retailers are department stores, specialty stores, supermarkets, convenience stores, superstores, mail order catalog firms, and discount houses.

Items of merchandise bought by retailers and wholesalers and then sold to others are called **resale products.** In most cases, resale products require no further processing; they are ready for shipment or resale to a buyer. Examples include clothing, household appliances, sports equipment, automobile parts, and canned food products. In other cases, some processing or repackaging may take place. For example, supermarkets buy sides of beef, divide them into individual cuts of meat, and package them for sale to consumers. Likewise, some fresh vegetables must be trimmed and washed before they are ready for sale in the produce department.

In addition to products bought for resale, resellers also buy products needed to carry on their business operations. A wholesaler, for example, may need fork lift trucks, delivery trucks, office furniture, and data processing equipment. Retailers may have the need for store fixtures, refrigerated frozen food cases, and sales registers. Both types of resellers may need light bulbs, floor cleaners, and office supplies.

---

[4]U.S. Bureau of the Census, *Statistical Abstract of the United States: 1989,* pp. 284 and 517.

▰ The Government Market

Another type of organizational market in the United States is the government market. This market consists of the federal government, which is the largest customer in the country, fifty state governments, and 83,186 local governments.[5] The local government category includes the various cities, towns, and counties from across the nation.

Federal, state, and local governments spend billions of dollars every year for products and services. Some examples of these would be computers, highway equipment, and accounting services.

▰ TYPES OF INDUSTRIAL PRODUCTS

Industrial products are used in the production of services and other products. Because firms in the industrial market use products to produce other products and services, they are the primary buyers of industrial products. While various organizations in the reseller and government markets buy industrial products, they are not major purchasers of those goods.

Industrial products and services can be classified into three broad categories: (1) raw materials, processed materials, and parts; (2) supplies; and (3) installations and accessory equipment.

▰ Raw Materials, Processed Materials, and Parts

Raw materials are the basic elements of the manufacturing process. They are supplied by mines, farms, forestry companies, or other extractive enterprises. Raw materials can be used in the production of end products (finished products) with little or no alteration. Examples are timber, minerals, wheat, crude petroleum, and cotton.

Materials that are the end product of one business but which will undergo further treatment by other manufacturers are called **processed materials.** These materials cannot be recognized in the finished product. A food manufacturer may buy a variety of ingredients—flour, sugar, salt—and combine them to make different cake mixes. Other examples of processed materials are sheet metal, chemicals, and plastics.

---

[5]U.S. Bureau of the Census, *Statistical Abstract of the United States: 1989,* pp. 284 and 517.

Illustration 7-2   Cotton is a raw material. It can be used in the production of end products with little or no alteration.

United States Department of Agriculture

Parts are manufactured items that become components of other products without modification. Examples are electric motors, switches, refrigerator thermostats, screws, nuts, and bolts. Tires and batteries are considered industrial products when they are purchased by automakers and used in the production of automobiles. They are consumer products, however, when they are sold to car owners as replacement parts. Likewise, buttons and zippers that are sold to a clothing manufacturer are industrial products, but when they are sold to a customer in a fabric store they are consumer products.

Supplies

Supplies do not become part of the finished product but are used up in the daily operations of a business. Items such as paint, oil, grease, and cleaning materials keep plants and equipment running. Other supplies used in day-to-day operations include stationery, cash register tapes, shipping cartons, mailing labels, and pencils.

Illustration 7-3   Tires are considered industrial products when they are used in the production of automobiles.

American Motors Corporation

Installations and Accessory Equipment

Installations are major items such as buildings, large machines, or pieces of equipment that are used to produce finished products or provide services. The **useful life** of installations—the period of time during which they can be used effectively—is longer than for any other group of industrial products. Generally speaking, installations are purchased by companies infrequently. Examples are printing presses owned by newspaper companies, jet airplanes owned by airlines, and mainframe computers belonging to banks.

Machinery used in the operation of a business that has a shorter useful life than installations is called **accessory equipment.** Microcomputers, store display cases and racks, cash registers, small power tools, forklifts, tractors, desks, and chairs are examples of accessory equipment. Companies typically buy accessory equipment more frequently than installations.

Illustration 7-4   File cabinets and office furniture are examples of accessory equipment.

UNIQUE FEATURES OF THE INDUSTRIAL MARKET

As we discussed earlier, the industrial market is the largest and the most diverse of the three types of organizational markets. It also has some features that distinguish it from the consumer market. Some unique features of the industrial market are the following: (1) derived demand, (2) fluctuating demand, and (3) a relatively small number of buyers.

Derived Demand

Demand means the amount of a product or service that people are willing and able to buy. Once demand has been determined a business can decide which products and services, and how much of each, to provide. The demand for industrial products and services is called **derived demand** because the amount purchased is determined by the demand for related products or services. For example, the demand for sheet metal is derived from the demand for products made of sheet metal as is the demand for machines that will cut sheet metal. The number of tires purchased by an automobile manufacturer depends on the number of cars demanded by consumers and organizational buyers. The demand for elevators is largely derived from the demand for new multi-story buildings.

Illustration 7-5

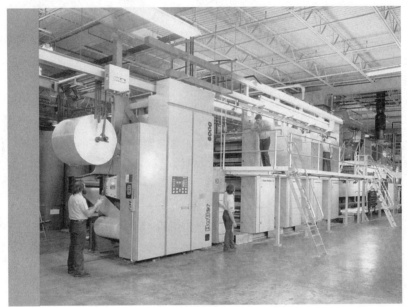

The demand for books and newspapers requires installations of large printing presses.

Webcrafters, Inc.

◣ Fluctuating Demand

Because it is derived from the sale of other goods, the demand for industrial products and services may fluctuate sharply when the pace of business activity changes. For instance, when car sales are brisk, automakers order tires from tire manufacturers and maintain an inventory in their warehouses. When an automobile manufacturer experiences a slowing of car sales, however, tire orders are reduced or even canceled altogether. The automaker may also reduce the size of its tire inventory. The demand for its product may decline so sharply that a tire manufacturer will close several of its plants. These plants will be reopened when automobile sales rebound and the demand for tires begins to increase.

Relatively Small Number of Buyers

Consumer products and services are purchased by millions of individuals and households. The number of organizational buyers for a given type of industrial product or service, however, is often limited. When an industrial product or service is used by only a small number of industries, it has a **vertical market.** There are few potential buyers of jet airplanes, diesel locomotives, or steel-making machinery.

An industrial product or service has a **horizontal market** when it is purchased by many kinds of businesses in different industries. Supplies such as stationery, pencils, paint, and cleaning materials are in this category. Power tools, microcomputers, and forklifts are further examples of industrial products with horizontal markets. While horizontal markets contain more potential users than vertical markets, they are still small when compared with the markets for most consumer products and services.

CHARACTERISTICS OF ORGANIZATIONAL BUYING BEHAVIOR

Organizational and consumer markets differ in several ways, as discussed in this chapter. Organizational buying behavior also differs from consumer buying behavior. Specifically, organizational buying has the following characteristics: (1) a rational process, (2) large orders, (3) involvement of many people, and (4) direct purchasing.

Rational Process

While consumer buying is sometimes done on impulse, organizational buying is rational and deliberate. This means that the purchasing activity of an organization is guided by objective factors such as price, operating costs, ease of repair, strength, replacement costs, and accompanying services. Although consumers may consider these factors when making purchasing decisions, they are also influenced by the emotional buying motives described in Chapter 6. Organizational buyers are concerned about obtaining the necessary products with the best service at the lowest possible cost.

Large Orders

The typical order placed by a business or other organization is considerably larger than the normal consumer order. Consumer purchases of individual items are usually small. For instance, although consumers might buy toothpaste frequently, they usually purchase only one or two tubes at a time. In the organizational market, purchases are larger and less frequent. For example, to keep production lines running, manufacturers must maintain an inventory. Thus, they buy quantities of the necessary products and store them. When this inventory falls to a predetermined level, they place new orders.

Involvement of Many People

In large companies or government agencies, one person is rarely totally responsible for the purchase of products and services. Many people in several different departments or units may be involved. For example, the purchase of a large computer by a manufacturer may be discussed by representatives from accounting, marketing, manufacturing, purchasing, information systems, and other departments that will use the machine. High-level executives are consulted when substantial sums of money are to be invested in equipment. Even in small businesses where owners or managers make all the major decisions, it is likely that they will discuss major purchases with other people in the company. Administrative assistants, for example, may be consulted regarding the purchase of word processing software or filing systems.

Direct Purchasing

With few exceptions, consumers usually do not buy directly from producers; however, it is a common practice in organizational buying. For example, automakers purchase steel directly from steel manufacturers. Large pieces of industrial machinery, such as those used in making paper, are sold directly to business users by the companies that produce them. Grocery wholesalers, and government agencies on some occasions, buy directly from food processing and packing companies.

Marketing to organizations is not the same as marketing to consumers. Not only are there major differences between organizational and consumer markets, there are also unique organizational buying activities that marketers need to understand if they want to participate successfully in this field.

APPLYING MARKETING TERMS

Name _____

Match each term with the statement that best describes an application of that term. Write the letter in the space provided.

a. accessory equipment
b. derived demand
c. raw materials
d. installation
e. parts

f. organizational buyer
g. supplies
h. resale products
i. processed materials
j. useful life

_____ 1. Tires purchased by automakers.

_____ 2. Products supplied by mines, farms, forestry companies, or other extractive enterprises to be used in manufacturing.

_____ 3. These cannot be recognized in the finished product.

_____ 4. Cash registers and small power tools used by a business.

_____ 5. A hospital that purchases supplies and equipment to provide care to patients.

_____ 6. The number of IBM and IBM-compatible computers in operation determines the number of IBM-based software packages supplied.

_____ 7. We must get that new shipment of books opened, organized, and on the shelves before the doors open. Our customers have been asking for those titles.

_____ 8. An electrical power generator at a plant that produces asphalt shingles.

_____ 9. "This machine will run for fifteen years."

_____ 10. Envelopes used to mail bills to credit customers.

MASTERING KEY CONCEPTS

Name _____

Answer each of the following questions in the space provided.

1. Buyers of products and services can be divided into two large groups. Name the two groups and describe the difference(s) between them.

2. Products and services bought by organizational buyers can be classified into three categories. List these categories.

3. What are the three major types of organizational markets?

4. Most companies in the industrial market fit into one of seven different industry groups. List these groups.

5. What are the three broad categories of industrial products?

6. How can you tell whether a particular item is a raw material or a processed material?

7. What are the differences between installations and accessory equipment?

8. Are the buyers of fax machines part of a vertical market or a horizontal market? Why?

9. Compared to consumer buying, organizational buying is said to be a rational process. Explain this statement.

DEVELOPING PEOPLE SKILLS

Read the following description of a human relations situation. Then complete your answers on a separate piece of paper.

Setting Goals

Continental Medical Supply (CMS) offers a complete line of medical and surgical items to hospitals. CMS requires all sales personnel to meet once a year with their supervisors to discuss their sales goals for the coming year. At this meeting, their sales performance in relation to the previous year's goal is also reviewed.

Ron Walker, a CMS sales representative for six years, met with his supervisor, Keisha Lewis. Ron's goal had been to surpass his previous year's sales volume by 15 percent. He achieved that goal. Due to increased competition, Ms. Lewis suggested that a 10 percent sales increase would be a reasonable goal for Ron for the coming year. However, Ron said he was motivated by higher goals and he was sure he could increase his sales by 20 percent. Ms. Lewis reluctantly agreed with Ron.

Within a month after he had set his new goal, Ron discovered that Memorial Hospital, his biggest customer, was considering changing to a new supplier who could deliver orders faster than CMS. Ron did not want to lose this account to a competing firm. He promised Susan Green, Memorial Hospital's purchasing manager, that CMS would meet or beat any other firm's delivery schedule. Green agreed to continue buying from CMS as long as deliveries were as fast as the competitor's. Green emphasized, "We must have prompt deliveries so we can provide quality medical care to our patients."

Ron knew that CMS's warehouse was not equipped to speed up deliveries to Memorial Hospital or to any other customer. He was hoping that Green would forget his promise. If the subject did come up again, Ron was confident that he could convince her once more not to change suppliers.

1. Is Ron Walker setting realistic sales goals? Explain.
2. Why do you think Ron insisted on setting such a high sales goal?
3. If you were Keisha Lewis, what would you have said to Ron about his sales goal for the coming year?
4. What action(s), if any, should Susan Green take if she discovers that Ron lied to her?
5. If you were one of Ron's friends, what advice would you give him?

MARKETING PROJECT 7

Use your own paper to complete this project.

Marketing to the Organizational Market

Assume that you are the owner of a small printing shop specializing in personalized items for weddings such as announcements, invitations, book matches, and napkins. To increase your sales volume you are going to offer a new product line. You will print business cards, letterhead, envelopes, and booklets. You hope your customers will be some of the larger businesses in town.

Explain how an understanding of each of the characteristics of organizational buying behavior will help you in marketing your new product line.

MARKETING INSIGHT

Read the following description of real-life marketing practices. Then complete your answers on a separate piece of paper.

The Federal Government as a Buyer

As the nation's biggest customer, the federal government buys vast quantities of goods and services. Military services, postal services, education, public welfare, natural resources, and day-to-day operations account for some of the largest expenditures.

Some companies, such as Boeing and Lockheed in the aircraft industry, make more than half of their sales to the federal government. Smaller firms now are doing more and more business with the U.S. government. According to an article in *Marketing News*, "Increasingly, the government contracts with private firms for jobs it once did in-house. About half of all sales of technology in the Washington, D.C., area are government-related. The technology is focused on such research areas as aerospace, weapons, biotechnology, agriculture, and telecommunications."[6]

Doing business with the government is different than selling to another business firm. Many firms are unaccustomed to the bureaucracy, institutional barriers, political sensitivities, technical requirements, competitive bidding, and financial constraints of the government.

Help is available to those not experienced in dealing with the federal bureaucracy. A government agency, the Business Service Center (BSC) in Washington, D.C., advises companies on selling to the federal government. The BSC, for example, issues publications listing the products purchased by various government agencies and the standards those products must meet.

1. Of the three categories of industrial products, which category do you believe accounts for most of the federal government's spending? Explain.
2. What industrial products would the Internal Revenue Service purchase? What industrial products would the Postal Service purchase?
3. What should companies expect when they start selling to the federal government?
4. Why would companies want to do business with the federal government, given the extra constraints and restrictions involved?

---

[6]John C. Franke, "Marketing to the Government," *Marketing News* (9 October 1989), pp. 1, 7.

CHAPTER 8
DIVIDING A MARKET INTO SEGMENTS

After you read this chapter and complete the activities at the end, you will be able to:

1. **Distinguish between mass marketing and market segmentation.**
2. **Describe four ways of segmenting consumer markets.**
3. **Identify three methods used to segment organizational markets.**
4. **Explain three benefits of market segmentation.**

Walk into any supermarket and you will be struck by the selection of available products. For example, you will find breakfast cereals sweetened, unsweetened, made from oats, with fiber, made from corn, bite-sized, spoon-sized, with nuts and fruits, with a prize inside, uncooked, and ready-to-eat. Some brands appeal to dieters, some to children, some to health buffs, and some to cost-conscious shoppers. Cereal companies have developed products with different marketing mixes to satisfy the needs and wants of different groups of consumers. This is just one example of market segmentation.

◢ MASS MARKETING VS. MARKET SEGMENTATION

Markets consist of customers—people and organizations—who are both willing and able to buy. Business firms can choose from two alternative approaches for defining, reaching, and satisfying these markets: mass marketing and market segmentation.

◢ Mass Marketing

A company that chooses **mass marketing** aims its marketing program at a large, broad consumer market, known as the mass market. Marketers who believe that most consumers have very similar preferences for their product often use mass marketing. Henry Ford, who founded the Ford Motor Company, 1903, used mass marketing during the company's early years. Ford's idea was to sell one standard car at a reasonable price to many people. The original Model T came in one color—black. Optional equipment was not available.

For mass marketing to be successful, a large group of consumers must desire the same product features. The company can then use a single marketing program to appeal to those customers. Mass marketing is used to sell *TV Guide* magazine. Millions of copies are sold each week through supermarkets, convenience stores, drug stores, other retail outlets, and by subscription. People of differing backgrounds, lifestyles, ages, and income groups buy *TV Guide* on a weekly basis. Many of these consumers see the magazine's advertisements on television, a common way for marketers to reach the mass market.

In recent years, the use of mass marketing has declined as companies have found it difficult to market one product that appeals to the masses. Consumers are demanding products tailored to their individual needs and wants, and marketers are responding to those demands.

Market Segmentation

Rather than trying to appeal to the entire consumer market, firms generally choose to focus their efforts on only a part of it. Within the total market, groups of customers with similar characteristics are called **market segments.** The process of dividing the total market for a product or service into market segments based on similarity of demand is called **market segmentation.** The market segment at which a company chooses to direct its marketing efforts is called the **target market.**

Differences Among Buyers

The market segmentation process divides a large market into segments comprised of buyers with similar needs or characteristics. Buyers differ in their need for various product or service characteristics, information, technical assistance, delivery, and credit services. For example, a consumer who buys computer software from a catalog may have a different set of needs than one who purchases the same item in a store. Catalog customers must wait for delivery, but they can shop without leaving home. Shoppers who buy in stores can compare different software packages and prices and take their purchases home immediately.

The process of dividing a market into segments starts with the firm finding out as much as it can about the consumers of its products or services. Various ways of obtaining marketing information, discussed in Chapter 4, must be undertaken to gather the needed information.

The starting point in segmenting a market is to identify differences among buyers. One approach that marketing managers can use to carry out this task is to ask a series of what, how, where, when, why, and who questions. You should realize that these questions are not actually used to segment the market. Instead, answers to these questions can help marketers understand the market well enough to decide if the market should be segmented, and if so, how it should be segmented.

What. What needs do buyers wish to satisfy with the purchase of a particular product or service? What influences their demand; that is, what causes buyers to purchase more or less? What risks do they perceive in buying the product or service? For example, are they concerned that it will go out of style or become outdated?

How. How do consumers or organizational users buy the particular product or service? How long does it take them to make their purchasing decisions? How is the product used? How much are buyers willing and able to spend? How much do they buy?

Where. Where do buyers purchase the product or service? Do consumers, for example, buy from catalogs or stores? Do organizational buyers purchase directly from manufacturers or from wholesalers? Where do customers obtain product or service information? Do they read advertisements and talk to salespeople, or do they rely on word-of-mouth recommendations?

When. When do people decide to buy? For example, do consumers compare the products offered by other stores before making a decision? Do organizational buyers purchase only after their companies have used a sample of the product? When do buyers purchase more of the product or service?

Why. Why are people motivated to buy? Why do they prefer a particular company's products or services?

Who. A business will want to know who its customers are, who buys from competing firms, and who is included in each of the marketing segments identified by the previous questions.

◣ Criteria for Segmenting Markets

In order for market segmentation to be useful, the targeted segments must meet criteria based on size, reachability, and responsiveness to a company's marketing program.

Size. A market segment must be large enough and have sufficient purchasing power to generate a profit for a firm. Segmentation is useless if a business cannot earn a profit by serving its selected market segments. Sometimes it is possible to treat each buyer as a segment and still earn a profit. This occurs with large purchases such as passenger airplanes or heavy equipment. Most of the time, however, a company must determine if there are enough potential customers to justify treating a group as a separate market segment. For example, two consumers may inform a company that they want toothpaste with a particular flavor. If they are the only consumers who want that flavor, sales will not justify spending the money to develop the product.

Reachability. In order to be profitable, a firm must be able to reach the selected market segment. This means that the segment must be accessible through existing channels of distribution and that the people included in the segment can be exposed to advertising for the product or service. For example, people in rural areas usually have different clothing needs from those living in urban areas. Because it is difficult to reach rural areas through its usual channel of distribution, however, a clothing manufacturer may decide that it is not profitable to sell to this segment.

Responsiveness. When compared with other market segments, a specific segment should respond differently to changes in the marketing of a product or service. If the response does not differ, there is no need to treat it separately. For example, consumers may be grouped into segments according to preference for cars in various price ranges—low price, medium price, and premium price. Assume that a company adds a low-priced car to its line. The low-price segment is responsive if its members purchase the car, but people in the other two segments do not. Consumers in the low-price segment then will continue to be treated as a distinct group. However, if the low-price consumer group does not respond to the low-priced car, then that segment will have to be redefined or combined with another segment.

◣ SEGMENTING CONSUMER MARKETS

The purpose of dividing the consumer market into segments is to enable businesses to target specific segments in an effort to reach buyers in the most efficient manner. Almost any factor that distinguishes consumers can be used to segment the market. There is no one best way to segment a market. Factors that are helpful in segmenting the market for vitamins might not work for furniture. Four widely used methods of segmenting the consumer market are geographic segmentation, demographic segmentation, lifestyle segmentation, and usage rate segmentation.

◣ Geographic Segmentation

Geographic segmentation involves dividing the consumer market into groups by location. Differences exist among consumers living in various geographic regions of the country, as well as between consumers living in cities, suburbs, and rural areas.

Regional Differences. Regional differences that affect consumer purchases include climate and social custom. Snowblowers, snowmobiles, and sleds are purchased by people who live in the northern section of the country. Residents of the sunbelt states spend more money on air-conditioning systems than on heating systems. People living in the South, Southwest, and West spend a lot of time outdoors. Thus, these regions are important markets for camping equipment, sporting goods, patio furniture, and barbecue equipment.

First time visitors to various parts of the country are introduced to popular regional foods. For instance, many restaurants in New England specialize in fresh seafood. In Texas, New Mexico, and Arizona many restaurants feature Mexican food.

City, Suburban, and Rural Differences. Where a person lives—city, suburb, rural area—also affects his or her buying patterns. People who live in suburbs are regular buyers of lawn mowers, grass seed, and weed killer. City apartment dwellers, on the other hand, do not need these items; but they do buy houseplants.

Illustration 8-1   Snowmobiles are popular recreational vehicles in the snowy northern region of the country.

Courtesy of North Dakota Tourism Office

Suburbanites who commute to work in the city need frequent automobile maintenance and repair. They may also prefer to buy cars that are economical to operate. City residents can use bus service or cabs for transportation to and from work.

Rural residents who are without conveniently located stores may buy groceries in larger quantities than people in cities or suburbs. Many buy freezers for storing food.

Many companies make it their business to stay a step ahead of . geographic changes, such as population shifts between regions. Cities that are growing rapidly often provide a firm with a new market opportunity. Out of the twenty-six metropolitan areas expected to experience the highest percentage increases in population between 1988 and 1993, 11 are in Florida and 6 are in California. While the population of the United States is expected to grow by 4.6 percent, for example, it is estimated that the Florida cities of Naples and Ocala will each grow by 17.1 percent.[1]

---

[1]"A User's Guide to the Survey of Buying Power: Part II," *Sales and Marketing Management*, vol. 141, no. 14 (13 November 1989), p. 9.

Demographic Segmentation

Demography is the study of population using such factors as age, sex, and income. Demographic segmentation is the process of dividing the consumer market into groups using population data.

Age. Age may indicate whether a person might be interested in buying a particular product or service. The consumer market can be divided into the following age groups:

- Children – 0 to 12 years of age
- Teenagers – 13 to 19 years of age
- Young adults – 20 to 34 years of age
- Younger middle-aged adults – 35 to 49 years of age
- Older middle-aged adults – 50 to 64 years of age
- Senior adults – 65 years of age and older

Children have a threefold impact on marketing. First, many have their own money to spend on products and services. Second, children influence their parents' purchasing decisions. A child's interest in camping may persuade parents to buy a tent instead of patio furniture. Children are also a factor in the decision to purchase home sound systems and swimming pools. Finally, billions of dollars are spent each year for clothing, toys, books, child care, pediatric services, school supplies, and other items for children.

Pets are often purchased for children. Buying a dog, for example, leads to many other purchases. Dog food is bought as regularly as groceries. Toys, collars, leashes, and visits to the veterinarian are necessary for dogs. Boarding at a kennel might be necessary when the family is on vacation.

Teenagers buy fast food, automobiles, automobile insurance, cassette tapes, stereo equipment, personal grooming products, and clothing. As they approach their twenties, teenagers begin to think about their future careers and make plans to further their education or acquire job training. Many marketers believe that the habit of buying products by brand name is developed during the teenage years. Thus, teenagers are used regularly in television and magazine advertisements in an effort to reach this market segment.

Young adults buy products and services that are needed to set up a household. A **household** consists of one or more persons who, as a unit, consume products and services. New households are formed when young people leave home and move into their own apartments or houses, either alone or with a spouse or roommate.

Households have many needs. Each requires furniture, appliances, linens, cookware, curtains or draperies, and so on for day-today comfort and convenience. All of these purchases are in addition to the expense of renting an apartment or buying a house or condominium.

Young middle-aged adults spend time and money replacing items, such as furniture and appliances, that they bought when they were in their twenties. They may look for larger homes or build additions to their present homes. They often buy additional or better cars. Young middle-aged adults are interested in purchasing or providing for additional life insurance, college education for their children, and retirement planning services.

Consumers in the older middle-aged segment are often financially secure and at the peak of their earning power. They have uncommitted leisure time and additional spending power because their children have left home and are financially independent. Thus, older middle-aged adults are prime purchasers of high-priced, high-quality products and services. They are interested in travel and hobbies of all kinds. Prior to retiring from full-time employment, some spend time visiting retirement communities in order to help them decide if and where they should relocate after retirement.

Because of the longer life span of most Americans, the senior adult market segment is expanding. Marketers of various products and services recognize the importance of this group, and many have developed advertising programs directed specifically toward senior adults. These consumers purchase travel services, medical services, health products, and housing that requires little maintenance. Senior adults also buy products and services for their children and grandchildren. Some people are surprised to see a toy store or a children's clothing store located near a retirement community. Some merchants have found success, however, in selling children's goods to senior adults who have money to spend on gifts for grandchildren.

Sex. One of the most obvious ways to segment the market is by sex. This is why there are so many products for women or men only. A retailer of women's clothing who plans to open a new store in Denver is not interested in the total population of that city but rather in the number of women living in the area. The health and grooming aids departments in supermarkets and drugstores contain a number of products for women only or for men only.

Income. Income levels also can be used to segment the consumer market. What, where, and how much people buy is related to their income. Income alone is no assurance that a person will buy a certain product. When it is combined with another factor—age, for example—a marketer can get a clearer picture of consumer-buying activity. For example, people buying their first home are usually between the ages of twenty and thirty-four. However, they must have sufficient income for the cash down payment and monthly payments.

In the last few decades, because of favorable economic conditions, more and more families have moved into higher income groups. This has brought about increases in **discretionary income** which is the money remaining after taking care of the basic needs of life—food, clothing, and shelter. Large numbers of individuals and families can now afford to buy products and services that were once considered luxuries, such as high-priced home appliances, fashionable clothing, cable television, better cuts of meat, meals in fine restaurants, and European vacations.

Illustration 8-2   In the last few decades, more and more individuals and families have moved into high-income groups and can afford to buy large homes.

Insilco Corporation

▲ Lifestyle Segmentation

Lifestyle segmentation divides consumers into groups according to their activities, interests, and opinions. In other words, it considers how people live their lives. To segment the market according to lifestyle, marketers seek answers to these questions about consumers:

1. How do they spend their time? How much time do they spend at work, on hobbies, or at social events?
2. What areas of interest are most important to them? What importance do they place on family, community, or personal achievements?
3. How do they see themselves and the world around them? What are their opinions regarding politics, education, culture, and the future?

Marketing experts have used answers to these types of questions to divide consumers into four main groups: outer-directed, inner-directed, need-driven, and integrated.[2] Firms can then show in their advertising how a product or service fits into a consumer's life.

Consumers in the **outer-directed group** buy products and services that will make them fit in with people they admire. Advertisements might picture people having fun with their friends and showing how the product, such as an item of clothing or a car, helps satisfy the need to fit in. Outer-directed people also see themselves as being goal-oriented and confident about their ability to make decisions.

Those in the **inner-directed group** value self-expression. Rather than being influenced by other people, they are motivated by personal wants and values and social responsibility. Many of them are people in their early twenties who prefer to live a simple life and have little interest in material possessions. They prefer natural products and the outdoors. These consumers are interested in products that are safe for the environment. When buying a car, they rate economy of operation high.

The **need-driven group** consists of consumers who live at or slightly above the poverty level. They have little enjoyment in their lives and they often feel left out of things. They only buy when they have a real need. Their purchases include used cars and lower quality products. Because they have little money to spend, many marketers do not try to attract this group of consumers.

Consumers in the **integrated group** have qualities of the outer-directed group blended with qualities of the inner-directed group. The best way to describe them is to say that they are decisive, goal-oriented people who are socially-conscious and responsible.

Lifestyle segmentation is more difficult to use than geographic or demographic segmentation where at least some of the necessary in-

---

[2]Arnold Mitchell, *The Nine American Life-Styles: Who We Are & Where We Are Going* (New York: Macmillan, 1983).

formation can be found in reference materials at the library. However, there is no information readily available on the number of consumers in the inner-directed group. Therefore, marketers generally use lifestyle segmentation in combination with other types of segmentation.

◣ Usage Rate Segmentation

Usage rate segmentation is the practice of dividing the market into segments based on how much of the product or service consumers buy. The segments are heavy users, light users, and nonusers. **Heavy users** are people who account for a small fraction of the number of a firm's customers, but a large fraction of its sales volume. For example, research on Pet Evaporated Milk found that 17 percent of its customers account for 87 percent of its sales.[3]

Light users comprise the largest number of buyers, but account for a small portion of its sales. **Nonusers** never buy the product.

Once a firm has divided its market into heavy, light, and nonuser segments, the business selects the group, or groups, toward which it will direct its marketing efforts. Some firms may decide to focus their marketing efforts on the heavy users and pay little or no attention to light users and nonusers. Other businesses are interested in pursuing all three segments. However, they develop different promotions for each one. A fast food restaurant, for example, may use advertising to keep heavy users coming back. Contests or games where customers get a game piece on each visit might encourage light users to come more often. The most difficult to attract are the nonusers. It may take entirely new menu items to convert some of them into customers.

The geographic, demographic, lifestyle, and usage rate factors discussed above are just four methods of dividing consumer markets into segments. Practically any factor that links or associates a consumer with the purchase of a specific product or service can be used—for example, occupation, dietary habits, size of household, and so on.

A manufacturer of work clothes and uniforms may find it useful to segment its markets by customer occupation. Construction, law enforcement, and health care professions have different uniform requirements. A processor and packer of canned vegetables may decide

---

[3]William F. Schoell and Joseph P. Guiltinan, *Marketing: Contemporary Concepts and Practices* (Boston: Allyn and Bacon, Inc., 1988), p. 231.

to serve that segment of consumers who prefer salt-free foods. The growing number of one-person households has created a market for one-bedroom apartments and for small packages of food, such as cans of soup containing one serving or individual slices of pie.

SEGMENTING ORGANIZATIONAL MARKETS

Like the consumer market, the organizational market is of little value to a business until it has been divided into segments. Three common methods of segmenting the organizational market are (1) product or service segmentation, (2) geographic segmentation, and (3) usage segmentation.

Product or Service Segmentation

Products and services must be defined precisely in order to segment the organizational market. For example, a steel manufacturer might group potential buyers by the type of steel they use, such as structural steel, steel plate, or cold-finished steel bars. A developer of computer software may segment users by type of computer—microcomputer or mainframe—for which they purchase software. End use should also be considered. How the buyer plans to use the product (i.e., in an expensive car or in an inexpensive radio) may determine what marketing methods a firm should use.

Geographic Segmentation

Segmenting the organizational market in terms of geographic location is important because users are not evenly distributed throughout the United States. Different types of organizational users are often concentrated in various regions. A marketing manager must recognize this fact or the marketing effort may be exerted in areas where no demand exists, while little or no effort is expended in areas having the greatest potential. A company selling parts to automobile manufacturers has a concentrated market for its products; assembly plants are located in a small number of states such as Michigan, Ohio, Wisconsin, Missouri, California, and New Jersey. On the other hand, a manufacturer of shipping cartons can find potential buyers in thousands of locations across the country.

Illustration 8-3   Rural areas are the principal markets for farm equipment.

Deere & Co.

Usage Segmentation

The rate at which a product or service is used can be the basis for segmenting the organizational market. For instance, an industrial chemical company may have two potential market segments: heavy users and light users. The company might find it more profitable to concentrate its marketing efforts on the light user market because it has been neglected by other chemical manufacturers.

All consumers or organizational users do not have the same needs. The consumer and organizational markets should be divided into segments consisting of buyers who share the same characteristics and needs. A company will then be in a position to target one or more of these segments and focus its marketing efforts.

BENEFITS OF MARKET SEGMENTATION

Businesses use market segmentation in order to achieve one or more of the following benefits: (1) define the total market, (2) focus marketing efforts, and (3) identify market opportunity.

Define the Total Market

By dividing the total market into segments a company can improve its understanding of why consumers or organizational buyers do or do not buy certain products or services. The market segmentation process helps a company stay abreast of changing needs and wants and provides an understanding of how to meet current market demands. Segmentation encourages an awareness of who is buying a product or service, where, and when.

Focus Marketing Efforts

Identifying potential buyers is the first step in planning a marketing program that will satisfy their needs. For example, television, radio, and newspaper advertisements can be better focused. This will enable buyers in the selected segment(s) to be reached with advertising appeals that are directed specifically at them.

Identify Market Opportunity

Companies that segment their markets are better prepared to assess their strengths and weaknesses in relation to those of competing firms. They are, for instance, able to determine how deeply another company's product is entrenched in the market. With this information a company is able to avoid a head-to-head battle with a competitor by marketing its product to a different segment.

APPLYING MARKETING TERMS

Name _____

Match each term with the statement that best describes an application of that term. Write the letter in the space provided.

a. discretionary income
b. demographic segmentation
c. market segments
d. markets
e. mass marketing

f. geographic segmentation
g. outer-directed group
h. lifestyle segmentation
i. heavy users
j. household

_____ 1. Designing a television commercial that appeals to children and broadcasting it on Saturday morning.

_____ 2. Making sure the product's features are the ones practically all consumers want.

_____ 3. They buy most of the product.

_____ 4. Money available to take a vacation.

_____ 5. Deciding to sell a new suntan lotion only in the sunbelt states.

_____ 6. People who are willing to buy the product or service and who have the money to buy.

_____ 7. People who buy a product to gain acceptance by those whom they admire.

_____ 8. Customers who are in the same age group, who enjoy the same sports, or who live in the same area.

_____ 9. Roommates buying furniture for their apartment.

_____ 10. Dividing consumers into segments according to their hobbies.

MASTERING KEY CONCEPTS

Name _____

Answer each of the following questions in the space provided.

1. What is the difference between mass marketing and market segmentation?

2. What are the six questions marketing managers can ask to help them identify differences among buyers?

3. What criteria must market segments meet to be useful?

4. Identify four widely used methods of segmenting consumer markets.

5. Geographic segmentation is based on what types of consumer differences?

6. Name three demographic factors that are used to segment consumer markets.

7. What are three common methods of segmenting organizational markets?

8. Describe the three benefits of market segmentation.

DEVELOPING PEOPLE SKILLS

Read the following description of a human relations situation. Then complete your answers on a separate piece of paper.

Getting Started in the Insurance Business

When Bill Baker received his license to sell insurance, he went to work for an independent agency that had an office across town. Although Bill knew that he would one day become his parents' partner in their independent insurance agency, he thought he should gain some experience working for someone else first. His parents agreed.

Independent insurance agents sell many kinds of insurance policies from a number of different companies. When they sell a policy, they charge a fee, called a commission, to the insurance company issuing the policy. Bill made enough sales during his first few months on the job to give him confidence that he could become a successful agent. He was selling property insurance to people living in apartments and homes near his office. He had much in common with these people and he enjoyed talking to them. Most of the customers, like Bill, were in their mid-twenties.

Bill's employer opened a second office and when Bill was given the opportunity to move to the new office, he accepted. Helping to establish a new office was the kind of challenge he liked. The new office was located in a suburban area where many of the residents were older, retired people.

Shortly after starting work at the new office, Bill realized that he was having trouble making sales. He told his friend, Dan, "I don't understand it. I'm doing everything here that I did at the other office, but it's not working. I call a lot of people every day, but I'm not getting very many of them to make an appointment with me to talk about their insurance needs. You know what that means: No appointments—no sales."

Bill explained that he selected the names of people living near his office from the telephone directory and called them to make appointments. Bill continued, "When people answer the telephone, I address them on a first name basis. I talk to them like we've been friends for years. After all, aren't you more likely to buy insurance from a friend?"

1. Why do you believe Bill is having difficulty making sales?
2. Is the market segment Bill is selling to now the same as the one he sold to when he started in the insurance business? Explain.
3. As Bill's friend, what suggestions would you give him for contacting prospective customers?

MARKETING PROJECT 8

Use your own paper to complete this project.

The Market Segment Memo

In Marketing Project 2 you were asked to assume that you were the marketing manager of a new chain of quick oil change and lube shops. Your assignment was to write a memo convincing the president of the company of the importance of selecting the appropriate marketing mix.

Write another memo to the company president. This time your task is to explain how the idea of geographic segmentation would be helpful in deciding where the company should locate new shops.

MARKETING INSIGHT

Read the following description of real-life marketing practices. Then complete your answers on a separate piece of paper.

Selling Blue Jeans in the '90s

Selling blue jeans was simple during the 1960s when marketers advertised to the broad market. Back then, blue jeans were blue jeans. Consumers often ended up buying the brand that was on sale.

According to one industry executive people's behavior has changed and niche strategies are making more sense. A niche is a specific market segment consisting of customers with similar characteristics. The VF Corporation, manufacturer of Wrangler, Lee, and Rustler jeans, has selected a specific niche for its Wrangler brand. This niche consists of blue-collar family men who wear jeans daily, who are over 30, who love the outdoors, and who live in small towns.

Wrangler has developed a marketing that focuses product, price, place, and promotion decisions on a single niche. For the product element of the marketing mix, Wrangler has introduced a new blue jean that is cut a bit fuller for what they are calling the "mature" man. In terms of price, Wrangler jeans sell for slightly less than Levi jeans. And as a result of place decisions, Wrangler jeans are sold through low-price mass merchandise retail outlets.

In aiming its promotion efforts at the blue-collar market, Wrangler advertisements will not have much in common with those of Levi's or Guess. Ads for those brands are designed for young, urban residents, and use few models who appear to be older than 20. In contrast, Wrangler ads show people who are 30 years of age or older.

According to the executive in charge of Wrangler's $10 million advertising campaign, "We wanted to talk to people in a different way than Levi's and Lee are talking to people. We want people to know that Wrangler's are good-looking jeans, but we also want it to be more real."[4]

1. Do you believe Wrangler's marketing mix matches its target market? Explain.
2. Describe a television commercial that Wrangler could use to attract the interest of its target market.
3. Choose a brand of jeans other than Wrangler. Describe the target market for these jeans and the marketing mix being used to reach that market.

---

[4]Joanne Lipman, "From '60s Uniform to '90s Niche: Wrangler Targets the Family Man," *The Wall Street Journal* (3 July 1989), p. 11.

UNIT 3
PROMOTION AND SELLING

9 OVERVIEW OF PROMOTION

10 PROMOTION: PERSONAL SELLING

11 PROMOTION: ADVERTISING

12 PROMOTION: VISUAL MERCHANDISING, SALES PROMOTION, AND PUBLIC RELATIONS

CHAPTER 9
OVERVIEW OF PROMOTION

After you read this chapter and complete the activities at the end, you will be able to:

1. **Define promotion and describe its role in the marketing process.**
2. **Explain the importance of promotion.**
3. **Explain how the communication process relates to promotion.**
4. **Explain the differences between a push strategy and a pull strategy in promotion.**
5. **Identify the five principal methods of promotion.**
6. **Explain the three steps included in promotional planning.**

As consumers, we are bombarded on a daily, hourly, and sometimes even a minute-by-minute basis with the promotional efforts of businesses and other organizations. When you read the local newspaper you notice that much of it is made up of advertising. As you watch TV you see commercials at least every 8-10 minutes. When you get home from school, you notice that your parents received a number of direct mail advertisements. Among these was the new Lands' End Catalog promoting fashionable men's and women's clothing.

As you drive to the nearby supermarket you pass two billboards on the roadway, one promoting a political candidate and a second promoting a new model of an automobile. At the same time, you undoubtedly listen to your favorite radio station as it finishes an advertisement for a rock concert. Finally, when you get to the supermarket you notice that there is a new visual merchandise display of your favorite brand of soft drink at the end of one of the aisles. As part of this display the soft drink company is promoting a contest where you can win a free trip to Hawaii. As you pay for your merchandise at the check-out counter, you take advantage of a special sale price by using a coupon that you clipped out of last night's paper. All of these activities and many other similar ones are classified as promotion in marketing.

◢ PROMOTION AND ITS ROLE IN THE MARKETING PROCESS

As discussed in Chapter 2, the marketing mix includes decisions on product or service, price, place, and promotion. A business cannot simply provide the right product or service at the right place and price; it must also convince consumers to make a purchase. **Promotion** is persuasive communication about products and services. In order to persuade consumers to purchase products or services, businesses must communicate their availability and benefits through various methods of promotion. Some common methods or elements of promotion are personal selling, advertising, visual merchandising, sales promotion, and public relations. Businesses combine these methods to create a **promotional mix.**

Illustration 9-1   Businesses use promotion to communicate the availability and benefits of products and services.

It is estimated that businesses in the U.S. will spend $315 **billion** on total promotion in 1992. Figure 9-1 shows the dollars spent on promotion in the U.S. for the years 1987–1989 and the estimate for 1992.

Figure 9-1   The amount of money spent on promotion in the U.S. is expected to top $315 billion in 1992.

YEAR	AMOUNT SPENT IN U.S. ON PROMOTION
1987	$205,900,000,000
1988	221,800,000,000
1989	239,000,000,000
1992 (estimated)	315,000,000,000

Source: "Ad Promotional Spending Expected to Rise 9.4%," *Marketing News* (4 December 1989), p. 21. Courtesy of American Marketing Association.

Promotion creates demand for products and services along the producer-to-consumer chain. The ultimate goal of all promotional activities is to stimulate the sale of products or services. Through promotional activities companies provide information that will convince potential buyers of the benefits that will result from the purchase of their products and services

Promotion can be divided into two major categories: personal and nonpersonal. **Personal promotion** means that a marketer deals directly with consumers. Personal selling falls into this category. **Nonpersonal promotion,** on the other hand, means that a marketer deals indirectly with consumers. Examples of nonpersonal promotion include advertising, visual merchandising, sales promotion, and public relations.

THE IMPORTANCE OF PROMOTION IN MARKETING

Not long ago small businesses relied on word of mouth to increase sales. A store owner might place a notice in the shop window to attract buyers who would then tell friends about their purchases. In today's fast-paced world of advanced technology and instant communication, sign-in-the-window promotion is not enough.

The promotional efforts of a marketing business are important for several reasons. First, they are critical if products and services are to move along the channels of distribution. Mass production depends on mass distribution, and promotional activities are an important part of making mass distribution possible. By stimulating the demand for goods and services, efficient promotional techniques contribute to economic strength, growth, and the high standard of living enjoyed by many people in the United States. When demand is increased, employment opportunities are provided for workers who produce and distribute the items involved. Increased employment means that more people are earning money that can be spent on goods and services. This cycle makes possible a higher standard of living through increased consumption.

Second, promotion plays a key role in introducing new products or services to the marketplace. The value of new products or services is often unknown. A company must demonstrate their usefulness and persuade buyers to purchase the new items through promotional activities. Think of some of the new products—cellular telephones, camcorders, color copiers, and facsimile machines—that have become an important part of American life in the past few years. The companies that are leaders in these new product fields and the supporting service firms have active, well-organized promotional plans.

Finally, promotion provides employment opportunities. Millions of people are employed in careers in advertising, visual merchandising, public relations, personal selling, and sales promotion. For in-

Illustration 9-2   A career in advertising is one of many employment opportunities available in the field of promotion.

stance, in 1980 there were nearly seven million people employed in personal selling careers in the United States. By 1990, nearly nine million people were employed in this field. This figure is expected to grow to eleven to twelve million by the year 2000. Promotion will become increasingly important and career opportunities in this field will continue to expand as marketing becomes more critical to the United States and world economies.

◢ THE COMMUNICATION PROCESS AND ITS RELATIONSHIP TO PROMOTION

Since the days of the cave dwellers, individuals have been using hand signals, vocal patterns, facial expressions, and symbolic drawings on walls for one purpose: to communicate with one another. Now we exchange information by telephone, letters, computer networks, fax machines, and an endless variety of other methods in order to accomplish the same goal.

Promotion is essentially a communication process. Marketers send persuasive messages to consumers through various channels or media in order to communicate reasons why they should buy particular products or services. Marketers represent the senders in this communication process; consumers represent the receivers. A **sender** (seller) must put information into a form that a **receiver** (buyer) can understand. The sender uses verbal or nonverbal symbols to transmit ideas. This process is called **encoding.** The sender also selects the **channel or medium of communication**—personal selling, direct mail, telephone, radio, newspaper, television, visual display—through which these ideas will be sent to the receiver. The consumer receives the symbols sent by the seller and, through a process called **decoding,** interprets the message. The seller hopes that the consumer will interpret the message as it was intended, having the impact that the seller desired. Figure 9-2 shows how the different parts of the communication process fit together.

Nonpersonal promotion, such as advertising or visual merchandising, is one-way communication. In one-way communication the sender or seller cannot be sure if the receiver or consumer has gotten the desired message. Thus, it is often difficult to measure the effectiveness of nonpersonal promotion.

When communication becomes a two-way process, such as during a sales presentation, the seller is able to receive a message or **feedback** from the buyer. Thus, a salesperson can determine how the message has been interpreted by the prospective buyer and respond accordingly.

Figure 9-2   The communication process is a very important part of promotion.

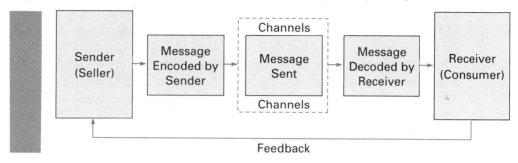

PULL OR PUSH STRATEGIES IN PROMOTION

The promotion of products or services generally follows either a push strategy, a pull strategy, or a combination of the two. With a **push strategy** the majority of promotional efforts undertaken by the manufacturer or supplier are directed toward getting intermediaries such as agents, wholesalers, and retailers to carry the products or services. Under this strategy each member of the channel of distribution is encouraged to promote the product or service to the next respective channel member. Thus, the promotional efforts of manufacturers are directed at wholesalers, wholesalers' efforts at retailers, and retailers' efforts, in turn, at final consumers. A push strategy includes promotional activities such as personal selling, advertising, and sales promotion that are designed to push the products or services through the marketing channels. Examples of products where a push strategy is frequently utilized include home improvement products, auto parts and accessories, garden supplies, and many industrial products.

When a **pull strategy** is utilized by a manufacturer or supplier, the majority of the promotional efforts are directed toward the ultimate consumer. Thus, manufacturers or suppliers are attempting to directly influence consumers to pull their products or services through the marketing channels. A pull strategy necessitates the development of a high level of consumer demand in order to pull the product or service through the marketing channels. Mail order catalogs that are sent directly to large numbers of ultimate consumers provide a good example of this type of strategy.

Many promotional efforts combine a push and a pull strategy. Procter and Gamble (P&G), a leading producer and marketer of consumer food, personal care, and pharmaceutical products, advertises its merchandise in trade magazines read by food wholesalers and retailers. P&G also has a sales force which makes calls on these channel members. This push strategy encourages the stocking of P&G products on the shelves at the retail level. At the same time, the company promotes heavily to ultimate consumers through magazines, television, and point-of-purchase displays. These activities help create consumer demand which pulls the P&G products through the marketing channels. Figure 9-3 displays a flow chart example of both a push and a pull promotional strategy.

Figure 9-3   Push and pull promotional strategies both have the same objective: increasing demand for a product or service.

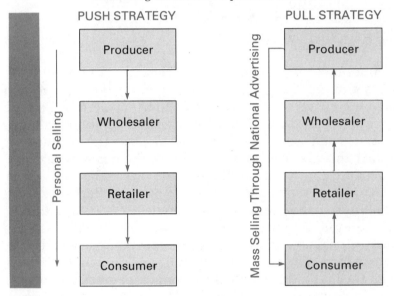

THE METHODS OF PROMOTION

Promotion includes many different forms of personal and nonpersonal selling activities. All these activities are designed to help marketers maximize sales and obtain exposure for products or services. The five principal methods or elements of promotion—personal selling, advertising, visual merchandising, sales promotion, and public relations—will be discussed briefly in this chapter and in more detail in the remaining chapters of this unit. As you have already learned, the specific combination of these methods chosen by a company to promote an item is often referred to as its promotional mix.

Personal Selling

Personal selling is direct, personal contact between a seller and a buyer for the purpose of effecting action on the part of the buyer. Direct contact permits the marketer to talk personally with the consumer in a persuasive fashion. This type of promotion is designed to help consumers buy products or services that fulfill their needs and wants. Almost all marketing businesses utilize some form of personal selling.

The main advantage of personal selling is that messages can be tailored to specific buyers. Thus, the success rate of this method is high. The major disadvantage of personal selling is its high cost.

People involved in personal selling must be well informed about their product or service in order to achieve success. They must also have good interpersonal skills. Sales representatives who set their own schedules and work on commission must be self-motivated. Finally, personal selling requires a clear understanding of the sales process.

Advertising

Advertising is the use of nonpersonal paid messages promoting a service, product, image, or idea directed at an audience through various mass media by an identified sponsor. Examples of typical advertising media include newspapers, radio, direct mail, television, and outdoor advertising. The primary goal of advertising is to create mass demand for products or services. Through advertising, marketers can reach thousands or even millions of potential buyers.

The advantages of advertising are that messages can be widely distributed and their content and timing controlled. The main disadvantage is the difficulty of reaching a specific target audience with a persuasive message.

There are ways to help advertisers reach their target market. A seller can choose to place an advertisement in a particular newspaper or magazine and often specify the section or page on which it should appear. A sporting goods store might purchase space for its advertisement on the back cover of an outdoor and leisure magazine. This gives the store a better chance of reaching a specific audience with its message. Some newspapers and magazines are available in zoned editions, which contain advertisements and articles of particular interest to readers within specific geographic boundaries. Businesses which use direct mail as an advertising strategy frequently purchase mailing lists for special target audience groups. Mailing lists are available for almost every conceivable market segment.

When purchasing advertising time in the broadcast media, a company can target a message to a specific audience by its choice of a particular television or radio station and the program. The director of a retirement center will not advertise on a local rock station but will purchase time on a station that attracts an older audience with an all news or talk show format.

Visual Merchandising

Visual merchandising is the visible presentation of products, services, or a business itself for the purpose of attracting attention, creating desire, and stimulating consumers to buy. Exterior and interior displays in retail businesses are one aspect of visual merchandising. Decorative glass storefronts, colorful signs, creative window displays, plush carpeting, and brightly painted walls are all elements of visual merchandising. Visual merchandising helps establish a company's image, which in turn, influences sales.

Point-of-purchase displays are another important element of visual merchandising. They increase demand, attract attention, or stimulate a desire for more information about a product. We have all stood in check-out lines and looked at the merchandise on the racks nearby. How many times have you idly thumbed through a magazine, then added it to your purchase? Few people go to the store solely to buy a magazine, but many start reading one while they are waiting in line and then buy it. This impulse buying is one of visual merchandising's main advantages, but to be effective such merchandising must be limited so that the consumer is not overwhelmed by too many competing messages.

Packaging is also a part of visual merchandising. Although the main function of a package is protection, it also influences sales. When trying to maximize sales, a firm cannot overlook the promotional possibilities of creative packaging.

Sales Promotion

Sales promotion is any activity that supplements advertising, personal selling, and visual merchandising. Sales promotion activities can be divided into consumer promotions and trade promotions. Consumer promotions are directed at the ultimate consumer and include coupons, rebates, premiums, contests and games, trading stamps, free samples, and many other activities. Most of these pro-

motions give consumers an extra incentive to purchase a product or
service, over and above the benefit of the product itself.

Illustration 9-3   Product demonstrations give buyers an extra incentive to purchase a
product.

Trade promotions are promotional activities directed at intermediaries such as wholesalers, industrial distributors, agents, retailers,
and sales representatives. These activities are designed to get these
various intermediaries to buy and sell large quantities of products or
services.

◣ Public Relations

Public relations is the total process of building goodwill toward a
business on the part of customers, employees, suppliers, stockholders, creditors, the community, and government. The direct selling of
products or services is not the main objective. Public relations activities are used to build a positive image of a business. Many businesses
employ specialists who perform public relations activities. In addition, every marketing worker who has contact with customers has an

opportunity to help a business develop and maintain a positive image and thus is involved in public relations.

Public relations includes such activities as membership and participation in civic and other organizations that provide community services, lobbying for or against legislation that affects business, dealing efficiently and fairly with customer complaints and problems, sponsoring special events, and preparing news releases that present the business in a favorable light. Good public relations activities emphasize activities that are of interest to the public.

Obtaining positive publicity is one of the major goals of a public relations program. **Publicity** is like advertising in that messages are carried by some of the same media—newspapers, radio or television stations, and magazines. Publicity differs from advertising in that a business does not have to pay for the message. Through publicity a business distributes information that will have a positive impact on its image. News items concerning a company's products, employees, or community involvement are examples of publicity.

◢ PROMOTIONAL PLANNING

The primary objective of promotional activities is to increase demand for products and services and to stimulate sales by making it easy for consumers to buy. Careful planning is the key to a successful promotional effort. Promotional planning should include (1) defining the objectives, (2) choosing the appropriate promotional mix, and (3) evaluating the effectiveness of promotional efforts.

◢ Defining the Objectives

The first step in the promotional planning process is to define the objectives. Without clear objectives it is practically impossible for a marketing business to determine if its promotional efforts are working. Objectives will vary depending on the type of business; the type of product or service; whether the business operates on a national, regional, or local level; the competitive environment; and many other factors. The promotional objectives for a typical marketing business may include one or more of the following:

1. Increase the sales of new products or services.
2. Increase product or service information.
3. Prepare the way for personal selling.
4. Maintain market position.
5. Expand the market geographically.

6. Expand the market to include new groups of people.
7. Convince present buyers to increase their purchases.
8. Convince customers to use an established product in a new way.
9. Stimulate immediate demand or sales.
10. Stimulate long-term demand or sales.
11. Create goodwill.

Choosing the Appropriate Promotional Mix

After a company has defined its promotional objective(s), the next step in the promotional planning process is to choose the specific promotional mix of personal selling, advertising, visual merchandising, sales promotion, and public relations that will help it achieve its objective(s). In order to select the most appropriate promotional mix, marketers often conduct marketing research that might include studying the potential market, defining the target market, analyzing advertising channels, planning the advertising media mix, testing advertising messages, or analyzing the results of various personal selling or visual merchandising programs.

When choosing a promotional mix, the scope of a marketing business must be considered. For example, a local neighborhood convenience store may choose to promote its merchandise through the distribution of inexpensive flyers to homes in the surrounding area. A regional or national food supplier, on the other hand, may use television and newspaper advertisements and elaborate point-of-purchase displays.

Another factor that must be considered in the selection of an appropriate promotional mix is the type of product or service. Unlike a department store, a business that sells its products to organizational buyers will not promote them by advertising in community newspapers or on popular radio stations.

A third important factor is the promotional efforts of competitors. Many marketing businesses are forced to design promotional mixes that insure their efforts against their competitors. Large food stores, for example, usually run major newspaper advertisements on one particular day of the week. A food store that does not advertise on that day may be at a competitive disadvantage.

A fourth factor that affects the selection of a promotional mix is the amount of money a marketing business has available to spend on promotional activities. Some advertising media, such as television and magazines, are much more costly than others and are usually too expensive for many small marketing businesses. Promotion budgets are often arbitrarily based on the amount of money available or what the competition is spending. Marketers, therefore, must carefully plan a promotion mix that will maximize results and remain within the budget.

The final factor that affects the choice of a promotional mix is the stage a product or service has reached in the product life cycle. When a product or service is introduced to the market, the emphasis is on its brand name and advantages. During the mature stage, emphasis is placed on product or service features that make it better than competing items. When a product or service reaches the decline stage (sales begin to weaken), emphasis is on cutting expenditures in order to get the last spurt of sales with minimum promotional dollars.

Evaluating Effectiveness

The final step in the promotional process is evaluating the effectiveness of promotional activities. It is very difficult to determine the effects of promotion, especially nonpersonal promotion. However, an organization must attempt to evaluate the effects of its promotional activities in order to plan future promotional programs. The goal of evaluation is to determine if the organization's promotional efforts have had a positive effect on helping the organization reach its particular goals.

In for-profit businesses, the major goal of most promotional activities in to increase sales. It is necessary for the sales increase to be worth the expense involved in undertaking the promotion. There are numerous techniques used in the evaluation of the effectiveness of promotional efforts. For example, a national television campaign can be evaluated with audience reaction data provided by the A.C. Nielson Company. Nielson can provide specific estimates on the number of people in the country who saw a particular commercial during a specific time period.

Sales promotion activities such as rebates and coupons can be evaluated by examining the number of rebates and coupons that have been redeemed. Many businesses and organizations attempt to determine the effect their efforts will have prior to the actual promotional campaign by **pretesting.** The use of groups of people to evaluate a promotional idea prior to its use is a good example of pretesting. Testing performed after the campaign is referred to as **posttesting.** This might include asking people if they recall seeing a specific ad after they have read the newspaper. This type of posttest is called a newspaper ad recognition test.

APPLYING MARKETING TERMS

Name _____

Match each term with the statement that best describes an application of that term. Write the letter in the space provided.

a. pull strategy
b. sales promotion
c. visual merchandising
d. decode
e. promotional mix
f. advertising
g. encoding

h. receiver
i. channel of communication
j. push strategy
k. public relations
l. sender
m. personal selling
n. promotion

_____ 1. A newspaper article that describes a scholarship program sponsored by a local business.

_____ 2. Coupons fit into this category of promotional activities.

_____ 3. The consumer who decodes the promotional message of the business or organization.

_____ 4. The combination of various methods of promotion used by an organization to reach the stated objective(s).

_____ 5. Attempting to convince various intermediaries along the channels of distribution to carry your products or services.

_____ 6. A point-of-purchase display at the local supermarket is included in this category of nonpersonal promotion.

_____ 7. Paid messages promoting a service, product, organization, or idea that fill up nearly two-thirds of the space in your local newspaper.

_____ 8. Creating demand for goods and services at the ultimate consumer level.

_____ 9. The person or organization in the communication process that tries to get a message across to consumers.

_____ 10. Newspapers, radio, television, and direct mail are examples of this part of the promotional communication process.

_____ 11. The consumer must do this to interpret the promotional message sent by the business or organization.

_____ 12. The type of promotion undertaken by a sales representative when calling on a retail business account.

_____ 13. Includes personal and nonpersonal forms of persuasive communication about products and services.

_____ 14. The process the sender must undertake to put information into verbal or nonverbal symbols the receiver can understand.

Name _____

Answer each of the following questions in the space provided.

1. What is the major goal of promotional activities?

2. Identify three reasons why promotion is important.

3. What is the relationship between the communication process and promotion?

4. Explain the major difference between a push strategy and a pull strategy in promotion.

5. List the five principal methods or elements of promotion.

6. What is the main advantage of personal selling?

7. What is the primary goal of advertising?

8. Define visual merchandising.

9. Give four examples of typical sales promotions.

10. Define public relations.

11. Why is planning important to the promotional process?

12. What are the three steps that should be included in the promotional planning process?

13. When choosing a promotional mix, which five factors should be considered?

Read the following description of a human relations situation. Then complete your answers on a separate piece of paper.

Dealing with a Stubborn Boss

Stacey Jackson, a high school senior, is employed as a part-time customer service representative at Travel Express, a small, privately-owned travel agency. Stacey's job responsibilities include answering the telephone, greeting customers, answering customers' questions, and delivering tickets to customers.

Stacey is enrolled in Advanced Marketing at her high school. One of her class requirements is to complete a marketing research project. Stacey is analyzing the promotional efforts of Travel Express. Stacey thinks that Mr. Strong, the owner, is spending money on promotional activities that are having very little effect on the sale of travel services. Stacey knows that her agency is spending about 5–8 percent more (as a percentage of sales) on promotional efforts than the industry standards for this size of travel agency.

In her research study Stacey is using a survey of present and prospective customers to determine the impact that the promotional activities of Travel Express have on the customers' decision making. Specifically, she is interested in finding out if customers purchase their travel service from Travel Express as a direct result of promotional activities.

The findings of her study appear to indicate that the agency could save a considerable amount of money if it would cut back on some of its promotional efforts. For example, the company spent $10,000 last year on sales promotion items such as calendars, travel bags, pens, and attendance at the local county fair. However, 90 percent of those surveyed responded that these efforts had very little impact on their decision to purchase travel services from Travel Express.

Stacey would like to share this information with Mr. Strong, but in the past he has not been overly receptive to ideas or suggestions proposed by younger staff members. On another occasion Stacey made a minor suggestion to Mr. Strong and he suggested that she should wait until she had more experience before she made any further suggestions.

1. Discuss the major problem that you see in this case.
2. What suggestions would you make to Stacey Jackson regarding how she could present this information to Mr. Strong?
3. What objections do you think Mr. Strong might raise regarding Stacey's recommendation?

MARKETING PROJECT 9

Using the five steps given below, develop a promotional plan for a dance to be held next month at your school. This project can be completed individually or in small groups (3–4 students). Small groups should select a recorder and a group leader. Use your own paper.

Developing a Promotional Plan for a School Activity

1. Develop at least three different promotional objectives for the dance's campaign.
2. Create a list of the different possible promotional activities that could be used to meet the objectives listed in Step 1.
3. Evaluate the different activities and select the top three. This is your promotional mix for this event. Identify the factors that impacted on your selection of this promotional mix.
4. Identify the approximate budget that would be required to implement this promotional campaign.
5. Explain how the effectiveness of this promotional campaign will be evaluated.

MARKETING INSIGHT

Read the following description of real-life marketing practices. Then complete your answers on a separate sheet of paper.

The Media Jungle

The "it's a jungle out there" phrase is being used to describe the advertising bombardment experienced daily by consumers. Advertisers are discovering that even superior advertisements may not hit the mark if they are not delivered on the best media channel at the most appropriate times and places.

Overburdened consumers are ignoring the jungle. Some advertisers believe it is time to rethink the advertising process. Keith Reinhard, chairman and CEO of the advertising agency, DDB Needham Worldwide, says advertisers are going to have to develop strategies that tune in to consumer "media networks."

Reinhard explains that a typical day of programming on his media network begins when the clock radio wakes him with music and commercials. He then checks the television for weather and news before leaving for the office. Outside, he grabs the *New York Times* and *The Wall Street Journal* and notices posters on buses. At the fitness center he looks through magazines while pedaling an exercycle machine. By the end of the day, advertisers have had 50 opportunities to tap into Keith Reinhard's media network.

DDB Needham knew they would have to tap into consumers' networks when they advertised Amtrak's Auto-train service, which allows passengers to travel with their cars on board. A mid-winter radio campaign aimed at harried travelers at the end of a long car trip was broadcast along the Florida-Georgia border. The campaign produced a 358 percent increase in Auto-train bookings.

Reinhard predicts that to stand out, advertisers must begin advertising campaigns by asking where prospective customers can be found in the media jungle.[1]

1. What is meant by the term "media network" as used in this article?
2. List the advertising activities that would typically make up your own daily "media network."
3. Where does this article predict advertising campaigns of the future will begin?

---

[1]Bickley Townsend, "The Media Jungle." Used with permission © *American Demographics*, December 1988.

CHAPTER 10
PROMOTION: PERSONAL SELLING

After you read this chapter and complete the activities at the end, you will be able to:

1. **Define personal selling and discuss its relationship to the promotional mix.**
2. **Explain what is meant by professionalism in selling.**
3. **Identify six categories of selling careers.**
4. **Explain the five psychological stages of a sale.**
5. **Describe the eight steps in the sale process.**

It is estimated that close to 10 million people in the United States earn their living by selling to organizations or individual consumers. It's difficult to find an organization that does not employ personal salespeople. Even nonprofit organizations employ sales representatives, though their job titles may read "marketing representative" rather than "salesperson." Most organizations spend more money on personal selling than on any other single element in the promotional mix.

On a personal basis you are probably involved in selling every day of your life. Perhaps you are trying to convince one of your friends to go to a movie on Saturday night. Or maybe you would like to persuade your parents to pay part of your car insurance. Maybe you would even like to talk your marketing teacher into an "A" in your marketing class this term. In all of these examples you are trying to sell your ideas to someone else—your friends, parents, or teacher. If you are currently employed, you are probably involved in personal selling in some way at work, too. Instead of selling your ideas you might be selling products or services to prospective customers.

PERSONAL SELLING

Personal selling is considered one of the most important parts of the promotional mix. It brings the marketer into direct contact with the consumer. **Personal selling** is defined as personal, persuasive communication between a marketing employee and a consumer that is designed to convince the consumer to purchase products or services. Selling takes place when a marketer determines the needs and wants of a consumer and then helps to satisfy those needs and wants for the mutual benefit of both parties. The key term in this statement is *mutual benefit;* both buyer and seller must be satisfied if effective selling is to occur.

Personal selling involves matching a consumer's needs and wants with the goods or services offered by a business. The better the match, the more satisfied the consumer. In the long run a good match means a lasting relationship between a business or organization and a consumer.

PROFESSIONALISM IN SELLING

Perhaps you have been exposed to a salesperson who tried to convince you to buy something that you didn't think you wanted or needed. Undoubtedly this salesperson was very persuasive, maybe even pushy, and you probably became somewhat irritated by these pressure selling techniques. This salesperson, unfortunately, violated the major premise of customer-oriented selling. That is, a professional salesperson's role is to assist customers in making a quality purchase decision.

Salespeople represent the product or service expert, and their role is to match the features of their product with the needs of consumers, as depicted in Figure 10-1. Professional selling by definition means that the sales process results in the mutual satisfaction of both the buyer and the seller. If either party involved in the sales process is dissatisfied, then professional selling did not take place.

Figure 10-1   Professionalism in selling requires matching the features of the product or service with the needs of the consumer.

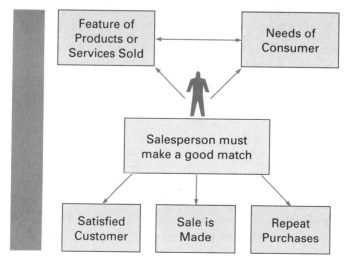

Sales personnel have long been misunderstood and frequently mislabeled as either unethical or unprofessional. Fortunately, the majority of salespeople are honest and have the best interest of the consumer in mind. Most have received advanced training and education and follow a strong code of professional ethics. They can operate on an unethical or unprofessional basis for a short period of time, but in the long run their success will be limited. It's not possible to survive on a long-term basis as a salesperson if you don't insist on satisfying the needs of consumers.

◢ CLASSIFICATION OF SELLING CAREERS

The classification of selling careers is not a simple task because there are so many different factors that influence how they are classified. One way to classify selling careers is by type of employer. For example, is a salesperson employed by a manufacturer, a wholesaler, a service business, or a retailer? A second way to classify sales positions is by the type of customer. Does a salesperson sell to ultimate consumers, wholesalers, service businesses, retailers, or manufacturers? Selling careers can also be classified by the type of product or service sold. Does the salesperson sell products or services, consumer goods, or technical services?

Sales and Marketing Executives International (SMEI) have identified six categories of selling careers.

1. **Industrial sales personnel** usually sell expensive products such as heavy equipment, computer and electronic equipment, machinery, and other technical products. These types of products are sold to purchasing agents in various industries. Industrial sales personnel usually must have a technical or engineering background.
2. **Retail sales personnel** generally do not seek buyers but rather buyers come to a fixed location to purchase products and services. Thousands of different items are sold by retail sales personnel. Approximately 50 percent of all sales personnel are employed at the retail level.
3. **Consumer route sales personnel** usually sell and deliver goods to a predetermined list of consumers. They sell such items as milk, bread, laundry supplies, and other convenience goods.
4. **Business route sales personnel** sell and deliver a wide variety of products and services including food products; office, factory, restaurant, and medical supplies; and many other items to a predetermined list of organizational users that buy on a regular basis.

5. **Consumer specialists** engage in direct selling by establishing personal contact with consumers. Door-to-door and telephone sales personnel fall into this category. Examples of items sold by this group include insurance, real estate, home repair products and services, financial services, household products, and other related products and services. Sales personnel in this category contact new prospects constantly.

6. **Business specialists** are similar to consumer specialists except that they sell to organizational users and are likely to be engaged in more creative selling. Examples of products or services sold by business specialists include business machines and small computers, business insurance, advertising, and commercial real estate. Like consumer specialists, sales personnel in this category must constantly prospect or canvas for new business.

PSYCHOLOGICAL STAGES OF A SALE

A salesperson should attract the prospective customer's attention, arouse interest, create desire, develop conviction, and invite action. These five elements—attention, interest, desire, conviction, and action—are referred to as the **psychological stages of a sale.** All buyers go through these stages consciously or unconsciously. A salesperson needs to understand how a buyer's mind works when she or he is making a purchasing decision. If a salesperson can estimate which stage a buyer has reached in the buying process, he or she will be able to tailor the sales presentation to that buyer's needs. For example, some customers know exactly what brand, color, and size they want to buy, where they want to buy it, and how much they have to spend. They have reached the action stage. A prospective customer at the other extreme has not expressed an interest in buying a particular product or service. He or she may not be planning to make a purchase right now. A salesperson must, therefore, be able to lead that person through all five psychological stages. The eight steps of the sales process (which are discussed later in this chapter) are designed to lead the prospect through these psychological stages.

Attract Attention

In the first psychological stage of a sale a customer becomes aware of the goods and services that are available, but does not necessarily appear interested in learning more about them. A salesperson cannot begin a sales presentation until the customer's attention has been focused on a product or service. The approach used by the salesperson is important in attracting the customer's attention and arousing interest.

Arouse Interest

This stage begins after the customer's attention is focused on a product or service. A buyer begins to look at the product or service as a way to satisfy a need or want. The salesperson's opening statement, which is part of the approach, may arouse buyer interest. This initial interest permits the salesperson to continue with the sales presentation and present or demonstrate the features and benefits of the product or service.

Create Desire

As the salesperson involves the buyer in the sales presentation by emphasizing the major selling points of the product or service, showing how it meets the buyer's needs and wants, and answering questions or responding to objections, the buyer's interest grows. She or he enters the desire stage. In this stage, the customer wants the product or service. A creative salesperson can heighten this desire by showing how each product or service feature translates into customer benefits.

Develop Conviction

If the salesperson's presentation is effective, a customer moves naturally into the conviction stage. In this stage the salesperson may need to answer questions again and overcome objections. A buyer in this stage is interested in making sure that the product or service will really meet his or her needs. Also, the buyer must be convinced that she or he will gain more satisfaction from this particular product or service than from other items that could be purchased with the same money.

Invite Action

The final psychological stage of the buying process is action, the point at which the customer makes a purchasing decision. If the four preceding stages have gone smoothly, the action stage is frequently automatic. A salesperson can use persuasive techniques to help the buyer make a purchasing decision. (These closing techniques will be discussed later in this chapter.) In some instances, however, the buyer may have difficulty making up his or her mind. When this happens, the salesperson may have to review the sales process in order to determine what went wrong. In many cases the salesperson will discover that the buying process broke down in the interest or conviction stage.

STEPS IN THE SALES PROCESS

People who sell goods or services follow a sales process that includes eight different steps. The salesperson should begin at the step that corresponds to the stage the buyer has reached in the buying process. For example, if a customer knows exactly what he or she wants to buy, the salesperson may have little to do except write up the order. Most sales transactions, however, require that the salesperson understand and follow the eight steps included in a sound sales process when helping buyers make purchasing decisions. In Figure 10-2, note how the psychological stages of a sale relate to the eight steps in the sales process.

Figure 10-2 Salespeople need to understand the steps and psychological stages in the sales process.

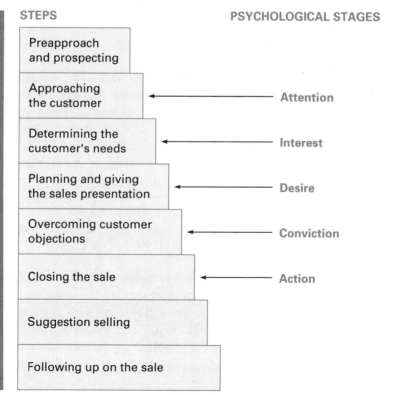

◤ Preapproach and Prospecting

The first step in the sales process is called the **preapproach.** It occurs before the salesperson establishes direct contact with buyers. The preapproach includes prospecting or locating potential customers, collecting and analyzing information about them, and developing a thorough knowledge of the products or services sold by the business. The fact-feature benefit analysis you studied in Chapters 5 and 6 is a useful technique for learning more about the products or services you are selling.

Prospecting is the process of locating or finding potential buyers who are capable of purchasing the products or services offered by the business. The importance of prospecting depends on the type of selling position. For example, insurance and real estate sales agents cannot sit and wait for clients to come into the office; they must actively seek potential customers. Prospecting is not as important to retail sales personnel since most consumers come into the business to purchase merchandise.

◤ Approaching the Customer

The **approach** begins when a salesperson first meets the customer. The most effective way to approach a customer or to open a sale is to create a positive first impression. A courteous, creative initial contact with a customer will go a long way towards promoting the final sale. A good approach will gain the customer's attention and arouse his or her initial interest in the product or service. The salesperson's opening statements are also considered part of the approach. These opening comments should increase the buyer's interest in what the salesperson has to say. Through the approach a salesperson can also help a customer discover that she or he has a buying problem (a need or want) that the salesperson can help to solve. It is estimated that the first 30 seconds are the most critical moments in the sales process.

◤ Determining the Customer's Needs

Once the salesperson has gained favorable attention and has created an initial interest in the product or service, the next step is to **determine the needs and wants** of the customer. This is usually accomplished by asking questions regarding the buyer's interests, expected uses, and experience with a product or service. As the salesperson asks these questions, the buyer's interest should increase.

The specific questions asked during this step depend on the type of product or service as well as the type of buyer. Some typical questions are as follows:

- Retail salesperson: Are you familiar with the features of the Hoover microwave oven?
- Industrial salesperson: Have you read the recent article in *Machinery Today* that explains how our new Model 3-X will increase your plant's productivity?
- Wholesale salesperson: Would you be interested in carrying a new line of nationally known men's shirts that has led the industry in average stock turnover?

Questions such as these help the salesperson involve the customer in the sales process. They will also help the salesperson determine what stage the buyer has reached in the buying process.

Planning and Giving the Sales Presentation

The purpose of the **sales presentation** is to create desire for a product or service. This step is the heart of the sales process and flows naturally from the previous steps. A salesperson should organize the sales presentation in advance. During the actual presentation, the salesperson should emphasize customer benefits, involve the customer, and skillfully present the product or service in an exciting or dramatic way.

Organize the Sales Presentation. Knowing what to say about products or services during the sales presentation is important in making a successful sale. A sales presentation that is not organized gives the customer a chance to dominate it and allows the salesperson to be sidetracked. A well-planned presentation, on the other hand, helps the salesperson maintain control over the sales process and leads the customer through the psychological stages of the sale.

A well-organized sales presentation requires advance planning, organization, and practice. The salesperson, however, should be flexible and adjust the presentation to the individual buyer's needs. The sales presentation should be tailored to the level of the customer's experience. The salesperson should not bore the customer with facts and information he or she already knows.

Emphasize Customer Benefits. Although it is important to talk about product or service facts and features, it is more important to translate this information into customer benefits. A customer will be more interested in how fast a snowblower will clear a driveway of snow than in technical facts concerning its five horsepower motor. Articles of clothing may be made of 50 percent cotton and 50 percent polyester, but it is important to point out that this means that they will not wrinkle and do not need ironing. A salesperson can prepare for this part of the sales presentation by reviewing the fact-feature benefit analyses forms prepared in the preapproach and prospecting step.

Involve the Customer. Product or service knowledge can help a salesperson get a customer involved in the sales presentation. If you were selling automobiles, for example, you would first discuss the features and benefits of a particular model and then invite a customer to test drive it and experience those benefits firsthand. If you were selling clothing, you might help customers try on merchandise and offer advice on colors and styles. The best way to present any product or service is to get the customer involved.

Use Skill to Dramatize. Dramatization is important during sales presentations. The salesperson's enthusiasm about a product or service often helps convince a customer to buy. Dramatization includes product demonstrations, handling products with respect, and choosing the correct words to describe features and benefits.

◣ Overcoming Customer Objections

Objections can occur at any point during the sales presentation, and the salesperson must be ready. Buyers must be convinced that a product or service will really meet their needs and provide satisfaction. **Objections** are honest points of difference between the buyer and the salesperson over issues such as price or quality. **Excuses,** which are often mistaken for objections, are not based on facts and are difficult for a salesperson to overcome. Excuses are false reasons why customers decide not to buy.

Examples of typical types of objections follow.

1. *Need:* My stereo system still works; I can't see that I really need a new one.
2. *Product:* I like the interior layout of this refrigerator, but I am afraid that it will be too small for my family.
3. *Source or brand:* I've always had good luck with Brand X shoes. I am just not sure about this new brand.
4. *Service:* According to other people I've talked with, I won't get good service from you.

5. *Price:* It's just too expensive.
6. *Time:* I don't see how I can charge anything else to my account right now.

A salesperson should always handle objections politely and professionally and not get defensive about them. A salesperson should view them as an opportunity to answer the customer's questions and provide more information about the product or service being sold. It is important to anticipate the types of objections customers may raise beforehand. One way to do this is to prepare an objection analysis sheet for each major product or service. Preparing an objection analysis sheet will help a salesperson identify in advance potential customer objections as well as possible response techniques. Figure 10-3 provides an example of an objection analysis sheet.

Figure 10-3   Potential customer objections and possible responses can be prepared in advance with an objection analysis sheet.

PRODUCT OR SERVICE: STEREO

Objection	Technique	Suggested Response
My stereo system still works; I can't see that I really need a new one.	Yes, But	Yes, it may work OK; but does it give you the quality sound of this new system?
It's just too expensive.	Direct Denial	No, not when you consider all the additional features and benefits of this product.

There are many techniques a salesperson may choose from in handling customer objections. Some of these are the yes, but, restate objection, superior point, and direct denial techniques.

Yes, But Technique. With this technique the salesperson begins on a positive note and then answers the objection.

Customer: My stereo system still works; I can't see that I really need a new one.

Salesperson: Yes, it may work OK; but does it give you the quality sound of this new system?

Restate Objection Technique. When using this technique, the salesperson restates the customer's objection in the form of a question.

This technique tends to reduce the magnitude of the objection in the customer's mind.

Customer: I like the interior layout of this refrigerator, but I am afraid that it will be too small for my family.

Salesperson: What makes you think that it will be too small for your family? How many cubic feet of storage space does your present refrigerator have?

Superior Point Technique. This technique allows a salesperson to agree with a customer's objection and then counter with a superior feature or benefit.

Customer: I've always had good luck with Brand X shoes. I am just not sure about this new brand.

Salesperson: I agree that Brand X has been around for a long time. This new brand, however, has several features that will make it more comfortable and durable.

Direct Denial Technique. With this technique the salesperson simply denies the customer's objection.

Customer: It's just too expensive.

Salesperson: No, not when you consider all the additional features and benefits of this product.

Closing the Sale

Many salespeople are unsuccessful because they fail to ask the customer to buy or **close the sale.** Timing is critical to a salesperson in closing a sale. A salesperson should learn to watch for and recognize buying signals. **Buying signals** are things that are done or said by customers that indicate they are close to reaching buying decisions. Buying signals indicate a readiness on the part of a customer to purchase a product or service. Examples of some typical buying signals include the following: (1) Can I get the sleeve length altered on this sport coat? (2) I think this chair would go well with my other furniture. (3) What type of buying terms does your firm provide?

There are techniques sales personnel can use to help customers make buying decisions. These closing techniques include the assumption close, the choice close, closing with an incentive, closing on a minor point, closing on an objection, closing by reviewing the selling points, and the direct close.

Assumption Close. With the assumption close the salesperson assumes that the customer is going to purchase the product or service and proceeds to write up the sale. A question concerning how a customer intends to pay for an item means that the salesperson is assuming the customer is buying it. Assumption oriented questions that are useful in this type of close include the following: (1) Did you want us to alter these slacks? (2) Will you be paying cash? (3) Did you want the item gift wrapped? (4) This is the model you want, isn't it? (5) When would be a convenient time for us to deliver the item?

Choice Close. The choice close is used when a salesperson has several closely related products or services to offer buyers. The choice offered by a salesperson always implies that a consumer will select and purchase an item from among the alternatives. The choice given may relate to such things as price, style, or color. For example: (1) We have three different models to choose from. (2) Each of these models has distinctive features. (3) Which of these colors do you prefer?

Closing with an Incentive. This technique is as old as selling itself. The salesperson offers the buyer an additional reason to make a buying decision. Examples of this technique are: (1) If you buy now, you will get 15 percent off the already low price. (2) If you purchase this encyclopedia set you will also receive a free atlas. (3) When you join you will get six free visits.

Closing on a Minor Point. When a salesperson uses this technique, a customer is asked to make a minor decision regarding a purchase. This technique assumes that it is easier for customers to make minor decisions than immediate major purchasing decisions. For example, if you were selling automobiles, you might ask a buyer questions such as the following: (1) Would you prefer the standard or deluxe interior? (2) Do you want a four or five speed transmission? (3) Are you interested in the two- or four-door model?

Closing on an Objection. With this technique the salesperson and the customer agree that an objection raised by the customer is the only barrier to the sale. When the salesperson answers the objection adequately, the customer will no longer have any reason to delay buying the product or service. If, for example, a customer objects that an item is too expensive, a salesperson might respond, "Is price the only factor that is stopping you from buying?" If the customer agrees, the salesperson closes on this objection by explaining the store's easy credit terms.

Closing by Reviewing the Selling Points. This technique involves summarizing or reviewing the major selling points of a product or service in a closing statement. The salesperson may say, "Let me summarize what we have discussed today. The major benefits of this product include. . . ." The salesperson then briefly reviews each of these benefits and closes by asking a question such as "Don't you agree that this is worth the price?"

Direct Close. This is one of the most frequently employed techniques used by salespeople to close a sale. The salesperson politely and directly asks the customer to buy. Examples of a direct close include questions such as these: (1) May I write up the order? (2) Should I have it wrapped for you? (3) Would you like us to deliver it?

Suggestion Selling

After a customer has made a buying decision, a salesperson should use **suggestion selling;** that is, make positive suggestions regarding the purchase of additional or supporting products or services. Suggestion selling can increase the sales volumes of many businesses by 25 percent. A question such as "Will there be anything else?" is not an example of suggestion selling; it does not make a positive suggestion. Examples of suggestion selling include the following: (1) How about a carrying case for that new camera? (2) You will need some shoe polish for your new shoes. (3) Let me explain our extended warranty service contract that is available with your new appliances.

Following up on the Sale

The sales process does not end after a customer has made a buying decision. The follow-up is an important part of every sale, although this is not always apparent to most salespersons. An enthusiastic and sincere closing statement that thanks the customer for his or her purchase is part of the follow-up. The follow-up also includes carrying out any promises that were made to the customer during the sale. If the salesperson promised delivery on Friday, she or he should check to make sure that this promise is fulfilled. If this is not possible, the salesperson should notify the buyer. Some sales personnel telephone customers after they have had an opportunity to use the product or service to see if they are satisfied with its performance. An organization with a reputation for following up on its sales is likely to obtain additional business because of its obvious concern for its customers. Customers who make purchases time after time are the life blood of the organization.

APPLYING MARKETING TERMS

Name _____

Match each term with the statement that best describes an application of that term. Write the letter in the space provided.

a. psychological stages of a sale
b. buying signal
c. closing the sale
d. suggestion selling
e. industrial salesperson
f. prospecting
g. consumer route salesperson
h. excuses
i. approach
j. business specialist
k. objections
l. sales presentation

_____ 1. Consciously or unconsciously, all customers go through attention, interest, desire, conviction, and action when making a purchase.

_____ 2. Asking the customer to make a purchase decision.

_____ 3. A sales career that requires the salesperson to have a technical or engineering background.

_____ 4. An action or statement by a customer which indicates a strong interest in buying a product or service.

_____ 5. A salesperson who is searching through the yellow pages of a phone directory to locate potential buyers for a product or service is at this step in the sales process.

_____ 6. This shirt and tie would go perfectly with that new suit.

_____ 7. Considered by many to be the most critical 30 seconds in the sales process.

_____ 8. False reasons why customers decide not to buy.

_____ 9. A salesperson who sells milk, bread, and other convenience goods to retail grocery outlets.

_____ 10. Honest reasons why customers decide not to buy.

_____ 11. Considered to be the "heart" of the sales process where the features and benefits of the product or service are explained to the customer.

_____ 12. A salesperson who sells copy machines and copy machine supplies to organizational users.

MASTERING KEY CONCEPTS

Name _____

Answer each of the following questions in the space provided.

1. Define personal selling and explain why it is important in your personal life as well as in your career.

2. What factors contribute to making selling a professional activity?

3. List and describe three categories of selling careers as identified by Sales and Marketing Executives International.

4. Why is it important for sales personnel to understand the psychological stages of a sale?

5. What is a salesperson trying to accomplish during the approach step of the sales process?

6. Why is advance planning important to a good sales presentation?

7. Describe two techniques for overcoming customer objections.

8. Why is timing critical to a salesperson when she or he is closing a sale? How do buying signals relate to the close of a sale?

9. Describe two closing techniques.

10. Why is suggestion selling an important part of the sales process?

11. What is included in the follow-up step of the sales process?

Read the following description of a human relations situation. Then complete your answers on a separate piece of paper.

Sales Incentives

Susan Green has been working as a sales associate at the Altamount Appliance Store since the beginning of the school year. Susan works approximately 20 hours per week after school and on Saturdays. Altamount sells primarily large appliances, such as refrigerators, stoves, washers, dryers, and television sets. However, two years ago the store manager decided to open up a new department, which carries a complete line of smaller appliances and electronic items. Susan is assigned to do sales and stock work primarily in the Small Appliance and Electronics Department.

Susan enjoys her job in this department and has been the top part-time salesperson for the last two months. Recently Susan's department manager, Marilyn Stauber, conducted a Saturday morning sales training session before the store opened at 10:00 A.M. In this session she indicated that the store was overstocked with cordless telephones, especially the expensive EZ2210 Model. To promote sales of this particular model, Ms. Stauber indicated that the store manager was willing to pay an incentive to the salespeople for each EZ2210 telephone unit sold.

Susan has sold several of these cordless telephones before and they appear to operate in a satisfactory manner. However, they are complicated for the user to operate and they cost much more than comparable units sold in the department. Susan suspects that the overstock of this particular model is due, at least in part, to these two customer factors—complexity of use and cost.

During the Saturday morning sales meeting Susan identified these two problems and the other salespeople agreed with her. However, after a few moments of discussion, Ms. Stauber made the following statement: "It's not your job to evaluate your products, Susan. What we want is sales and we want each of you to push this particular model. Don't you think the $5.00 incentive for each unit sold should be enough to buy your loyalty to Altamount?"

1. What do you see as the major problem of this case?
2. What alternatives could Susan have considered before she spoke out at the sales meeting?
3. Do you think that there is an ethical issue in this case?
4. If you were Susan, what would you do after the sales meeting?

MARKETING PROJECT 10

Prepare a complete sales presentation for a product or service of your choice. Please include the elements listed below.

Developing a Complete Sales Presentation

1. Pre-approach—Complete a fact-feature benefit analysis for your product or service.
2. Approach—Write out the exact wording of your approach.
3. Determining customer needs—Identify at least two questions you might ask the customer.
4. Overcoming objections—Prepare an objection analysis form for your product or service. Identify at least two possible objections and corresponding techniques to overcome these objections.
5. Closing the sale—Write out the exact wording you would use in closing the sale for your product or service.

MARKETING INSIGHT

Read the following description of real-life marketing practices. Then complete your answers on a separate piece of paper.

Selling to Your Customers

Once you lose a customer's attention, it's difficult to get it back. It is much easier to close a sale if you hold the customer's attention through your entire sales presentation. Here are six steps to make it easier:[1]

- Organize your thoughts before you start talking. If what you want to say is not clear in your mind, it will be worse when you say it. Don't make the customer struggle to understand you because if it doesn't make sense they stop listening.
- Get right to the point. Don't force your customer to wonder "So what's the point?" Don't keep them in suspense. Give them some meat to chew on while you elaborate with the details.
- Translate what you have to say into benefits for the customer. People seldom ignore what you say if they think there is something in it for them.
- Ask questions to involve the listener and create a dialogue. Determine the customer's interests, job, family status, hobbies, or areas you may have in common. Find out if they are listening by asking questions. Let them contribute to the conversation.
- Don't be afraid to let the real you shine through. Each of us has a unique personality. Don't try to copy someone else's style. You weaken what you are saying if you try to say it in a way that is unfamiliar to you. Your message is weakened if you have the added burden of playing a role. Just think about what you are saying and you'll be more comfortable.
- Be enthusiastic. If you aren't excited about your product, how can you expect your customers to be? Be animated and lively. Try to get through your customer's filters. If you don't have their attention and give your attention to them, you are not communicating.

1. Why is it important to hold a customer's attention throughout the sales process?
2. Why is customer involvement important in the sales process?
3. Which of the six suggestions in this article do you consider to be the most important? Why?

---

[1]Nido R. Qubein, "Six Steps to Get and Keep Your Customers' Attention," *Personal Selling Power* (September 1989), p. 12.

CHAPTER 11
PROMOTION: ADVERTISING

After you read this chapter and complete the activities at the end, you will be able to:

1. **Define advertising.**
2. **List and discuss the four major purposes of advertising.**
3. **Discuss four major criticisms of advertising.**
4. **Describe the three ways that advertising can be classified.**
5. **Discuss print and broadcast media and the advantages and disadvantages of each for advertisers.**
6. **Explain outdoor and specialty media.**
7. **Identify and explain the five steps of the advertising planning process.**
8. **Explain the major function of an advertising agency.**

American businesses spent over $118 billion dollars on advertising products, services, and ideas in 1988.[1] Advertising is part of all of our daily lives. The information and entertainment provided by newspapers, magazines, radio, and television are all made possible by the dollars spent advertising.

Advertising influences our purchasing decisions on a daily basis. Examine something you recently purchased such as a pair of jeans, a stereo, or a pair of snow skis. What influenced your decision to purchase these particular items? Perhaps you saw the jeans advertised in the local newspaper as being on sale. Before you purchased your stereo, you may have heard a radio ad promoting a local retail electronics store that carries the brand of electronic equipment you like. You may have been influenced in your decision to purchase new skis because of the advertising you recently saw in a popular ski magazine. Obviously other factors such as need, influence of your friends, reputation of the product, color, or cost were also involved. However, advertising probably had an impact on your decision to buy a particular product or service.

---

[1]*Advertising Age* (15 May 1989), p. 24.

If you doubt the power of advertising consider the fact that our very image of Santa Claus as a chubby, rosy-cheeked, grandfatherly fellow in a red coat was largely shaped by advertising. In 1931, an artist for Coca-Cola drew a picture of a twinkly-eyed figure who had a soft drink in his hand. And why? To convince people to drink Coke in the wintertime.

Advertising has been an important business activity since ancient times. Town criers proclaimed messages for those who made or produced more than they could consume or use. They announced sales of livestock and agricultural products. They called out rhymes and slogans for tradespeople who realized the value of letting others know about their products. The development of signs provided a second form of advertising. Then, as now, a sign gives potential customers some idea of the nature of the business, price, and where they are located. Using signs as a form of advertising dates back to at least 3000 B.C., when the Babylonians inscribed sales pitches on bricks.

With the advent of the printing press and the subsequent development of newspapers, businesses found a way to communicate with large numbers of potential buyers. Advertising became a permanent feature of the American system. The development of the radio, which could reach large numbers of potential customers instantaneously, gave a voice to advertising and made regional and national marketing a fact of life. Television provided the opportunity of using moving pictures and gave advertisers a medium that had an even greater impact.

Illustration 11-1

Advertising is part of our lives. It helps inform, educate, and entertain us.

The California Raisin Board

Each of these historic communications developments meant changes in the way advertising was presented. Newspapers and magazines allowed the display of products and detailed descriptions. Because of the limited time (thirty seconds to one minute) available on radio, advertisers could convey only important benefits or features. Television allowed advertisers to display and explain a product in a manner that was similar to a door-to-door salesperson's presentation.

ADVERTISING

Advertising is a vital ingredient of the American economic system. It would be pointless for a business to offer a product or service if there were no way to tell people about it. **Advertising** can be defined as the use of paid nonpersonal messages promoting ideas, goods, or services directed at an audience through various mass media by an identified sponsor. An identified sponsor is the business or individual who pays for an advertisement. Advertising is a means of communication. It is used to inform, to persuade, and to encourage people to act. Simply stated, it is the way a business talks with mass numbers of potential buyers. Advertisements tell customers that a product or service is available and point out the advantages it offers. The 10 top U.S. advertisers spent over $10 billion on ads in 1988. Figure 11-1 lists the 1987 and 1988 expenditures by these top 10 advertisers.

THE IMPORTANCE AND PURPOSES OF ADVERTISING

Advertising is an important part of the promotional mix. It is important to the total marketing effort of a business or organization because it aids the movement of goods and services along the channels of distribution. Thus, one of the major purposes of advertising is to stimulate demand and increase sales of goods and services at all levels in the distribution process.

In addition to stimulating demand and increasing sales, advertising also serves several other major purposes. Advertising serves an informational purpose; people learn from advertising. They find out what products and services are available and what they will do or how they function. Advertising relates the benefits of these products and services and explains how they will improve people's lives.

Advertising also serves an important social purpose. It is indirectly responsible for the high standard of living enjoyed by many people in the United States. By stimulating demand, advertising pro-

Figure 11-1   The top 10 U.S. advertisers spent over $10 billion on ads in 1988, up from about $9.5 billion in 1987.

TOP U.S. ADVERTISERS
(In Millions)

Company	1987	1988
Phillip Morris	$1,920	$ 2,058
Procter and Gamble	1,466	1,507
General Motors	966	1,294
Sears, Roebuck and Co.	1,001	1,045
RJR Nabisco	843	815
Grand Metropolitan PLC	790	774
Eastman Kodak Co.	678	736
McDonald's Corp.	658	728
PepsiCo Inc.	703	712
Kellogg Co.	561	683
Total	$9,585	$10,352

Source: Reprinted with permission from *Advertising Age* (27 September 1989), Copyright Crain Communications, Inc. All rights reserved.

motes the sale of more goods and services. This translates into increased employment opportunities and thus increased income or wages that can be spent on goods and services. This increase in consumption results in a higher standard of living.

Finally, advertising is a major contributor to the entire communications process. One of its basic functions is the transmission of information. Without advertising, newspapers, magazines, radio, and television would not exist in their present forms because advertising is their primary source of income.

In addition to these major purposes, advertising also serves a number of related but more specific purposes including the following:

1. Producing immediate sales of products or services.
2. Increasing the quantity purchased by those who are already buyers of the products or services.
3. Promoting the purchase of more than one unit of a product or service at a time.
4. Appealing to those who do not yet buy a product or service.
5. Familiarizing consumers with the uses of products or services.
6. Stressing the exclusive features of products or services.
7. Introducing new styles to the marketplace.
8. Getting customers to come into a business.
9. Preparing the way for a personal selling program.
10. Increasing sales during the off-season.

Advertising efforts are undertaken by producers as well as by various intermediaries along the channels of distribution. Using the push strategy, for example, manufacturers advertise so that wholesalers and retailers will know what products or services are available and where they can be obtained. Wholesalers, in turn, advertise so that retailers will have information on which to base their buying decisions. As the last step in the distribution process, retailers are responsible for making consumers aware of available goods or services, their benefits, and where they can be purchased.

In addition to advertising directed to various intermediaries, under the pull strategy producers or manufacturers also frequently engage in advertising programs aimed at consumers that encourage them to purchase various products or services from available sources. (See Chapter 9 for more detail on the push and pull strategies of promotion.)

THE CRITICS OF ADVERTISING

As one of the most visible business activities, advertising is often an easy target for criticism. Four of the most frequent objections to advertising are:

1. Advertising makes people buy things they don't want.
2. Advertising makes products and services cost more.
3. Advertising helps sell bad or inferior products or services.
4. Advertising is a waste of money.

Improving the image of advertising was the object of a recent nationwide newspaper and magazine campaign sponsored by the American Association of Advertising Agencies. This association addressed the above four objections in the advertisement shown in Illustration 11-2.

TYPES OF ADVERTISING

Advertising can be classified in many different ways. It is useful to classify advertising based on its purpose, its coverage, and its type of appeal.

Purpose of Advertising

Advertising can be classified according to purpose as promotional, institutional, or advocacy advertising. **Promotional advertis-**

Illustration 11-2   The American Association of Advertising Agencies used this creative advertisement to respond to some objections.

LIE #1: ADVERTISING MAKES YOU BUY THINGS YOU DON'T WANT.

Advertising is often accused of inducing people to buy things against their will.

But when was the last time you returned home from the local shopping mall with a bag full of things you had absolutely no use for? The truth is, nothing short of a pointed gun can get *anybody* to spend money on something he or she doesn't want.

No matter how effective an ad is, you and millions of other American consumers make your own decisions. If you don't believe it, ask someone who knows firsthand about the limits of advertising. Like your local Edsel dealer.

LIE #2: ADVERTISING MAKES THINGS COST MORE. Since advertising

costs money, it's natural to assume it costs *you* money. But the truth is that advertising often brings prices down.

Consider the electronic calculator, for example. In the late 1960s, advertising created a mass market for calculators. That meant more of them needed to be produced, which brought the price of producing each calculator down. Competition spurred by advertising brought the price down still further.

As a result, the same product that used to cost hundreds of dollars now costs as little as five dollars.

LIE #3: ADVERTISING HELPS BAD PRODUCTS SELL.

Some people worry that good advertising sometimes covers up for bad products.

But nothing can make you like a bad product. So, while advertising can help convince you to try something once, it can't make you buy it twice. If you don't like what you've bought, you won't buy it again. And if enough people feel the same way, the product dies on the shelf.

In other words, the only thing advertising can do for a bad product is help you find out it's a bad product. And you take it from there.

LIE #4: ADVERTISING IS A WASTE OF MONEY. Some people wonder why

we don't just put all the money spent on advertising directly into our national economy.

The answer is, we already do.

Advertising helps products sell, which holds down prices, which helps sales even more. It creates jobs. It informs you about all the products available and helps you compare them. And it stimulates the competition that produces new and better products at reasonable prices.

If all that doesn't convince you that advertising is important to our economy, you might as well stop reading.

Because on top of everything else, advertising has paid for a large part of the magazine you're now holding.

And that's the truth.

ADVERTISING.
ANOTHER WORD FOR FREEDOM OF CHOICE.
American Association of Advertising Agencies

American Association of Advertising Agencies

ing tries to convince potential buyers to purchase a specific product or service. It is also called immediate response or direct action advertising because it urges customers to buy a specific item. Most advertising falls into this category. **Institutional advertising** attempts to generate goodwill or bolster a company's image. It is also called attitude or indirect action advertising because its aim is to create a favorable impression and enhance a firm's reputation. Advertisements by oil companies that discuss their effort to help clean up the environment or utility company advertisements concerning energy conservation are examples of institutional advertising. **Advocacy advertising** is a form of advertising that presents an individual's or organization's viewpoint.

Coverage of Advertising

Advertising can also be classified according to coverage as local, national, or cooperative advertising. **Local advertising** is usually sponsored by retail businesses. It makes up the bulk of local newspaper and local radio station advertising. **National advertising** is sponsored by a manufacturer or other supplier whose products are distributed nationwide or in a large region of the country. Prime time television advertising is almost exclusively national. **Cooperative advertising** combines both national and local advertising. An advertisement is prepared and distributed by a manufacturer or supplier with space for local retailers that carry its goods to insert their names and addresses. Advertising costs are shared by the manufacturer and the local merchants.

Appeal of Advertising

A third way to classify advertising is by the type of appeal (rational or emotional) used in an advertisement. An **appeal** is an underlying message that is designed to arouse a response. In advertising it helps convince consumers to buy products or services.

An advertisement has a **rational appeal** if it is directed at a consumer's logical thought process. Such an advertisement contains facts about a product or service so that consumers can weigh its benefits and make a logical purchasing decision. An advertisement that describes an automobile's excellent gas mileage, rack-and-pinion steering, front-wheel drive, and suspension systems appeals to the rational thoughts of consumers and helps convince them to buy.

Advertising that appeals to a consumer's wants and needs has an **emotional appeal.** An automobile advertisement that shows the car's

Illustration 11-3   Local advertising makes up the bulk of local newspaper advertising.

sleek lines and luxurious interior and an attractive driver is designed to appeal to a consumer's emotions and desires.

People have many needs that advertisers seek to uncover. Major advertising agencies employ behavioral scientists who study consumer attitudes and motives. These agencies seek to develop advertisements that will appeal to these attitudes and motives.

◢◣ ADVERTISING MEDIA

Advertisers reach customers through various advertising media. **Advertising media** are the different methods—newspapers, radio, magazines, television, signs, billboards, direct mail—that companies use to send their advertising messages to potential buyers. An advertising medium is a single method such as radio or billboards. The combination of advertising media used by a business or organization is known as the **advertising media mix.** Figure 11-2 shows the total dollar volume spent on various advertising media in the U.S. in 1987 and 1988.

Figure 11-2   More advertising dollars are spent on newspapers than any other single medium. Direct mail, however, is growing at the fastest rate.

U.S. ADVERTISING DOLLARS BY MEDIA

Medium	1987 (In Millions)	1988 (In Millions)	Percentage Change 1987–1988
Newspaper	$ 29,412	$ 31,197	+ 6.1%
Magazine	5,607	6,072	+ 8.3
Television	23,904	25,686	+ 7.5
Radio	7,206	7,798	+ 8.2
Yellow Pages	7,300	7,781	+ 6.6
Direct Mail	19,111	21,115	+10.5
Outdoor	1,025	1,064	+ 3.8
Miscellaneous	16,085	17,337	+ 7.2
Total	$109,650	$118,050	+ 7.7%

Source: Reprinted with permission from *Advertising Age* (15 May 1989), Copyright Crain Communications, Inc. All rights reserved.

A business wants to develop an advertising program that will allow its message to reach the largest number of potential customers with the greatest impact and the least cost. It is possible at times to achieve all three objectives, but this is rarely the case. A particular medium may be capable of reaching more potential customers than any other medium, but its cost may also be higher. In this case, an advertiser must weigh the benefits of communicating with more people against the extra cost and decide which is more important. The advertiser should be familiar with the advantages and disadvantages of each medium in order to make such marketing decisions.

There are three major classifications of advertising media: print media, broadcast media, and outdoor and specialty media.

◤ Print Media

Print media includes newspapers, magazines, shoppers' guides, direct mail, the yellow pages, and other printed materials. A news-

Illustration 11-4

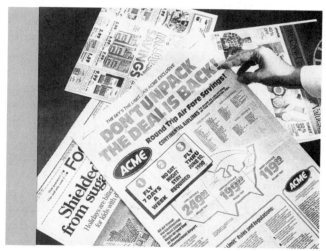

Advertisers
reach customers
through various
advertising
media.

Courtesy of The Goodyear Tire & Rubber Company

paper is considered a general use product because it reaches a very general widespread audience. Newspapers carry something of interest for nearly everyone; readership is quite diversified.

Newspapers carry both national and local advertising. More money is spent on newspaper advertising ($32 billion) than on any other single medium. Newspaper advertisements are either display or classified advertisements. Display advertisements are located throughout a newspaper and usually include a headline, illustration, body copy, price, and business identification. Classified advertisements, which are usually called want ads, are placed in a separate section near the back of a newspaper. Classified advertisements are less expensive than display advertisements but are not as visible.

Because daily or weekly newspapers are published in nearly every city, town, suburb, or rural area in the country, an advertiser has a great deal of geographic selectivity and can place advertisements in newspapers that will reach large numbers of potential customers. The advertiser can request that advertisements be run on special pages, such as the sports page, farm page, or food page, so that specific groups of readers will see them.

Newspapers offer the best time advantages of any medium because an advertisement can be prepared and placed in a newspaper in a very short time or quickly withdrawn if necessary. This allows an advertiser flexibility in case of emergencies such as changes in the weather or the availability of products. If a retailer, for example, prepares and submits an advertisement for a shirt sale and the shirts do not arrive from the supplier, the advertisement can easily be postponed.

Newspapers have several disadvantages for advertisers. One disadvantage is the short life of a newspaper. After a newspaper is a day old, it is usually discarded. Thus, advertisements do not receive secondary exposure. Another disadvantage is that newspapers are usually hastily read, and many people do not pay attention to advertisements that are placed on the bottom halves of newspaper pages. While improvements in equipment and paper stock have enhanced newspaper reproduction quality, it is still marginal when compared with magazine reproduction quality. Newspaper advertisements are usually printed in black and white although some color is now being used in most newspapers.

Magazines allow advertisers to reach consumers nationwide. Magazines have a prestige that is not associated with newspapers. They are published for general audiences as well as for specialized audiences. Indeed, the trend is towards more specialization in content. It is now possible to advertise in magazines published solely for homemakers, computer users, car enthusiasts, stamp collectors, sports fans, runners, campers, do-it-yourselfers, investors, or almost any other group. There are also magazines for doctors, lawyers, plumbers, retail store managers, interior decorators, computer repair personnel, restaurant owners, and many other groups of professional and business people.

Magazines are usually kept in homes or businesses for a period of time before they are discarded; therefore, advertisements receive additional exposure. Many national magazines make advertising space available to regional advertisers. A Colorado business, for example, can advertise in *Time* magazine. Since its advertisement will appear only in issues of *Time* distributed in Colorado, it will cost considerably less than a national advertisement but will still have the prestige associated with a national magazine. Magazine reproduction is excellent because of the high quality of the paper and the printing processes that are used.

A magazine advertisement must be prepared far in advance of the magazine's publication date. Last minute changes are almost always impossible. Magazine advertisements are more expensive than newspaper advertisements. Even though the cost of each potential buyer reached through a magazine advertisement is competitive, the overall cost is often too high for local advertisers. Another disadvantage is that a magazine advertisement, like a newspaper advertisement, often competes with the other material on the same page and may be skimmed over.

Shopper's guides are composed almost entirely of advertising. They contain both display and classified advertisements, but the majority of advertisements are classified. The guides are delivered door to door or are available at supermarkets and other stores. The reproduction quality of a shoppers' guide is similar to that of a newspaper. Guides are usually read by people who are interested in buying something in particular. Thus, they are typically discarded quickly. Entertainment guides are similar to shoppers' guides but contain advertisements for restaurants, theaters, and clubs.

Direct mail is an advertising medium that has a distinct place in the promotion of products or services. It includes advertising that is sent through the mail as well as catalogs. It may take the form of sales letters, coupons, circulars, postcards, or brochures. Mail order buying has become more prevalent, and a number of businesses do all their advertising and selling through the mail. Direct mail advertising has grown more rapidly than other advertising medium in the last ten years. Direct mail ranks behind only newspapers and television in terms of dollars spent by businesses and organizations. More than $21 billion were spent in 1988 on this advertising medium.

The advantages of direct mail include being able to select people by interest or geographic location and send advertisements directly to their homes or businesses. Mailing lists of people with specific interests are available as are lists of people who have demonstrated a willingness to purchase through the mail. Direct mail also allows an advertiser to describe a product or service in detail, to use extensive art for demonstration, and to personalize the message.

Direct mail also has several disadvantages. Many people immediately discard this kind of advertising as junk mail. Mailing costs may be high, and maintaining a mailing list can be expensive. The preparation of the art and cost for an advertisement may also be costly.

The yellow pages are located in the back of most telephone directories or as a separate directory. Space in the yellow pages is sold to businesses and organizations in a fashion similar to newspapers and magazine advertising space. Many communities will have several different competitive telephone directories containing paid advertising. The major advantage of yellow pages advertising is that this medium is generally widely circulated (one in each household) and has a relatively long life, lasting at least a year. Another advantage of yellow pages advertising is its ability to segment the market geographically. The major disadvantage of the yellow pages is the lack of customer utilization of this section of the telephone directory and the difficulty of measuring its effectiveness in terms of increasing business.

◢ Broadcast Media

Radio and television are **broadcast media.** They reach more homes than any other type of medium. There is a radio in approximately 99 percent of the homes and cars in the United States. It is estimated that 98 percent of all homes have television.

Radio is a flexible medium. Since it is portable, a radio can go just about anywhere—beaches, picnics, offices, backyards. Since radios are used extensively in automobiles, radio advertising is an excellent way to reach a large number of people. Because radio stations cater to various tastes by playing different types of music, such as rock, classical, country, or jazz, an advertiser can direct a message to a specific audience. An advertiser can also select the time of day that a radio advertisement will be broadcast. This provides flexibility because groups such as sports fans, homemakers, farmers, and business people generally listen to the radio during specific time periods.

The biggest disadvantage of radio is that an advertising message comes and goes very quickly; it is not available for rereading or review. There are also more radio stations in most towns than there are newspapers, so the competition is fierce. A radio does not require a listener's full attention; it serves as a background for other activities. This lack of attention means that radio advertisements are often missed.

Television's impact on consumers is stronger than any other medium's. Nearly $26 billion were spent on television advertising in 1988. It is like a door-to-door salesperson calling on a prospect. It allows the visual demonstration of products and services. Television does not require viewer literacy. As with radio, an advertiser can select the time of day that an advertisement will be broadcast and direct a message to a selected audience. Different groups of people watch television during specific time periods. In local markets across the country, advertisers have found that even low-budget productions can be a tremendous boost to business. One of the fastest growing areas of television advertising is on cable TV. Over $1 billion were spent on cable TV ads in 1988.

Naturally there are disadvantages. The cost of television advertising is one of them. Even though the size of the audience reached by prime time or local television advertisements makes the cost for each viewer quite low, overall costs can be very high. Many small business firms cannot afford to prepare a television commercial and run it enough times to have an impact on viewers. Cost also limits the selection of time periods during which local advertisers can run their commercials. The overall expense of prime time advertising eliminates all but the nation's largest companies. It is estimated that a single local television spot (30 seconds) costs an advertiser $500 to $10,000. National commercials cost much more. For example, a 30-second spot during Super Bowl XXIV cost $700,000.

Like radio advertisements, television advertisements are not available for review. Television commercial breaks are often looked on as a time to fix snacks or read the newspaper. Thus, in addition to competing with programs on other television channels, an advertiser often competes with some of the very activities that are the subject of the commercial message.

Outdoor and Specialty Media

Outdoor and speciality media include outdoor signs and billboards as well as specialty items such as matchbooks and other inexpensive novelties. Outdoor signs or billboards offer an advertiser space for a simple message. In some cases a sign may be located close to the business whose advertisement it displays. Since people often pass signs and billboards again and again, the repetition of an advertisement helps keep its message in their minds. Advertisements on the inside or outside of public transportation vehicles and taxicabs or in terminals and stations attract attention because they are located in places where people have little else to do besides read the messages. Transit advertising is relatively inexpensive and, if a public vehicle passes near an advertised business, it can be beneficial.

Specialty media are items that carry the advertiser's name and are given to selected people as a means of keeping the company name in front of the customer. In order to be effective, such items must be useful, of good quality, and easy to use. While expensive, specialty advertising can serve as a reminder for a long time if items are of lasting quality. Matchbooks, calendars, pencils, and other relatively inexpensive novelty items are examples of specialty advertising.

THE ADVERTISING PLANNING PROCESS

Advertising, like other promotional activities, requires advance planning in order to be effective. There are five steps in the advertising planning process: (1) setting the advertising objectives, (2) preparing the advertising budget, (3) selecting the advertising media, (4) implementing the advertising plan, and (5) evaluating the effectiveness of the advertising program.

Setting Advertising Objectives

The advertising planning process begins with setting realistic objectives. What does a business want to accomplish with its advertising program? Should the program sell specific goods or services, attract new buyers, remind current buyers of the products or services offered, introduce new products and services, develop and maintain goodwill, or improve the image of the business? Or should the advertising program accomplish some combination of these objectives?

Preparing the Advertising Budget

After the advertising objectives have been established, the next step is to prepare an advertising budget. In order to do this, a business must first decide what percentage of anticipated sales income will be allocated for advertising expenses. The percentage will vary depending on the type of business, previous advertising experiences, competition, and the nature of the products or services being promoted.

Comparative percentages for different types of businesses are usually listed in specialized trade journals. By multiplying the anticipated sales volume by this percentage, a business can determine the advertising budget for the year. A retail business, for example, may spend between 2 and 10 percent (5 percent is most common) of its gross sales on advertising. This means that if a small retail business anticipated gross sales of $350,000 for the coming year and decided to allocate 5 percent for advertising, the advertising budget for that year would be $17,500 ($350,000 $\times$ .05).

Once the advertising budget is set, it can be broken down into planned monthly expenditures. Some companies base their monthly advertising budgets on the anticipated sales volume for each month. These sales estimates are based on the previous year's sales records plus any projected increases or decreases. For example, if May contributed 10 percent of last year's sales and no changes are expected, a business would plan to spend 10 percent of this year's advertising budget in May. Thus, a business can base its monthly advertising program on the anticipated sales for each month.

The November to December holiday season is an exception to the monthly budgeting approach. Many retail and mail order businesses generate 25 to 50 percent of their annual sales during this period. It would be unwise to spend 25 to 50 percent of the advertising budget during the month of December. Budget allocations can also vary because of the objectives that the business has established for its advertising program. Special seasonal sales events, grand openings, clearance sales, and other promotional activities may also have an impact on how the advertising budget is allocated.

Advertising is a completely controllable business expense. This means that an owner or manager can control, through good planning and accurate record keeping, the amount of money that is spent on advertising. It also means that the advertising budget can be adjusted, for good reason, at any time during the year. Budget adjustments may be required in response to the actions of competitors or changing economic conditions. An owner or manager can keep track of advertising expenditures by using a monthly tabulation record such as the one shown in Figure 11-3 on page 250.

A completed monthly tabulation record will provide the following information for each advertising account: (1) the planned expenditure for a particular month, (2) how much was actually spent, (3) the planned year-to-date expenditure, and (4) the year-to-date amount that has been spent. The totals for the four columns will reveal (1) whether a business was over or under budget for a particular month and (2) if it is over or under budget for the year.

Figure 11-3   A monthly record of advertising expenses can provide valuable information to the business manager.

ADVERTISING BUDGET
MONTHLY TABULATION RECORD

ACCOUNTS	MONTH		YEAR TO DATE	
	BUDGET	ACTUAL	BUDGET	ACTUAL
Media Expense				
Newspaper				
Radio				
Television				
Direct mail				
Other				
Advertising Expense				
Salaries				
Supplies				
Travel				
Postage				
Subscriptions				
Entertainment				
Dues				
Totals				

Planning the Advertising Media Mix

After the objectives of an advertising program and an advertising budget have been established, the next step in the planning process is the selection of media that will effectively send a message to current and prospective customers. This is known in marketing as planning the media mix. Most local business firms will find that newspaper, radio, or direct mail advertising meets their needs. A regional or national business may want to consider magazine, television, or outdoor advertising.

The selection of a medium depends on a number of different factors. Will it reach the desired audience? Is it suitable for the type of advertising that a business would like to do? Will the advertising budget cover the expenses of this particular medium? What media are used by competitors? What other media are available to the business? Figure 11-4 provides a checklist that can be used to evaluate various advertising media.

Figure 11-4   This checklist contains some of the factors that should be evaluated when selecting an advertising medium.

MEDIA CHECKLIST

	Yes	No
1. Does the medium *reach* the largest number of prospects at the lowest cost per prospect?	_____	_____
2. Does the medium provide an opportunity for an adequate selling *message*?	_____	_____
3. Does the medium provide the opportunity to *illustrate* the merchandise or service being sold?	_____	_____
4. Does the medium *sell* merchandise or services, or does it merely *announce* them?	_____	_____
5. Does advertising in the medium present difficult or time-consuming *problems?*	_____	_____
6. What is the medium's *flexibility?* Can the copy message be changed easily?	_____	_____
7. Does the medium provide the opportunity to *repeat* the selling message?	_____	_____
8. Does the medium provide *excitement?*	_____	_____
9. Does the medium *fit* the type of business in terms of prestige and distinction?	_____	_____
10. Does the medium *cover* the entire market area with minimum waste coverage outside the market zone?	_____	_____
11. Does the medium have any characteristics that might *annoy* people and contribute to poor public relations for the business?	_____	_____
12. Is the total *cost* of advertising in this medium within the financial capacity or budget of the business?	_____	_____

Source: Adapted from Harland E. Samson and William T. Price, Jr., *Advertising: Planning and Technique*, 3d ed. (Cincinnati: South-Western Publishing Co., 1992), p. 22.

◣ Implementing the Advertising Plan

The next step in the advertising planning process is the implementation of the plan. In a small business this is often the responsibility of the owner or manager. Local newspapers and radio stations will often provide technical assistance to small businesses in planning and implementing their advertising programs. Large businesses employ advertising specialists or use advertising agencies to implement their advertising plans.

◣ Evaluating the Effectiveness of the Advertising Program

The final step in the advertising planning process is to evaluate the success or failure of the advertising program. The effects of advertising efforts are difficult to measure. The most common evaluation technique is the examination of sales records for the advertising period. An increase in sales can at least be partially attributed to advertising efforts.

Advertisers may conduct pretests and posttests. Pretests often involve showing advertisements to people who are wired to electronic equipment that measures pulse rates, eye movement, brain waves, and even perspiration. Although there is debate concerning the effectiveness of such pretesting, advertisers do use these methods to help them determine if a proposed advertisement is interesting, believable, or memorable. Major advertisers may also conduct posttests. These tests ask consumers what they remember about an advertisement and their attitudes towards it.

Since most pretesting and posttesting procedures are too complicated and expensive for many small businesses, direct mail techniques can be used. For example, a retail store manager mails an equal number of two different advertisements for the same product that include store coupons. The manager then determines which of the two advertisements has produced the best response.

After designing a personal finance program for microcomputers, a university professor sent flyers describing it to several hundred prospective customers. The flyers were of two types; one listed a higher purchase price than the other. This direct mail technique revealed that people were more interested in the program at the high price. They apparently believed that the low price represented a low-quality product. The professor could sell more programs and increase profits by using the flyers that listed the higher price.

Measuring the effects of an advertising program is extremely difficult for a number of reasons. Potential buyers may not respond to an advertisement immediately but may choose to purchase a product or service months later. When attempting to evaluate an advertising program, advertisers must also consider the weather, the actions of competitors, the season, and any other factor that influences buying patterns. Small advertisers do have an advantage because they are closer to customers and are better able to understand what advertising approach has the strongest appeal. They can strive to create advertisements that are tuned to the market, include the information that buyers need, and support their images and goals. In the final analysis, however, the evaluation of any firm's advertising efforts is an educated guess. There is no sure technique for determining whether an advertisement has accomplished the objectives of an advertising program.

USING AN ADVERTISING AGENCY

Many medium-sized and most large businesses and organizations utilize the services of an advertising agency. An **advertising agency** specializes in helping businesses and organizations in the planning, development, and implementation of their advertising plan. Most of the ads that you see on network television or in a national magazine have been produced by the personnel who work at an ad agency. These agencies employ advertising space buyers, artists, copywriters, account managers, and a whole host of other specialists in the advertising process. The advantage of using an ad agency is that the business or organization does not need to employ all of the specialists, but rather they rely on the expertise of the agency. Figure 11-5 gives the top 10 U.S. advertising agencies.

Figure 11-5   Top 10 U.S. advertising agencies in terms of gross income.

Y & R LEADS U.S. AGENCIES AGAIN
IN 1988 WORLDWIDE GROSS INCOME

RANK	AGENCY	GROSS INCOME		BILLINGS	
		1988	1987	RANK	1988
1	Young & Rubicam	$758	$736	1	$5,390
2	Saatchi & Saatchi Advertising Worldwide	740	683	2	5,035
3	Backer Spielvogel Bates Worldwide	690	601	3	4,678
4	McCann-Erickson Worldwide	657	513	4	4,381
5	FCB-Publicis	653	NA	5	4,358
6	Ogilvy & Mather Worldwide	635	564	6	4,110
7	BBDO Worldwide	586	550	7	4,051
8	J. Walter Thompson Co.	559	488	8	3,858
9	Lintas Worldwide	538	418	9	3,586
10	Grey Advertising	433	369	12	2,886

Notes: Dollars are in millions. U.S.-based agencies are ranked based on worldwide gross income and billings. D'Arcy Masius Benton & Bowles is ranked 10th by billings.

Source: Reprinted with permission from *Advertising Age*, (20 March 1989), Copyright Crain Communications, Inc. All rights reserved.

APPLYING MARKETING TERMS

Name _____

Match each term with the statement that best describes an application of that term. Write the letter in the space provided.

a. specialty media
b. institutional advertising
c. cooperative advertising
d. advertising media mix
e. promotional advertising
f. outdoor advertising

g. newspaper advertising
h. local advertising
i. advertising agency
j. national advertising
k. advocacy advertising
l. direct mail advertising

_____ 1. A service business that specializes in developing and implementing advertising programs for organizations.

_____ 2. An advertisement which presents the viewpoint of a political party or candidate.

_____ 3. A 30-second television spot advertisement shown during the World Series or Super Bowl.

_____ 4. A J. C. Penney or Sear's catalog sent to consumers' homes is an example of this type of print medium.

_____ 5. A billboard positioned along a major thoroughfare is an example of this type of advertising.

_____ 6. An advertisement for a small delicatessen in a rural area.

_____ 7. A type of advertising in which the advertising costs are shared by a manufacturer and the local business(es) that market its products or services.

_____ 8. In the U.S., the greatest amount of money is spent by businesses and organizations on this advertising medium.

_____ 9. A type of advertising that attempts to generate goodwill or bolster an organization's image.

_____ 10. The combination of television, direct mail, and specialty items used by an organization to accomplish its advertising goals.

_____ 11. Items such as matchbooks, pens, and calendars that carry the advertiser's name for the purpose of keeping the organization's name in front of the customer.

_____ 12. A type of advertising that tries to convince potential buyers to purchase a specific product or service.

MASTERING KEY CONCEPTS

Name _____

Answer each of the following questions in the space provided.

1. What are the four major purposes of advertising?

2. How does advertising relate to the high standard of living enjoyed by many people in the United States?

3. Critics of advertising say that it makes people buy things they do not want. How would you respond to this criticism?

4. What are the differences between a rational and an emotional advertising appeal?

5. List two advantages and two disadvantages of each of the following advertising media.

Media	Advantages	Disadvantages
Newspaper		
Direct Mail		
Television		
Radio		
Magazines		

6. Describe the five steps in the advertising planning process.
   a. Setting the advertising objectives

   b. Preparing the advertising budget

   c. Planning the advertising media mix

   d. Implementing the advertising plan

   e. Evaluating the effectiveness of the advertising program

7. What is the advantage of an organization using an advertising agency?

DEVELOPING PEOPLE SKILLS

Read the following description of a human relations situation. Then complete your answers on a separate piece of paper.

Advertising Ethics

Michael Valdez has worked on a part-time basis at Riverside Sporting Goods for nearly two years. During his two years at Riverside he has been responsible for selling in all areas of the store and for ordering and stocking in the athletic shoe department.

Michael is enrolled in an advanced marketing class at his high school and has also completed two years of art classes. The area of marketing that has always been of most interest to Michael is advertising.

For several months Michael has been asking store manager Robin Huffman to let him get involved in the store's advertising program. The promotional program for Riverside Sporting Goods consists of weekly newspaper advertisements, sponsorship of the radio broadcast of the local high school's football and basketball games, direct mail coupons, and rebates offered by manufacturers. Last week Michael was given his first opportunity to lay out the newspaper advertisement for this Thursday's edition. Ms. Huffman provided Michael with a list of products to be included in the advertisements, product fact sheets, an ad layout sheet, and the manufacturer's suggested ad layout.

Michael immediately noticed that one of the products to be included in this week's ad was a line of specialty shoes sold in his department. The inventory of these particular shoes is extremely limited and they have been on back order for nearly six months. When Michael asked Ms. Huffman if advertising this line of shoes might not be misleading to consumers, he was informed that as far as she was concerned, it really didn't matter much if they ran out of stock. "After all," Ms. Huffman said, "the major goal of our advertising program should be to get customers into the store; not to sell a particular product."

With these directions from Ms. Huffman, Michael finished the ad and it appeared in the Thursday newspaper. Michael, however, did not feel good about the entire process.

1. What do you see as the problem facing Michael in this case?
2. What would you do if you were in Michael's shoes?
3. Do you think it is ethical for a store to run an advertisement for a product when limited stock is available? Defend your position.

MARKETING PROJECT 11

Look through some newspapers or magazines and find an example of each of the following types of advertising: (1) promotional, (2) institutional, (3) local, (4) national, and (5) cooperative. If possible, cut out these advertisements and mount or tape them on posterboard. For each of the five advertisements, prepare a written report answering the questions below.

Types of Advertisements

1. What is the major purpose of this advertisement?
2. Why did you classify it as promotional, institutional, local, national, or cooperative advertising?
3. What type of appeal does the advertisement use?
4. How effective do you think the advertisement will be? How did it attract your attention? What do you like or dislike about it?
5. What suggestions would you make concerning ways to improve the advertisement?

MARKETING INSIGHT

Read the following description of real-life marketing practices. Then complete your answers on a separate piece of paper.

Three-Dimensional Print Ads

Three-D glasses may soon become the latest rage among advertisers if the new three-dimensional ad system, Anaglifics, is successful. Developed by 3DMark Company of Los Angeles, the Anaglifics System employs a full-color capability to three-dimensional print advertising. "We've broken the traditional two-color limit on 3-D advertising, opening up a new avenue for magazine inserts, direct mail pieces, and P-O-P [point-of-purchase] displays. Before [this new process], advertisers generally had to settle for red and blue images only," said Dick Rick, chairman of the company.

This new technology combines a complex system of photography, processing, and printing using special inks in six colors which are printed on two sides of the paper. The 3-D glasses accompany each ad. What distinguishes this new process is that even without the glasses, consumers see a beautiful full-color image, making it an effective marketing tool even if the glasses get separated from the ad.

3DMark is the same company that produced the Stereo Viewer, a high-tech paper viewer with full-color, stereographic transparencies. The viewer, which can be folded and packed flat for magazine insertion or direct mail advertising, was used by Toyota to introduce one of its new car models in *Time, People,* and *Cosmopolitan* magazines. Since then several companies, including Hewlett-Packard and an ad agency for Pepsi, have expressed interest in using the Stereo Viewer. A new version of the viewer featuring a scent strip that permits a fragrance to be released will be introduced by the company in the near future.[2]

1. What do you see as the major advantages of three-dimensional print advertising?
2. What do you see as the major disadvantages of three-dimensional print advertising?
3. What is the potential impact on the consumer of adding fragrance or aroma to the advertisement?
4. Would the new technology used to produce three-dimensional ads be of any value to the smaller business? If so, what do you see as the application for the smaller business?

---

[2]Cyndee Miller, "New Process Creates Full-Color 3-D Print Ads," *Marketing News* (1 February 1988), p. 3. Courtesy of American Marketing Association.

CHAPTER 12
PROMOTION: VISUAL MERCHANDISING, SALES PROMOTION, AND PUBLIC RELATIONS

After you read this chapter and complete the activities at the end, you will be able to:

1. **Define visual merchandising and explain its major purposes.**
2. **Identify the three major types of visual merchandising activities.**
3. **Explain the four principles of visual merchandising that business firms should follow.**
4. **Define sales promotion and explain its major purposes.**
5. **Explain the difference between consumer sales promotions and trade promotions.**
6. **Identify typical sales promotion activities.**
7. **Define public relations and explain its major purposes.**
8. **Describe how a business can gain favorable publicity.**

The next time you enter a supermarket, take a close look at the way the store is laid out. Notice the displays of popular merchandise at the end of the aisles. Go through the produce department and check out how the various produce items are attractively displayed. Notice the location of such staple items as milk, bread, and meat. These items are frequently positioned at the back of the store for the purpose of drawing customers past other merchandise. When you get to the check-out counter, notice the point-of-purchase displays featuring "impulse" items. Impulse items are unplanned purchases that customers make at the last moment as they prepare to leave the store. These activities are all examples of visual merchandising.

This same supermarket is also heavily involved in sales promotion and public relations activities. For example, the store manager serves on the advisory committee for marketing education at the local high school. The employees and management of the store have decided to make contributions of damaged and surplus food products to a nearby shelter for homeless people.

Every Thursday in the local newspaper the supermarket offers a variety of coupons for cents off selected merchandise. The store also carries a number of products that include rebates offered directly to customers. At another level, the supermarket receives money from wholesalers and other intermediaries for stocking and selling new merchandise. The store can also receive payment from manufacturers or suppliers in the form of an advertising allowance for buying certain quantities of a particular item of merchandise.

These various visual merchandising, sales promotion, and public relations activities are designed to support the other parts of the promotional mix—personal selling and advertising.

VISUAL MERCHANDISING

Visual merchandising is the practice of displaying products or services in a way that will attract the attention of potential buyers, arouse their interest, and heighten their desire to purchase these products or services. Visual merchandising reminds people to buy by attractively presenting products or services at a critical juncture in the buying process. Visual merchandising includes window displays, interior displays, and outside displays. Decorative glass storefronts, colorful signs, creative window displays, effective store layout and design, lighting, plush carpeting, and brightly painted walls are all elements of a total visual merchandising program. Although visual merchandising is usually associated with retail businesses, it is also part of the promotional mixes of other types of businesses that market goods or services. Retailers, wholesalers, and manufacturers use many of the same visual merchandising techniques.

Purposes of Visual Merchandising

Like personal selling and advertising, the major purpose of visual merchandising is to stimulate demand and increase the sales of goods or services. This method of promotion is designed to bring potential buyers into a business. Window displays and signs are used to attract people's attention and arouse their interest in the merchandise that is offered for sale inside the business. Interior displays enable a business to show new products in use, which helps arouse interest and increase immediate sales. The National Retail Merchants Associa-

Illustration 12-1   Visual merchandising is the practice of displaying
products or services in a way that will attract the
attention of potential buyers and arouse their
interest.

tion estimates that 25 percent of all fashion merchandise is sold
primarily because of how it is displayed.[1] On the other hand, shelf
space is the name of the game in the supermarket business.[2] Figure
12-1 shows the average linear feet of shelf space occupied by specific
categories of products. It also gives the dollar sales per month for each
linear foot of shelf space occupied.

---

[1]Ray Marguart, "Merchandise Displays Are Most Effective When Marketing,
Artistic Factors Combine," *Marketing News,* vol. 17, no. 17 (19 August 1983), p. 3.
[2]"Space Hogs," *U.S. News and World Reports* (14 August 1989), p. 70.

Figure 12-1   Supermarkets measure sales of products in dollar sales per month per linear foot.

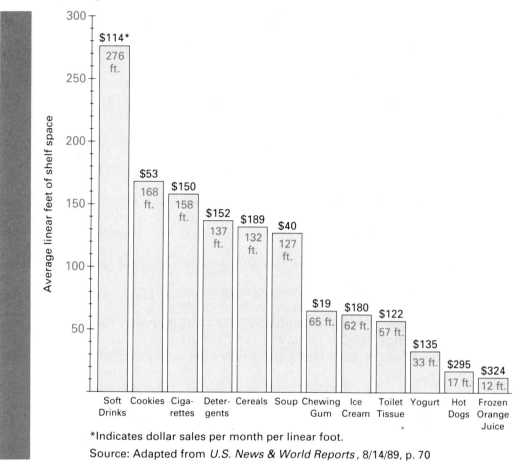

Source: Adapted from *U.S. News & World Reports*, 8/14/89, p. 70

Finally, a visual merchandising program includes the interior layout, lighting, and decoration of a business. The fixtures, colors, lights, and signs used in the interior layout of a business should be practical as well as aesthetically pleasing. Carpeting, fixtures, width and pattern of the aisles, and the intensity and color of the lighting affect the atmosphere of a business. These factors influence the mood of prospective buyers and their purchasing decisions.

Types of Visual Merchandising Displays

Visual merchandising displays can be classified as window displays, interior displays, and outside displays.

Window Displays. Many buildings have windows that face the street. Stores in shopping malls often have interior windows. **Window displays** are designed to attract attention and persuade potential buyers to come into a business. The way merchandise is displayed in a window allows people passing by to form an impression of a business. A firm's image can be partially created by the type and quality of its window displays.

Window displays may feature a single item, an assortment of related items, seasonal products such as bathing suits or graduation gifts, or merchandise that supports special sales events, such as Easter sales or dollar days. In order to be effective, window displays should be changed frequently, usually every two or three weeks.

Interior Displays. Interior displays are located within a business. Like window displays, this type of visual merchandising can promote single or related products, sales items, or seasonal merchandise. Interior displays are designed to permit prospective buyers to see and handle merchandise, to see how articles of clothing look when displayed on lifelike mannequins, or to see how items appear when combined with complementary or related products. The major purpose of interior displays is to attract attention and stimulate interest in purchasing the displayed merchandise. It is estimated that consumers spend an average of only eleven seconds observing a display. Thus, in order to be effective, interior displays must convey their messages quickly and be balanced, properly proportioned, and hard-hitting. Interior displays are often designed to produce impulse buying. The trend toward self-service or minimum service at the retail level is increasing the importance of in-store merchandising.

Basically, there are six kinds of interior displays: island displays, end displays, wall displays, platform displays, shadow box displays, and point-of-purchase displays.

Island Displays. Island displays are usually large open tables stacked with merchandise and separated from surrounding displays. They are most effective when located in heavy customer traffic areas.

End Displays. An end display is an open display of merchandise on a rack, table, or bin at the end of an aisle. Displays of timely and specially priced merchandise are the most common types of end displays.

Wall Displays. Wall displays are frequently used to show clothing and apparel items that can be pinned or hung on walls.

Platform Displays. When platform displays are used, merchandise is shown on raised platforms or stands. The height of the platforms increases the visibility of the merchandise.

Illustration 12-2   Platform displays increase the visibility of merchandise.

Shadow Box Displays. Shadow box displays are small closed interior displays that are built into walls or placed on counters or ledges. They display items that are available for sale in various departments of a store.

Point-of-Purchase Displays. Point-of-purchase displays are placed with the merchandise being sold. They are usually coordinated with the manufacturer's or wholesaler's advertising program or are provided by the manufacturer or wholesaler. Point-of-purchase displays are easy for a retailer to set up and maintain. They include posters and counter cards that urge customers to buy products and, in addition, stands, racks, and other types of containers that display merchandise.

Outside Displays. Outside displays consist of signs, banners, pennants, and other attention-getting devices that identify a business. They draw potential customers into a business. For many firms, outside displays are more important than other types of displays. Automobile dealerships, mobile home dealers, real estate companies, and restaurants rely heavily on outside displays.

Principles of Visual Merchandising

In order to effectively display merchandise or services, businesses must follow several basic principles. First, designing effective displays requires planning. A basic rule of thumb is to keep the idea for a display as simple as possible. Display planning begins with a statement of the display's purposes or goals. Once these are clearly stated, a theme can be developed. The theme of a display may be based on the characteristics of a product or service, a news or sporting event, a special sale, or a holiday.

Planning also requires making decisions concerning the products or services to use in a display, where to locate it, and how to communicate the selected theme. Any products or services included in a display should be complementary. A sporting goods store would not display hunting or fishing equipment with skiing equipment. Various display elements, such as props, lights, signs, sizes, weights, textures, and colors, must be selected. Planning also includes an evaluation of a display to determine whether it is accomplishing its stated purposes or goals. Observing the behavior of consumers as they pass a display and keeping track of the sales of display items are two methods that can be used to measure a display's effectiveness.

A second principle of effective visual merchandising is that the products used in displays should be presented in a way that means something to viewers. For example, a display of men's suits is more effective if the suits are shown with matching accessories (shirts, ties, and pants) on lifelike mannequins. Effective displays show prospective buyers how products will benefit them.

The third principle of effective visual merchandising is that the design of a display should reflect the value of the merchandise being displayed. An expensive set of china should be displayed in a fashion that emphasizes its exclusive image. On the other hand, a large selection of men's slacks or shirts might be stacked neatly on a sale table. Highlighting a single item in a display usually means that it is a prestige product with a high price. If many different items are included, they are usually low priced.

The fourth principle of effective visual merchandising is that displays should be changed frequently. Consumers, for example, like to go window shopping and wander through businesses to see new merchandise displayed. If window and interior displays do not change, shoppers are less likely to continue visiting a business.

SALES PROMOTION

Sales promotion includes those activities other than personal selling, advertising, visual merchandising, and public relations that stimulate market demand for products or services. The major goal of sales promotion is to enhance or work with the other elements of the promotional mix.

Purposes of Sales Promotion

The main objective of sales promotion, like personal selling, advertising, and visual merchandising, is to increase sales. Remember, however, that most sales promotion activities must be coordinated with other promotional activities in order to be effective.

Different sales promotion activities serve different purposes. Trading stamps, contests, and games are designed to build customer loyalty. Product sampling is a strategy that is often used to introduce new products to the marketplace. The goal of special sales events is the stimulation of sales during slow seasons or the clearance of overstocked merchandise. Consumer premiums are designed to help a business attract new customers and increase the amount purchased by present customers. Many sales promotion activities are undertaken to keep a business competitive. For instance, if several supermarkets and grocery stores give coupons for Thursday specials, this may force other area stores to adopt the same practice.

Thus, sales promotion activities serve various purposes including the following:

1. Bringing new buyers into a business.
2. Introducing new products or services.
3. Increasing the amount purchased by present customers.
4. Increasing sales during slow seasons.
5. Allowing a business to remain competitive.
6. Keeping the name of a business and its products or services in buyers' minds.

▲ Types of Sales Promotion Activities

Sales promotion activities can be classified as consumer sales promotions or trade promotions. In 1988, $118 billion was spent on all sales promotions. Approximately $53 billion was spent on consumer promotion and about $65 billion on trade promotions.[3]

Consumer Sales Promotions. Consumer sales promotions include all sales promotion activities that are designed to stimulate consumer demand. Consumer sales promotion activities give consumers external reasons to buy products or services. Examples of consumer sales promotions include product sampling, consumer premiums, price deals, rebates, coupons, trading stamps, special events, special sales, consumer contests and games, and many other similar activities.

Product Sampling. Samples are an important form of consumer sales promotion. Product samples are things consumers receive free from manufacturers or retailers that allow them to try new products or services. You have probably received a sample of a new brand of toothpaste or shampoo through the mail. Or perhaps you have visited a supermarket or fast food restaurant where you had the chance to sample some new food. After tasting this sample, consumers may decide to purchase the new product.

Premiums. When premiums are used as a sales promotion strategy, consumers receive something free in or attached to a package or by returning a label, box top, or other proof-of-purchase symbol. Manufacturers of bubble gum, caramel corn, and cereal appeal to children by including premiums inside their packages. Gifts are also offered to adults who are willing to visit new recreational real estate developments or to consumers who open new checking or savings accounts with local financial institutions. Frequently automobile dealers offer free gifts to those who are willing to test drive one of their new car models. Supermarkets frequently offer dishware or cookware free to consumers who buy specific amounts of merchandise. Once a consumer has begun to collect a set of dishes, he or she is likely to return to a store to make other purchases to complete the set. Ideas for consumer premiums are limited only by the imagination of the marketer; they can take many different forms.

---

[3]"Sales Promotion: The Year in Review," *Marketing and Media Decisions* (July 1989), pp. 124–126.

Price Deals. Price deals are short-term discounts offered by manu-facturers that are designed to increase sales of particular products. Most price deals are printed on the package and offer so many cents off of the regular price of the item. Price deals are an effective way of meeting the competitions' coupon offers. The overuse of price deals, however, can tend to make consumers believe the cents off were built into the original price.

Rebates. Rebates allow the consumer to recover a certain portion of the cost of an item by simply completing and sending in a form to the manufacturer. Rebates have been widely used since the 1970s by automobile manufacturers.

Coupons. Coupons allow consumers to save money on a particular food item or to buy one item and get a second item free. Coupons are

Illustration 12-3

Coupons represent the largest expenditure of all sales promotions.

commonly offered by restaurants and supermarkets or grocery stores. Fast food chains as well as local restaurants frequently run coupons in local newspaper supplements. Many supermarkets and grocery stores run weekly coupon specials offering consumers small amounts off the prices of a variety of products. National manufacturers and distributors also run coupons in magazines with regional and national circulations. Coupons represent the largest expenditure of all consumer sales promotions, with approximately $40 billion spent annually on this activity in 1988.[4]

Trading Stamps. Retail businesses, such as supermarkets and grocery stores, service stations, car rental agencies, and some department stores, give trading stamps to consumers who purchase merchandise and services. Consumers paste these stamps in booklets that, when completed, can be redeemed for merchandise at a trading stamp redemption center. Trading stamps, which were very popular ten or fifteen years ago, are less widely used today. Nevertheless, a large number of businesses still give trading stamps. The major purposes of this type of consumer sales promotion are to attract new buyers and develop customer loyalty.

Special Events. Many companies sponsor a variety of special events as part of their overall sales promotion program. Examples of special events include sponsorship of a local golf tournament by a sporting goods store (entry blanks must be picked up at the store), the establishment of a teen board and periodic fashion shows sponsored by a department store, an art exhibit that is borrowed from a local art gallery and displayed in local stores and restaurants, and monthly fashion shows conducted by a bridal salon. Other examples are demonstrations of home appliances at county fairs or home shows and free investment seminars offered by a financial services broker. The goal of all special event promotions is to draw consumers into a business so that they will be exposed to the products or services being sold or when possible, see the products in use.

Special Sales. Special sales are considered part of the sales promotion program of a business. Examples of special sales are back-to-school sales, midnight madness sales, dollar day sales, founder's day sales, anniversary sales, holiday sales, and end-of-season clearance sales. One-cent sales enable consumers to buy one item at the regular price and obtain a second one for a penny. Special sales are one of the

---

[4]"Sales Promotion: The Year in Review," *Marketing and Media Decisions* (July 1989), pp. 124–126.

major sales promotion techniques used by retailers. Often these sales generate a large percentage of a year's sales volume.

Consumer Contests and Games. Consumer contests and games are popular types of sales promotion activities. They are sometimes called sweepstakes. A **contest** requires some skill on the part of participants. A contest participant may be asked to write a jingle or slogan, to create a name for a new product, to solve a puzzle, or to guess how many jelly beans or pennies are in a large container.

Games, which are usually sponsored by grocery stores, supermarkets, and restaurants, give customers a chance to win money, merchandise, or vacation trips to attractive places. Bingo and similar games are frequently used by grocery stores and supermarkets. Each time a consumer makes a purchase, she or he is given a number that must be pasted on a bingo card. When the card is filled with numbers in a certain pattern, a prize (cash or merchandise) is awarded. Another type of game is the prize drawing. A name is drawn from a container in which consumers have placed pieces of paper listing their names and addresses. The person whose name is drawn wins a prize such as merchandise or a gift certificate.

Consumer contests and games are designed to build consumer loyalty by encouraging repeat visits. Consumers often return to a business in order to increase their chances of winning a contest or game. Although illegal in some states, contests and games usually have a beneficial effect on the sales volumes of the organizations that sponsor them.

Trade Promotions. The second classification of sales promotion activities, **trade promotions,** include activities that encourage intermediaries—wholesalers, industrial distributors, agents, retailers, sales representatives—to buy and sell large quantities of products or services. Examples of typical trade promotions include trade premiums and gifts, premium or push money, slotting allowances, advertising allowances, contests, promotional allowances, and trade shows.

Trade Premiums and Gifts. Many manufacturers offer trade premiums and gifts to dealers, wholesalers, sales representatives, and retailers if they buy and sell more of certain products or services. For example, if a retailer orders one hundred cases of a product, the manufacturer may provide some type of free gift or an extra case of the same product at no charge. Some businesses even offer a free vacation to the dealer or retailer who buys a certain amount of merchandise.

Premium or Push Money. Some manufacturers offer push money or cash premiums to businesses that buy a specified quantity of merchandise. Push money is often used as an incentive to persuade dealers, wholesalers, sales representatives, and retailers to place more emphasis on selling a particular type of merchandise.

Slotting Allowances. A slotting allowance is a direct payment to a retailer, usually a chain of supermarkets or convenience stores, for carrying or stocking an item. Food manufacturers are increasingly willing to pay these allowances because of increased competition for shelf space.

Advertising Allowance. An advertising allowance is a reduction in the cost or price of merchandise that is given to dealers in return for the purchase of a certain quantity of merchandise. The savings that result from this price reduction are intended to help dealers pay for product advertising.

Contests. Contests are used to encourage dealers or other intermediaries to increase their sales volumes. Prizes are awarded to those who sell the most products or services. Insurance companies frequently use this technique and reward agencies that meet or exceed their goals.

Promotional Allowances. Promotional allowances often take the form of merchandise discounts that manufacturers or wholesalers give retailers in return for additional retail shelf space or the placement of their merchandise in desirable locations.

Trade Shows. Trade shows are used by manufacturers or suppliers to disperse information about their products or services to prospective customers. In a trade show, booths are set up by the various manufacturers or suppliers where they can display their merchandise or services. The Consumer Electronics Show is held annually in Las Vegas where hundreds of manufacturers and suppliers display their latest electronics product lines to prospective retail and wholesale buyers.

◣ PUBLIC RELATIONS

Public relations is the total process of building goodwill toward a business on the part of customers, employees, suppliers, stockholders, creditors, the community, and government. The direct selling of products or services is not the primary objective. Instead, public relations activities are undertaken in order to build a positive image for a business. Many businesses employ specialists who perform public relations duties. However, every marketing worker has the opportunity to help a business develop and maintain a positive image and thus is indirectly involved in public relations.

Activities that are usually considered part of public relations include (1) membership and active participation in civic and other organizations that provide community services, (2) lobbying for or against local, state, or federal legislation that will affect business, (3) preparing news releases for use in local and national media that show a business in a favorable light, (4) involvement and participation in special events such as sponsorship of a summer Special Olympics program, and (5) dealing efficiently and fairly with customers who have had a negative experience with a business. Other similar activities can also be considered part of public relations.

Purposes of Public Relations

The major goals of public relations activities are to determine the public's attitude toward a business and to create a program that will help develop the desired reputation for the business. Public relations is concerned with maintaining goodwill toward a business on the part of various groups—customers, employees, stockholders, creditors, the community, and the government. For example, a public relations department might take a leading role in helping the local city government sponsor a downtown renovation project. If a business is publicly owned (owned by stockholders), the public relations department may be responsible for preparing the annual report and organizing the annual stockholders' meeting. Public relations efforts vary from one business to the next, but all public relations activities are intended to help a business develop goodwill and maintain a positive image.

Obtaining Publicity

Obtaining positive publicity is one of the major goals of a public relations program. **Publicity** is like advertising in that messages are carried by many of the same media—newspaper, radio or television stations, and magazines. Publicity differs from advertising in that a business does not have to pay to have these media carry its messages.

Through publicity, public relations personnel attempt to distribute information that will have a positive impact on the company's image. Sometimes, however, negative publicity can come from outside a business. An article in a local newspaper describing a lawsuit against a local business may have a negative impact.

Positive publicity can be generated in a number of ways. A business may sponsor a local softball tournament, an owner or manager could volunteer to lead the annual United Way campaign, or a business could enter a float in the Fourth of July parade. These are all activities that are newsworthy and thus may elicit positive publicity.

Illustration 12-4

The sponsorship of special events such as athletic competitions may elicit positive publicity for a company.

Simon Bruty/ALLSPORT USA

In order to gain publicity, public relations personnel prepare news releases that are distributed to the various media. **News releases** are written articles that objectively describe a special event that is being sponsored by a business or the achievements of an employee who is making a special contribution to the community. News releases generate publicity that, over time, can help a business develop a positive reputation.

A news release should always include the name of the business, the name of the person who prepared it, and when it can be used by the media. The first paragraph of the news release should capture the reader's attention and should include the five *W's* of a good news story—who, what, when, where, and why. The liberal use of quotations (particularly of important persons) will make a news release more interesting for readers. Short sentences should be used. Since adjectives have a tendency to raise questions in readers' minds, their use should be avoided in preparing news releases. Finally, a headline can be written for the story, but the media will probably modify it to fit the available space or time.

APPLYING MARKETING TERMS

Name _____

Match each term with the statement that best describes an application of that term. Write the letter in the space provided.

a. slotting allowance
b. point-of-purchase display
c. interior display
d. sales promotion
e. outside displays
f. publicity

g. public relations
h. consumer sales promotions
i. special events
j. trade shows
k. trade promotions
l. coupons

_____ 1. The latest style of clothing displayed on mannequins in a major traffic area of a department store.

_____ 2. Money paid directly to supermarkets for stocking and selling a new product or product line.

_____ 3. Activities directed toward encouraging intermediaries in the marketing process to buy and sell more products and services.

_____ 4. A display of bookmarks located near the cash register at a bookstore.

_____ 5. The major goal of this activity is to enhance the other elements in the promotion mix by building customer loyalty, introducing new products, attracting new customers, and keeping the organization competitive.

_____ 6. These activities give the ultimate consumer external reasons to buy products or services.

_____ 7. The largest consumer sales promotion activity in terms of dollars spent by manufacturers and wholesalers.

_____ 8. A fashion show at a nearby shopping mall would be an example of this type of consumer sales promotion activity.

_____ 9. Where booths are set up in a large building, convention center, or room for the purpose of displaying new merchandise and services to prospective buyers at the wholesale and retail level.

_____ 10. A news release describing the opening of a new business would be an example of this type of public relations activity.

_____ 11. Maintaining overall goodwill of consumers is the goal of this promotional activity.

_____ 12. Banners and pennants announcing a sale at an automobile dealership.

Answer each of the following questions in the space provided.

1. What is the major purpose of visual merchandising?

2. How do window displays affect a firm's image?

3. Why is planning important to the success of a display?

4. List the four principles of visual merchandising.

5. List three purposes of sales promotion.

6. What are consumer sales promotions?

7. List and describe three examples of trade promotions.

8. How can marketing workers act in a public relations capacity?

9. List three activities that can generate positive publicity for a business.

DEVELOPING PEOPLE SKILLS

Read the following description of a human relations situation. Then complete your answers on a separate piece of paper.

Pay for Services Offered

Lisa Anderson has been employed by the Varsity Shop for nearly two years. The Varsity Shop specializes in women's fashion clothing and accessories. Like most small department stores and specialty stores, the Varsity Shop is not large enough to employ a visual merchandising specialist but instead relies on one of the sales workers in the store to design and set up displays. Since Lisa studied visual merchandising in high school, the manager asked her to take over these duties.

The Varsity Shop is located in a busy shopping mall and the display windows must be changed at least every two weeks. In addition to doing the mall windows, Lisa is occasionally expected to redo the interior displays which consist of wall displays and dressed mannequins. Lisa must also set up the signs and posters used in the store.

Although Lisa does not mind doing the display work, she must often stay a couple of hours after the store has closed to complete it. During regular business hours the store is usually too busy for her to do anything but help customers. Lisa spends an average of four hours of her own time each week doing the display work.

Last week Lisa decided that she was no longer going to do the display work without pay. At the end of the week she turned in her time card with an extra four hours listed. When she received this week's paycheck, she noticed that the manager of the Varsity Shop had disallowed the extra four hours and that the paycheck was for the same amount as in the past. When she asked the store manager about this, she was told that the store had a policy of not paying overtime and that she should try to find a way to get her display work finished during regular store hours. She was also told that a lot of other people in the store worked extra hours and were not paid for them. Lisa was displeased by what the manager told her but does not know what to do.

1. What is the major problem in this case?
2. What alternatives does Lisa have that may help her solve her problem?
3. If you were Lisa, what would you do in this situation?
4. What could Lisa have done to avoid this problem in the first place?

MARKETING PROJECT 12

Use your own paper to complete this project.

Preparing a News Release

Write a short (no more than one page) news release promoting an upcoming special event such as a Distributive Education Clubs of America (DECA) event or community event. Be sure to include the five *W's*—who, what, when, where, and why—and follow the guidelines given in the text.

MARKETING INSIGHT

Read the following description of real-life marketing practices. Then complete your answers on a separate piece of paper.

Video Advertising in the Aisles

Using point-of-purchase video advertisements to reinforce a product's marketing message can be effective and cost efficient. Five years of research on in-store videos established some basic guidelines:

- Exposure rates to a message can be determined by the number of people passing an in-store video display. Understanding store traffic patterns can effect the number as well as the quality of exposures. Adjusting the angle of the screen can increase exposure.
- People tend to respond first to sound, so a strong musical track is vital. After that they are attracted to quick, intimate exchanges between people. Programs should be at least 10 minutes long and should be changed every 10 days to two weeks.
- Video ads meant to address people waiting to check out have advantages. Besides generating income they can effectively cut the consumer's perception of waiting time, a frequent consumer frustration. Corridors with the heaviest customer traffic are not necessarily the best locations. While there may be fewer people in areas near the dressing rooms, the audience is captive and much more likely to watch.
- If not properly placed, in-store videos can actually reduce the effectiveness of a salesperson. At a cash register it should be visible to the waiting customer, not the person ringing in the sales. The volume should be adjusted during the day by a store manager.[5]

1. What do you think are the major advantages to a retail business of using an in-store point-of-purchase video display?
2. What do you think are the major disadvantages to the retail business of using an in-store point-of-purchase video display?
3. Why would an understanding of store traffic flow be useful in terms of the placement of in-store videos?
4. Why would a strong music track be important to in-store video displays?

---

[5]Paco Underhill, "In-Store Video Ads Can Reinforce Media Campaigns," *Marketing News* (22 May 1989), p. 5. Courtesy of American Marketing Association.

UNIT 4
PRICING AND DISTRIBUTION

13   PRICING

14   MARKETING CHANNELS AND INTERMEDIARIES

15   PHYSICAL DISTRIBUTION

CHAPTER 13
PRICING

After you read this chapter and complete the activities at the end, you will be able to:

1. **Discuss the meaning of price.**
2. **Distinguish between price and nonprice competition.**
3. **Identify factors affecting price.**
4. **Describe three basic pricing strategies.**
5. **Describe four popular pricing policies.**
6. **Discuss the pricing methods used by different kinds of businesses.**

What do the following terms have in common? Tuition . . . Fees . . . Fare . . . Rent . . . Toll . . . Interest . . . Premiums . . . You are correct if you said they are different terms used to describe price.

Tuition is paid to take courses at a school or college. Fees are paid for a service, such as that of a medical doctor or an attorney. Fares are paid for transportation on a plane or in a taxi. Rent is paid for a place to live or for the use of some piece of equipment for a period of time. A toll is paid for a long-distance telephone call or for traveling over certain bridges or roads. Interest is paid for the use of money. Premiums are paid for life, health, and other insurance policies.

◢◢◢ THE MEANING OF PRICE

The **price** of a product or service is its exchange value stated in terms of money. It reflects the cost of the good or service, various operating expenses, and, hopefully, a profit. For manufacturers, the cost of goods is equal to the expense of producing them. The cost of goods for wholesalers and retailers is the amount they originally paid for them. As discussed in Chapter 2, price decisions are one of four parts of the marketing mix. To successfully market any product or service, sellers must establish selling prices and also decide how much they will emphasize price.

PRICE AND NONPRICE COMPETITION

Products and services can compete with other products and services on either a price or a nonprice basis. The choice will affect not only pricing decisions and activities, but also decisions on product, promotion, and place.

Price Competition

Price competition occurs when sellers stress low prices. They call attention to their low price and match or beat the price of competitors who also emphasize low prices. Sellers using price competition may change their prices frequently or at least they must be willing and able to do so. For example, when a company reduces its price, its competitors must respond quickly and lower their price.

As is true with other marketing decisions, price competition has both advantages and disadvantages. Prices can be changed when the firm's costs change or when demand for the product or service changes. Also, if a competitor tries to gain a bigger share of the market by cutting prices, a company can react quickly by cutting its prices. A disadvantage of price competition is that competitors also have the flexibility to adjust their prices. If you lower your prices, your competitors can quickly match or beat your prices.

Nonprice Competition

Using **nonprice competition,** sellers emphasize factors other than price to distinguish their products and services from those of competitors. These nonprice factors include product quality, packaging, service, advertising, and product features.

One advantage of nonprice competition is that a company can build customer loyalty to its brand. When customers prefer a brand or a particular business because of nonprice factors, it may be difficult for competing firms or brands to lure them away. For example, when customers regularly patronize a store for nonprice reasons, such as the personal service of the salespeople, they are less likely to leave this store for a lower competitive price. However, when price is the primary reason why customers buy a particular brand, competitors can use price cuts to attract these customers.

Marketers planning to use nonprice competition must distinguish their brands from those of competitors. Buyers must be aware of these differences and they must see them as desirable and worth the additional price. The unique features that set a particular brand apart from its competitors should be difficult, and preferably impossible, for other companies to imitate.

A company attempting to compete on a nonprice basis cannot completely ignore competitors' prices. The firm must be aware of competitors' prices and will probably end up pricing its brand near or slightly above the other brands on the market. The more unique a product or service is, the greater the freedom of a marketer to set prices above competitors' prices.

FACTORS AFFECTING PRICE

The exact price charged for a product or service depends on several factors, including (1) costs, (2) competition, (3) nature of the product or service, (4) image desired, and (5) supply and demand.

Costs

The costs of raw materials, supplies, labor, advertising, insurance, and other items are often beyond the control of the company. These costs, however, have a great impact on the price the firm can charge.

Companies may choose from three courses of action when their costs are rising. First, they can pass along all of their cost increases to their customers in the form of higher prices. For example, the destruction of part of the orange crop by a winter freeze in Florida is often followed by higher orange juice prices in the stores. Second, they can pass along part of their cost increases and absorb part of them. For example, they can take less profit or switch to cheaper materials to reduce costs. Third, they can stop selling the product.

When cost declines occur, firms can reduce their selling prices and keep their profits the same. Another choice they have is to leave their prices unchanged and earn higher profits. Low sugar prices, for example, may allow a candy company to both increase the size of the package and earn more profit without raising the price.

Competition

The actions of competitors must be considered when setting prices. Sellers must ask: What will competitors do if we undercut their prices? Will they quickly meet the low price? Will they beat it and offer an even lower one? Will they leave their prices unchanged?

Or will they raise their prices and spend more for promotional activities?

Other questions to consider are: What will competitors do if we raise our prices? Will they raise their prices? Or will they leave their prices unchanged and advertise that their brand is a better value for less money? A firm cannot know exactly how competitors will react when it changes its prices. However, when competitors are affected, they will take some kind of action. For example, they may respond by cutting prices or by using some form of nonprice competition, such as launching a new advertising campaign.

Nature of the Product or Service

When prices rise or fall, the sales of some products and services are affected more than others. For example, a change in the price of steak is likely to affect sales substantially. If the price rises, people will probably buy less steak; if the price falls, people will probably buy more. On the other hand, a change in the price of table salt is not likely to affect salt purchases significantly. If the price of salt rises, people will probably not buy less; if the price falls, people will probably not buy more. They will continue to purchase the same amount of salt.

Marketing managers can determine whether a price change will cause people to buy more or less of a product or service by asking questions such as these: How much of a product or service do consumers purchase? Why do they purchase it? Is the product or service a luxury or a necessity? The answers to these questions will help marketing managers make better pricing decisions.

Image Desired

A firm's image is, to a certain extent, determined by the prices it charges for its products or services. For example, a company that wants to present itself as a firm that offers goods at the lowest prices in the field would set its prices accordingly. It may select a low-cost location in order to keep expenses at a minimum.

Supply and Demand

Supply and demand play a major role in determining price. **Supply** is the quantity of a product or service that firms provide at a given

Illustration 13-1   Changes in meat prices are likely to affect meat sales substantially.

time and at a given price. **Demand** is the amount of a product or service people are willing and able to buy at a given time and at a given price.

Changes in demand cause changes in prices. When demand for a product or service increases, its price generally goes up. For example, when a clothing style becomes a fashion or a fad, many people purchase clothing of that particular style. This usually causes a price increase. **Fashion** is a style that is generally accepted by a large group of people. An item that becomes a **fad,** however, is popular and sells well for only a brief period. As demand for the item decreases, its price generally goes down.

Changes in supply also affect price levels. Prices usually decrease when an abundant supply is available. This occurs, for example, when there are many competing businesses selling the same products or services or when seasonal fruits and vegetables are harvested. Conversely, prices generally go up when supply is low.

Marketing managers must consider supply and demand when making decisions concerning new products or services. If possible, they should choose to sell products and services that are in great demand because these items will command a high price.

PRICING STRATEGIES

Marketers must establish effective strategies for pricing their products and services. **Strategies** describe how managers plan to reach the company's objectives. **Pricing strategies** describe how marketers price their products and services relative to competing products and services. The three basic pricing strategies are (1) pricing above the market, (2) pricing below the market, and (3) pricing at the market.

Pricing Above the Market

A company pricing above the market is pricing its products and services higher than similar products and services sold by competitors. Companies using this strategy will try to win business based on such factors as quality, image, or location. Products and services must be distinct in the customer's eyes for this strategy to be effective. Because it's easier to lower prices than to raise them, the company can cut the price if it finds it made a mistake in charging the higher price.

When a new product or service is priced above the market it is known as **price skimming.** Firms following this strategy charge a high price that buyers who most desire the product or service will pay. This strategy was used successfully with calculators, microwave ovens, VCRs, and camcorders. This enables the company to recover its initial investment costs quickly. If competitors enter the market with a similar offering, the price can be lowered.

Pricing Below the Market

A company pricing below the market is pricing its products and services lower than similar products and services sold by competitors. Firms accomplish this by taking less profit for each unit and hoping to make it up with a higher volume of sales. This strategy is used when price competition is a major aspect of the business; that is, when the company is attempting to win business based on lower price. Discount stores have used this pricing strategy effectively.

When a new product or service is priced below the market it is known as **penetration pricing.** The objective is to gain a large market share quickly.

Pricing at the Market

Firms pricing at the market charge the same prices competitors charge for similar products or services. Companies price at the market when their products or services are not so outstanding that they can price above the market. They may also follow this strategy when their costs are not low enough to allow them to price below the market.

PRICING POLICIES

After marketing managers have decided on overall pricing strategies, they are ready to select the pricing policies they will use. **Policies** are guidelines to action and are related to attaining the firm's objectives. Some of the more popular pricing policies available are (1) odd-even pricing, (2) price lining, (3) promotional pricing, and (4) discounts.

Odd-Even Pricing

The odd-even pricing strategy is based on the belief that customers will respond more positively to prices ending in certain numbers. **Odd prices** are used by marketers, usually retailers, who believe the use of selling prices that end in odd numbers will improve sales. For this reason, they set their selling prices to end in 1, 3, 5, 7, or 9. Often, the price is just below some round number. For example, the price for a product may be set at $9.99, which marketers believe will be more attractive to customers than $10.00. Supposedly, customers will think that the product or service is a bargain and instead of paying $10.00, they will pay only $9.00 plus change.

Even prices are used to give a product an exclusive or upscale image. An even price supposedly will influence a customer to view the product as being a high quality, premium brand. For example, a handbag manufacturer may use a suggested retail price, which is printed on the tag, of $40 instead of $39.95.

Price Lining

Price lining describes the practice of offering products at a limited number of set prices. For example, a clothing retailer may offer men's shirts at $27, $40, and $55, and at no points in between.

In retail stores that offer many different types of products—with many brands of each product type and many different sizes within a brand—consumers may become confused about which item is the best price offer. Some of the confusion is removed by grouping products into price lines. For example, in the case of men's shirts described above, the three price levels tell the customer that the lower price line is for the economy-minded, the middle line is aimed at those who want medium quality, and the highest priced shirts are for those who want superior quality, with maybe a bit of prestige.

Price lining also enables marketers to serve different market segments through different prices. Prices must be set sufficiently apart so customers can see the differences in the various products. However, if the price lines are too far apart, no clear market segment will be served.

Promotional Pricing

Promotional pricing, often used in retailing, occurs when some products are priced very low to attract customers in the hope that they will buy other things at regular prices. Promotional pricing of this kind often involves the use of loss leaders. Items sold at very low prices, often below cost, to attract customers who may also buy regularly priced merchandise are called **loss leaders.** Supermarkets routinely practice promotional pricing of this kind, usually by offering low prices on standard items such as butter or selected cuts of meat.

It should be noted that some states or local areas have laws governing the use of loss leader pricing. Furthermore, some customers go to a particular store to buy only the advertised specials which defeats the marketers purpose of using promotional pricing.

Discounts

Setting prices for the organizational market is unlike setting prices for the consumer market. A major difference is the discount pricing structure used in the organizational market.

A common practice in sales made between businesses is to state a product's **list price,** which is the price normally quoted to potential buyers and sometimes preprinted on the package. Any **discounts,** which are reductions in the price, are then quoted. Some different discounts that are used in the organizational market are (1) trade discounts, (2) quantity discounts, (3) cash discounts, and (4) seasonal discounts.

Trade Discounts. Trade discounts, also called **functional discounts,** are reductions off the list price given by producers to resellers for performing certain marketing functions. Trade discounts are usually stated in terms of a percentage or series of percentages off the list price, such as: List price of $200 less 30/10.

The list price in this case is the manufacturer's suggested retail price. The numbers following the word "less" are the trade discount percentages. The first number refers to the retailer's discount and the second number refers to the wholesaler's discount. In this example, the manufacturer of a product with a retail price of $200 quotes trade discounts 30 percent and 10 percent. This means that the price paid by wholesalers is the retail price less discounts of 30 percent and 10 percent. This does not mean a total discount of 40 percent for the wholesaler. Each discount percentage is calculated on the amount remaining after the preceding percentage has been subtracted. The wholesaler keeps the 10 percent for performing the storage, selling, and transportation tasks. The 30 percent is passed on to the retailer for performing storage and selling tasks. A summary of this trade discount example is as follows:

Retailer pays wholesaler:	$200 less 30 percent
	$200 less $60
	$140
Wholesaler pays manufacturer:	$140 less 10 percent
	$140 less $14
	$126

Thus, the retailer's selling price to the consumer is $200; the wholesaler's selling price to the retailer is $140; and the manufacturer's selling price to the wholesaler is $126.

Quantity Discounts. Quantity discounts are reductions in price to encourage buyers to order larger quantities than normal. There are two kinds of quantity discounts: cumulative and noncumulative.

A **cumulative quantity discount** applies to purchases made during a specific period of time. The buyer's purchases are totaled up at the end of the period and the discount received depends on the quantity, in terms of either dollars or units, bought during the period. The discount percentage usually increases as the quantity purchased increases. For example, a retailer who buys $100,000 of merchandise from a wholesaler over a twelve-month period receives a three percent rebate; for purchasing more than $200,000 the retailer receives a six percent rebate. A cumulative quantity has a promotional impact because it rewards a buyer for being a loyal customer.

A **noncumulative quantity discount** applies to a single order rather than to the total volume of orders placed during a period of time. The size of the discount often increases with the size of the order. For example, a manufacturer of fax machines may offer retailers a price of $750 per unit if up to five units are purchased; a price of $725 per unit if between six and twenty units are purchased; and a price of $690 if more than twenty units are purchased. Sellers use noncumulative quantity discounts to reward buyers who help them reduce costs by buying in large quantities. For example, when buyers purchase in large volumes, they may be reducing the amount of warehouse space needed by the seller. It could also mean the costs of processing orders is reduced because the buyer is purchasing fewer times in larger amounts.

Cash Discounts. **Cash discounts** are reductions in price that reward buyers for paying their bills promptly. When cash discounts are available, two pieces of information are stated on the billing statement in addition to the amount of the bill: the amount of the price reduction and the time within which the bill must be paid to receive the reduction. For example, a bill may be quoted as $1,000, 2/10, net 30. This means that the bill for the product is $1,000, but that the buyer can take a 2 percent discount and pay $980 if payment is within ten days. Otherwise, $1,000 is due within 30 days.

Generally, the buyer should take the cash discount. For example 2/10, net 30 terms mean that if the buyer does not pay within 10 days, the buyer is paying 2 percent interest (the discount) to keep the money for twenty more days. There are 18 periods of 20 days in a year (i.e., 18 times 20 days = 360) during which the buyer could earn the 2 percent if the buyer paid within the 10 days. That equals an annual percentage rate of 36 percent. Because this rate of interest is so high, the firm could even consider borrowing money at bank interest rates to take advantage of cash discounts. The benefit to sellers of giving cash discounts is that they get their money sooner.

Seasonal Discounts. **Seasonal discounts** are used to encourage buyers to place orders and pay for products in advance of when they will need them. Manufacturers of products such as lawn mowers, air con-

ditioners, snow blowers, and toys use seasonal discounts to get retailers to stock up on their products ahead of their selling seasons.
These manufacturers are thereby able to produce these products at a
more constant level throughout the year, to decrease the amount of
inventory they must carry at any one time, and to receive cash payments from their customers sooner.

METHODS OF SETTING PRICES

The methods used to set prices for products and services differ
according to the type of business involved.

Pricing by Manufacturers

Manufacturers set prices for their products based on their production, administration, and selling costs. Production costs include the
cost of raw materials and parts as well as factory workers' wages and
costs related to the wear and tear of the machinery and equipment.
As shown in Figure 13-1, manufacturers select selling prices that
cover all these costs and also include a certain amount of profit.

Figure 13-1   Selling price set by manufacturers.

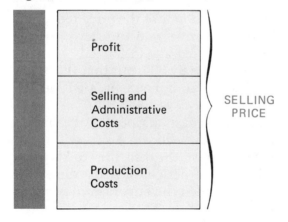

If no other companies produce the same good or if demand is
strong, a manufacturer may be able to raise its selling price. Before
increasing a price, however, a manufacturer should anticipate the
reaction of buyers. Some may decide not to purchase the product at
the higher price. Also, other firms may decide to enter the market.
Competitors may view the manufacturer's action as an opportunity
to increase profits or to attract customers by charging a lower price.

Pricing by Wholesalers

Wholesale prices are generally based on a mark-on that is established for each product line. A **markup** or **markon** is the amount that is added to a product's cost (the amount originally paid for it) in order to arrive at the selling price. As shown in Figure 13-2, the markup includes all operating expenses plus a profit.

Figure 13-2   Selling price set by wholesalers.

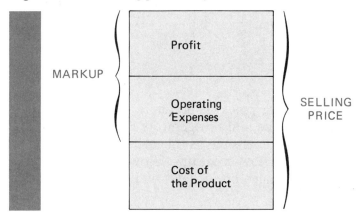

Wholesalers must set their prices carefully because retailers and other industrial users tend to base their purchasing decisions on price. Wholesalers can lose customers quickly if their prices are too high.

Wholesalers can also encounter problems because they buy in large quantities and are not always able to pass along increases in the prices of the goods they purchase to their customers. For example, if manufacturers raise their selling prices but retailers will not pay a higher price, wholesalers are caught in the middle. They may have to reduce profits or take a loss in order to remain in business.

Pricing by Retailers

As with wholesale prices, most retail prices are determined by adding a markup to cost as shown in Figure 13-3. The cost to a retailer of a product is called the **delivered cost** which is the amount paid for the product plus shipping costs.

Some retailers use the same markup for all products they sell. This is often the case in retail businesses that carry related products. Most stores, however, find it more practical to establish different

Figure 13-3   Selling price set by retailers.

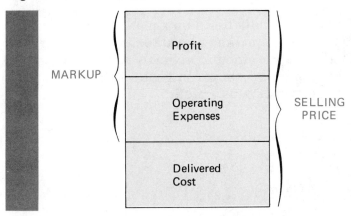

markups for different types or lines of products. In a department store, for example, men's socks and refrigerators probably have different markups. Fast-selling items such as magazines and many grocery products generally have low markups. Slow-selling products such as furniture and appliances often have high markups. These

Illustration 13-2

In a department store, clothing generally has a lower markup than furniture or appliances.

types of products usually tie up a store's money over a long period of time, involve extra storage expense, and must be delivered to their buyers.

Once a markup is selected, a retailer can determine the selling price of a product using the cost method of retail pricing. For example, if a retailer paid $10 for a product and wants to take a 40 percent markup on the delivered cost, the retail selling price is determined as follows:

$$
\begin{aligned}
\text{Retail Price} &= \text{Cost} + \text{Markup} \\
&= \$10 + (.40 \times \$10) \\
&= \$10 + \$4 \\
&= \$14
\end{aligned}
$$

After setting their prices, retailers should seek answers to various questions concerning their pricing decisions. For example: Do the prices cover costs and generate the desired profit? Do they reflect the appropriate image? How do they compare with the prices charged by competitors? Are customers willing and able to pay these prices?

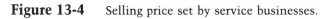 Pricing by Service Businesses

As shown in Figure 13-4, a service business sets prices based on the cost of any materials used to provide the service, the time and expertise required to perform it, operating expenses, and a profit allowance.

Figure 13-4   Selling price set by service businesses.

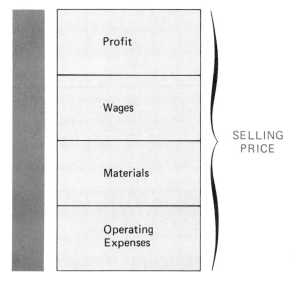

Some service enterprises charge by the hour (e.g., according to the actual number of hours needed to perform the service). Some companies, however, charge a standard fee. Preparers of tax forms often have a set fee for each type of tax form and do not charge according to the amount of time required to complete the task.

Pricing decisions are among the most important decisions that a marketing manager must make. Manufacturers, wholesalers, retailers, and service businesses use different methods to set prices. Nevertheless, the goal is the same. All businesses strive to set prices that are low enough to attract buyers yet high enough to cover costs and provide a profit.

APPLYING MARKETING TERMS

Name _____

Match each term with the statement that best describes an application of that term. Write the letter in the space provided.

a. price lining
b. seasonal discounts
c. price competition
d. loss leader
e. list price
f. cumulative quantity discounts
g. cash discount
h. nonprice competition
i. price skimming
j. trade discounts

_____ 1. A supermarket sells bread for ten cents less than it paid for the bread, hoping to attract customers who will buy regularly priced items.

_____ 2. A home builder receives a five percent rebate for buying $500,000 worth of lumber from a particular supplier over a twelve-month period.

_____ 3. A clothing manufacturer establishes a line of women's coats priced at $150, $250, and $400.

_____ 4. "Let's set the price on our new word processing program high enough to quickly recover the money we spent to develop it."

_____ 5. Advertising the product's features and packaging rather than its price.

_____ 6. A manufacturer of patio furniture gives discounts to buyers who purchase its products in January.

_____ 7. Giving the buyer a two percent discount for paying the bill within ten days.

_____ 8. An auto parts wholesaler normally charges $85 for a particular car battery.

_____ 9. A luggage retailer is offered a 25 percent discount for performing storage and selling tasks.

_____ 10. A service station reduces its gasoline price by one cent per gallon to match the price of the service station across the street.

Name _____

Answer each of the following questions in the space provided.

1. Explain the difference between price and nonprice competition.

2. What are five factors upon which the exact price for a product or service depends?

3. How do changes in supply and demand affect prices?

4. Describe the three basic pricing strategies.

5. What is the difference between price skimming and penetration pricing?

6. What are four pricing policies that marketing managers may use?

7. Explain how setting prices for the organizational market differs from setting prices for the consumer market.

8. What is a markup and how do wholesalers use it in setting prices?

DEVELOPING PEOPLE SKILLS

Read the following description of a human relations situation. Then complete your answers on a separate piece of paper.

Starting a Business with Spouse and Friends

Judy and Bob Marshall and Susan and Ken Gordon were about to see the results of their hard work. It had been almost a year since the two couples, who had been friends for ten years, started talking about starting an office supplies business together. Now their business was almost ready to open and they would face very little competition in the area.

The friends had several years of business experience between them. When the four owners got together to finalize the plans for opening their business, they realized they could no longer delay their decisions on a pricing strategy and cash discounts. They all agreed that prices should not be set at the market. However, Judy and Susan wanted to set prices above the market, while Bob and Ken preferred to price below the market.

Another point of disagreement had to do with cash discounts. Judy and Bob wanted to pay bills early enough to receive cash discounts offered by suppliers even if they had to borrow from the bank to do it. Most of their suppliers offered terms of 3/10, net 30. Susan and Ken agreed that they should pay their bills early, but not if they had to borrow the money.

After they had discussed the two areas of disagreement for almost two hours, Judy said, "We disagree on two important decisions and the business is not even open yet. I wonder how many other issues we'll disagree on in the future when the business is operating. I hate to say this, but I'm beginning to think that being in this business together may ruin our friendships, our marriages, or maybe both."

1. What do you believe is an advantage of friends going into business together? What is a disadvantage?
2. What do you believe is an advantage of a married couple going into business together? What is a disadvantage?
3. Regarding the selection of a pricing strategy, do you agree with Judy and Susan or with Bob and Ken? Explain.
4. Do you agree with Susan and Ken that they should not borrow money to take advantage of cash discounts? Explain.

MARKETING PROJECT 13

Use your own paper to complete this project.

The Pricing Memo

In Marketing Project 2 and Marketing Project 8 you assumed that you were the marketing manager of a new chain of quick oil change and lube shops. In each case you were asked to write a memo to the president of the company. Please refer to these projects for background information.

Your assignment for Marketing Project 13 is to write another memo to the company president. In your memo you will recommend that the company compete on a nonprice basis. Be sure to defend your recommendation with solid arguments about pricing strategies and the factors affecting price.

MARKETING INSIGHT

Read the following description of real-life marketing practices. Then complete your answers on a separate piece of paper.

Value Is in the Eye of the Beholder

True or false? *Low price is the most effective sales tool.* Many people answer "True." However, price is not the only factor that determines whether people buy a particular product or service. According to Allen Fishman, price sometimes plays a relatively unimportant role in the purchase decision.[1] In fact, in one study it was found that the company with the lowest prices actually had the lowest sales volume. So, if low price isn't the most effective sales tool, what is? The answer is *perceived value.*

The perceived value of a product or service is what a consumer believes it is worth. The value of things depends upon the judgment of those who want to own them. Fishman states, "Go, for example, to any rock concert, but don't consider the ticket cost. Instead, watch the fans buy souvenirs." Sweatshirts sold at these events have price tags of around $30.

Why would anyone spend that much money on a souvenir? The answer, according to Fishman, is the shirt is worth that much to them. Consumers spend more for a product when they receive intangible values in addition to the tangible product. The tangible part is the shirt itself, which may not be worth more than $5 or $6. The intangible part is the experience of the concert as well as giving concert-goers the opportunity to make their friends envious.

Price is important, but it is only one part of the marketing mix. Marketers need to find out what their products and services mean to customers; that is, they must determine their perceived value.

1. This Marketing Insight describes when low price is not the most effective sales tool. Describe an example of when low price is the best sales tool.
2. If high prices will scare some people away, shouldn't marketers always charge the lowest price possible? Why or why not?
3. Give an example of a product or service that consumers your age will spend more money for even though a product or service of similar quality is available at a lower price. Why are consumers willing to pay the higher price?

---

[1]Allen Fishman, "Perceived Value Beats Low Price as Sales Tool," *The Columbus Dispatch* (20 December 1987), p. 13H.

CHAPTER 14
MARKETING CHANNELS AND INTERMEDIARIES

After you read this chapter and complete the activities at the end, you will be able to:

1. **Describe five common marketing channels for consumer products.**
2. **Describe four common marketing channels for industrial products.**
3. **Describe different types of retail businesses.**
4. **Describe different types of wholesalers.**
5. **Explain how product and service marketing differ.**

Think about all the different products you buy: food, clothing, sports equipment, gasoline, videotapes, books, and magazines to name just a few. How many of these items do you buy directly from the producer? If you are a typical consumer, your answer will be that you buy very few products directly from the producer. Instead, you rely on **marketing channels,** also called **channels of distribution,** which are systems of individuals and organizations that direct the flow of products and services from manufacturers or producers to customers. Marketing channels are like pipelines that products flow through as they travel from producers to customers.

Most, but not all, channels of distribution have intermediaries. **Intermediaries,** sometimes called **middlemen,** are businesses that aid the movement of goods and services through the marketing channels. Intermediaries perform various functions and go by various names, but most can be classified as either a wholesaler or a retailer. This chapter focuses on these marketing channels and intermediaries and discusses the important role they play in a firm's overall marketing program.

MARKETING CHANNELS FOR CONSUMER PRODUCTS

Consumer products are items intended for use by individuals or families. They can be used by consumers without a great deal of further processing. Examples of consumer products are frozen and canned foods, clothing, household appliances, and automobiles. Five common marketing channels for consumer products are (1) producer to consumer, (2) producer to retailer to consumer, (3) producer to wholesaler to retailer to consumer, (4) producer to agent to retailer to consumer, and (5) producer to agent to wholesaler to retailer to consumer. Figure 14-1 illustrates the various marketing channels used for consumer products.

Figure 14-1   Marketing channels for consumer products.

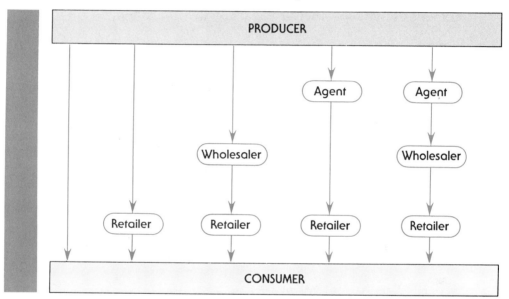

Producer to Consumer

This is the shortest channel of distribution for consumer products. Producers or manufacturers may sell their products directly to consumers in their homes either through a sales representative or direct mail. For example, fresh fruits and vegetables, cooking utensils, cosmetics, and food storage containers often flow directly from the manufacturer or producer to the consumer by way of a sales representative. Avon, Discovery Toys, and Tupperware products pass through this channel. Book publishers, record, CD, and tape companies and some clothes manufacturers sell products directly through the mail. L.L. Bean and Lands' End have both become very successful at using the direct mail, producer-to-consumer catalog as a marketing channel.

Almost all service businesses use this channel. Dry cleaners, dentists, and preparers of income tax returns provide services directly to customers.

Producer to Retailer to Consumer

Sometimes producers or manufacturers sell goods to retailers who, in turn, sell them to consumers. The retailers involved are usually large firms. For example, a food manufacturer might sell canned foods to a large supermarket company. A manufacturer of draperies might sell them to Sears or the J.C. Penney Company.

Illustration 14-1   Extractors may sell products to retailers who then sell them to consumers.

Producer to Wholesaler to Retailer to Consumer

Thousands of small producers and retailers use this marketing channel. For example, a manufacturer may sell a product to a wholesaler who also buys related products from other manufacturers. This wholesaler then sells an array of goods to retailers. Thus, a manufacturer of toothbrushes sells them to a drug wholesaler who, in turn, sells a group of products (including toothbrushes) to drugstores, supermarkets, and other retail stores.

Producer to Agent to Retailer to Consumer

Some producers sell their products through agents who help them reach large retailers such as national and regional supermarket chains. **Agents** are intermediaries who actively assist in the sale of products without taking title to them. This means that they do not own the goods involved. Agents are an important link in the marketing channel because they bring buyers and sellers together. Agents often work for producers who are looking for retailers to buy their products. Sometimes they work for retailers who are trying to find suppliers for certain goods. Hosiery and apparel are examples of goods commonly sold through agents.

Producer to Agent to Wholesaler to Retailer to Consumer

Agents are often used in industries where many producers supply products to a large number of wholesalers scattered around the country. Again, the job of the agent is to bring buyers and sellers together in order to make products available for purchase. Agents are widely used in industries such as canned fruits and vegetables and frozen foods.

MARKETING CHANNELS FOR INDUSTRIAL PRODUCTS

Industrial products are used in the production of services and other products. Because firms in the industrial market use products to produce other products and services, they are the primary buyers of industrial products. However, various organizations in the reseller and government markets also buy some industrial products. Machinery, tools, and raw materials used in manufacturing processes are examples of industrial products.

Four common distribution channels for industrial products are (1) producer to industrial user, (2) producer to agent to industrial user, (3) producer to industrial distributor to industrial user, and (4) producer to agent to industrial distributor to industrial user. Figure 14-2 illustrates the various marketing channels used for industrial products.

Figure 14-2   Marketing channels for industrial products.

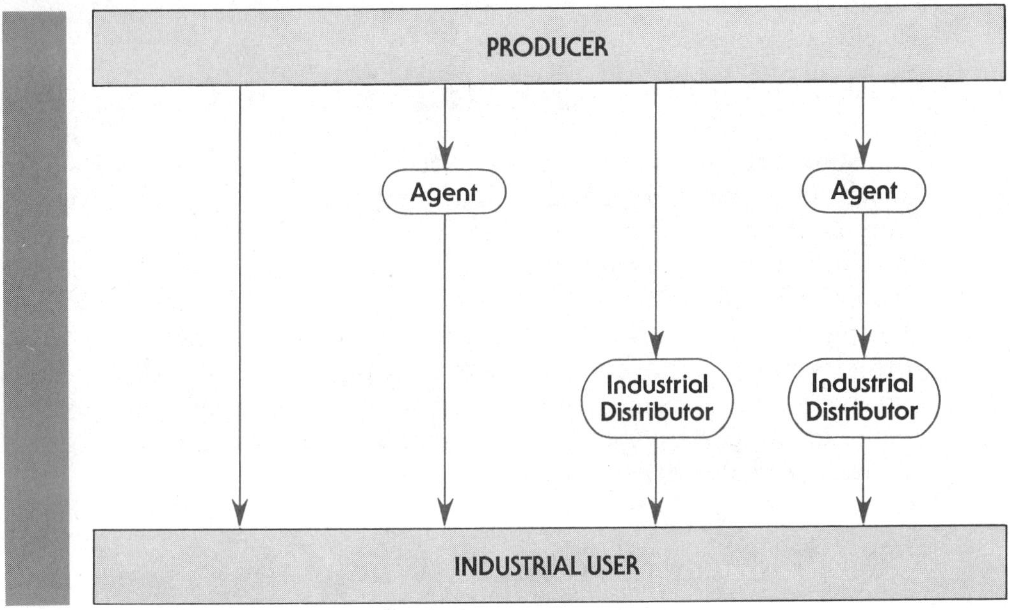

Producer to Industrial User

The majority of industrial products and services are sold by producers or manufacturers directly to industrial users. They are often designed for a specific use. Examples include an elevator for a factory building, aircraft for an airline, and refinery equipment for an oil company.

Producer to Agent to Industrial User

A firm without its own sales force might use this marketing channel. Also, because of their knowledge of an industry, companies may use agents rather than their own sales representatives to introduce a new product or enter a new market.

Producer to Industrial Distributor to Industrial User

Producers or manufacturers of some items use industrial distributors to help them reach their markets. **Industrial distributors** are wholesalers who buy goods from producers or manufacturers and sell them to industrial users. They usually handle lower priced goods such as accessory equipment and operating supplies. Accessory equipment includes items such as typewriters, small power tools, cash registers, and small lathes. Lubricating oil, pencils, and office stationery are examples of operating supplies. Industrial distributors often keep quantities of products on hand in order to supply numerous industrial users rapidly.

Producer to Agent to Industrial Distributor to Industrial User

Small manufacturers or producers often hire agents as an independent sales force to contact large industrial distributors. They do not have the resources to sell their goods directly to these distributors.

RETAILING

Retailing is that part of marketing in which goods and services are sold to ultimate consumers (the people who buy them for personal use). Most retailing occurs in stores where customers initiate the transactions. There are over 1.25 million retail businesses in the United States employing in excess of 17 million people.[1]

Consumers usually buy in small quantities. This results in a large number of individual sales transactions for each retailer. A music store might have annual sales of $1,000,000. This means that it has sold, for example, an average of $10 worth of cassette tapes 100,000 times that year.

Retail businesses can be classified by (1) ownership, (2) product lines carried, and (3) methods of reaching customers.

Ownership

One method of classifying retail businesses is according to ownership. The four major types of retail businesses by ownership are (1) independent retail stores, (2) chain stores, (3) franchise businesses, and (4) manufacturer-owned stores.

---

[1]U.S. Bureau of the Census, *Statistical Abstract of the United States: 1989,* 109th ed. (Washington, D.C.: U.S. Government Printing Office, 1989), p. 753.

Independent Retail Stores. The typical **independent retail store** is a small business that is managed by the owner or owners. Retailing in the United States consists of a large number of small stores, many medium-sized stores, and a small number of large stores. Generally independents are numerous but small; that is, they have small sales volumes. One in every ten retail stores is an independent, and these independent retail stores account for more than 50 percent of all retail sales.

Chain Stores. Chain stores are groups of retail stores that are centrally owned, centrally managed, and handle the same product lines. Chain stores are the major competitors of independent retail stores.

Illustration 14-2

An independent retail store is a small owner-managed business.

Many chain store organizations started as single stores. Having met the needs of consumers in local areas, the owner(s) decided to expand into other areas, usually nearby communities. These companies grew by buying already established stores or by building one or more new stores.

Chain store companies acquire merchandise by placing large orders with producers or other suppliers. For example, if a firm has fifty stores in various cities, it can place a large order for tires from one manufacturer and then have them shipped to its stores. By buying in large quantities, the chain can save money. This may also result in lower prices for the chain's customers.

Franchise Businesses. A **franchise** is an agreement by which a parent company gives an individual or a small company the right to do business in a standardized manner. The parent company is the **franchisor.** It can be a manufacturer, wholesaler, or service company. The person or company given rights by a franchisor is called the **franchisee.** These rights may include the authority to sell the franchisor's products and to use its name, trademark, and operating procedures. Rights may vary from franchise to franchise.

A franchise combines features of independent retail stores and chain stores. Franchise owners invest their own money in the business, enjoy the profits of success, and accept responsibility for failure. At the same time they are connected with a well-known company that can provide assistance in setting up and operating the business.

Manufacturer-Owned Stores. By having their own retail outlets—called **manufacturer-owned stores**—manufacturing companies can have complete control over the channel of distribution for their products. Some manufacturers of candy, shoes, and men's clothing prefer to sell their products only through their own stores. Other producers use manufacturer-owned stores but not as sole outlets for their products. For instance, they may have stores to test the sales of new products or to dispose of outdated styles or products that have slight defects.

◤ Product Lines Carried

Retail businesses may also be classified according to the product lines they carry. Most consumer products are sold through six different types of stores: (1) department stores, (2) specialty stores, (3) supermarkets, (4) convenience stores, (5) superstores, and (6) discount houses.

Department Stores. **Department stores** sell a variety of merchandise grouped into well-defined departments. The usual departments are men's and boys' wear, women's wear, jewelry, cosmetics, household linens and towels, home furnishings, appliances, and furniture. Department stores are large stores that usually offer many services including credit, delivery, merchandise returns, and personal assistance. J.C. Penney and Sears are two well-known national department store companies.

Specialty Stores. Stores that carry a limited variety of goods but a large assortment of each item are called **specialty stores.** An assortment refers to the range of choice for each kind of product offered. For instance, because it carries mainly furniture items, a furniture store will probably have a much larger assortment of lounge chairs than a department store. In most cases specialty stores are named according to the main product sold: bookstores, hardware stores, jewelry stores, and computer stores.

Specialty stores sometimes handle unusual imported or domestic items that are not found in other types of stores. The owner of a bookstore, for instance, may specialize in finding and selling rare books. A jewelry retailer may make trips to Europe to buy unique rings and bracelets to resell in the store.

Supermarkets. A **supermarket** is a large retail store that sells a wide variety of food and some nonfood items and features self-service and low prices. Supermarkets are divided into sections such as canned goods, frozen foods, meats, produce, and dairy products. Nonfood items such as toothpaste, magazines, kitchen utensils, pet supplies,

Illustration 14-3   In department stores, merchandise is grouped into departments such as women's wear.

shampoo, and cleaning supplies are also sold. It is estimated that supermarkets account for three-fourths of the grocery store business in the United States.

Prior to the 1930s, food retailing occurred in small neighborhood grocery stores. Customers were waited on by clerks who stood behind counters that separated the customers from the merchandise. Clerks filled customers' orders and sometimes delivered the groceries to their homes.

The first supermarkets were independent stores that opened in the 1930s. A large number of independent supermarkets remain; however, chain stores now dominate the industry.

Convenience Stores. Convenience stores carry limited varieties of food items—bread, milk, ice cream—that meet customers' needs between major shopping trips. They offer convenience rather than a wide selection of products. Convenience store prices are often higher than supermarket prices. Many shoppers are willing to pay higher prices when buying only a few items because they are able to make their purchases quickly and easily. Convenience stores are usually in easy-to-reach locations near residential areas.

Superstores. Very large stores that carry foods and numerous other products and services that consumers routinely buy are called **superstores.** The goal of superstores is to meet customers' ordinary needs at low prices.

Supermarkets fulfill consumers' needs for food items and a limited number of nonfood items. Superstores go beyond this by stocking complete lines of health and personal care products, hardware items, some clothing, lawn and garden products, greeting cards and stationery, books, toys, videotapes, and low-priced housewares. They also provide services such as dry cleaning and shoe repair. Some even have branch banks located inside the stores.

Discount Houses. Discount houses are stores that offer wide varieties of products at so-called discount or low prices. Their prices are somewhat, though not always, lower than the prices of other retailers such as department stores. Discount houses sell appliances, furnitures, clothing, health and beauty products, automobile accessories, and even food items.

Discounters are able to charge lower prices because they buy in large quantities from manufacturers and other suppliers at reduced prices. In addition, they lower their operating costs by emphasizing self-service shopping. Fewer salespeople are needed to assist customers. The stores are usually in low-rent locations and do not have the elaborate fixtures, decorations, or displays of many other retail stores. These savings can be passed on to customers through reduced prices.

◢◣ Methods of Reaching Customers

Finally, a retail business can be classified by the way it reaches its customers. There are four different methods of reaching consumers: (1) over-the-counter retailing, (2) mail order retailing, (3) direct retailing, and (4) vending machine retailing.

Over-the-Counter Retailing. Selling products in a store is called **over-the-counter retailing.** Customers go into a store to shop and select the products they wish to buy from the retailer's stock. Ninety percent of all retailing activity occurs this way. Food, clothing, home appliances, furniture—a seemingly endless number of products are sold through the over-the-counter method.

Mail Order Retailing. In **mail order retailing,** customers select the products they want from catalogs or advertisements. While most orders are mailed to the company, an increasing number of customers are placing orders by telephone or fax. In the future, customers will be able to place their orders over telephone lines using home computers.

Merchandise is delivered directly to customers by the United States Postal Service, United Parcel Service, or private freight lines. Some department stores also sell by catalog. In this case, merchandise is picked up by customers at catalog desks in the stores.

Many companies have successfully used mail order as their method of doing business. Some of them provide such large varieties of merchandise that they are called "department stores in print." Others concentrate on specific types of goods such as housewares, novelty items, vitamins and other health products, clothing, or food products.

Direct Retailing. In **direct retailing,** sellers contact prospective customers in their homes. There are two main types of direct retailing: door-to-door selling and party plan selling.

Some cosmetic, encyclopedia, and vacuum cleaner manufacturers have become famous for selling door to door and demonstrating products in prospective customers' homes. Others sell their products by the party plan. A salesperson asks someone to give a party and invite relatives and friends. The salesperson shows the manufacturer's product line to the group, demonstrates how each item is used, and takes orders. Food storage containers, jewelry, toys, home furnishings, and clothing are products that are sold this way.

Vending Machine Retailing. Vending machine retailing requires no personal contact between seller and buyer. The product is sold through a machine. This type of retailing has grown in popularity, and the variety of products offered has increased. Soft drinks, candy, and snack foods have been sold through vending machines for many years. In addition, vending machines now dispense refrigerated foods and foods that can be heated in microwave ovens located nearby. Toothpaste, toothbrushes, small toys, games, and road maps can often be found in service station vending machines. Vending machines at airports dispense insurance policies.

Probably the most familiar type of vending machine is coin operated. However, some machines now accept credit cards. In order to make purchases, customers simply insert their cards. The machines record transactions and electronically provide bills. Many banks now have asset machines that allow customers to access their bank accounts, pay bills, receive cash, and transfer funds between accounts.

WHOLESALING

Wholesaling involves selling products to buyers who are purchasing them for reasons other than personal or family use. Hence, wholesalers buy products from extractors and manufacturers and sell them to other businesses. They do not sell goods directly to consumers. Recent figures show over 4.5 million people working in over 400,000 wholesale businesses nationwide.[2] Wholesalers can be divided into two broad groups: merchant wholesalers and agents.

Merchant Wholesalers

Merchant wholesalers take title to the products they distribute which means that they own them. In other words, they buy and sell products on their own account. There are two types of merchant wholesalers: full-function wholesalers and limited-function wholesalers.

---

[2]U.S. Bureau of the Census, *Statistical Abstract of the United States: 1989,* 109th ed. (Washington, D.C.: U.S. Government Printing Office, 1989), p. 761.

Full-Function Wholesalers. Full-function wholesalers (also called **full-service** or **service wholesalers**), the most common type of merchant wholesalers, perform a wide range of marketing activities. They buy products from many manufacturers or suppliers and store them in warehouses, performing a valuable service for their customers (other businesses). Supermarkets, hardware stores, drugstores, and auto parts stores carry thousands of items. In fact, they stock so many items that it would be impossible for their managers to contact all the necessary suppliers in order to acquire these products. By bringing together all types of goods from thousands of suppliers, full-function wholesalers offer managers a single source of supply.

Full-function wholesalers sell on credit and provide their customers with information about new products. They have sales representatives who regularly call on customers and deliver goods.

Rack jobbers (a type of full-function wholesaler) place their own display racks in stores and stock them with merchandise. Rack jobbers keep their displays neat, clean, and well stocked. The merchandise is often provided to stores on **consignment.** This means that retailers either carry the items without buying them or purchase the goods with merchandise return privileges. Thus, retailers assume no

Illustration 14-4

Rack jobbers must keep their displays neat and well stocked.

risk if the products do not sell. Examples of products that are handled by rack jobbers include housewares or kitchen utensils in drugstores and hosiery or clothing in supermarkets.

Many full-function wholesalers specialize in a particular line of products such as food items, hardware, medicines, electrical supplies, or dry goods. Some even limit their operations to a narrow range of products such as frozen foods.

Some full-function wholesalers sell only to businesses that use the products in their daily operations and do not resell them in the same form. Examples are wholesalers of dental equipment and supplies, restaurant equipment, office furniture, barbershop and beauty shop equipment, machinery, and industrial chemicals.

Limited-Function Wholesalers. In addition to the full-function wholesaler, there is a second type of merchant wholesaler called a limited-function wholesaler. **Limited-function wholesalers** provide a narrow range of functions or marketing services for their customers. There are four kinds of limited-function wholesalers: (1) cash-and-carry wholesalers, (2) drop shippers, (3) truck jobbers, and (4) mail order wholesalers.

Cash-and-Carry Wholesalers. **Cash-and-carry wholesalers** sell on a cash only basis and do not make deliveries. Their customers typically are businesses that are too small to be serviced by full-function wholesalers. Small grocers, for example, go to the warehouse, select and pay for their goods, and transport them to their stores in their own trucks.

Drop Shippers. **Drop shippers** (sometimes called **desk jobbers**) take title to the goods they sell, but they do not take physical possession of these goods. They obtain orders for products from retailers, service organizations, industrial buyers, and other wholesalers. The drop shippers then arrange to have shipments sent directly from extractors or manufacturers to buyers. These wholesalers have offices—hence the name desk jobbers—but do not have warehouses or delivery equipment because they do not perform the storage and transportation functions. Drop shippers are of major importance when bulky goods such as coal, timber, farm products, or heavy machinery are involved.

Truck Jobbers. **Truck jobbers** sell and make deliveries to retailers from stocks they carry in their trucks. They specialize in the sale and delivery of perishable or semi-perishable products and are found mainly in the grocery field. Examples of truck jobbers are wholesalers who deliver candy, bread and bakery items, and potato chips to supermarkets and convenience stores. Unlike full-function wholesalers, truck jobbers do not usually sell on credit.

Mail Order Wholesalers. **Mail order wholesalers** sell through catalogs that are distributed to their customers—mainly small retailers and other businesses in rural areas that are not served by other types of wholesalers. Examples of products that are sold by mail order wholesalers include sporting goods, jewelry, and hardware. Mail order wholesalers account for only a small part of the nation's total wholesaling business.

Agent Wholesalers

Agents are wholesalers who actively assist in the sale of products (or services) without taking title to them. They bring buyers and sellers together. Generally agents perform fewer services than limited-function wholesalers. The most important types of agent wholesalers are (1) brokers, (2) selling agents, and (3) manufacturers' agents.

Brokers. In a typical transaction, a **broker** negotiates the sale of a product and then allows the seller to accept or reject the prospective buyer's offer. When such transactions are completed, brokers are paid by whoever hired them. They are paid a **commission**—a percentage of the dollar amount of products sold. Most brokers work for sellers, although a small number do represent buyers. They furnish valuable information about products, prices, and general market conditions. Brokers do not physically handle products.

Brokers often deal in products that are seasonal which means that sellers cannot offer them year-round. Examples of seasonal products are fruits, vegetables, and seafood. A broker is hired for a single transaction or to sell a specific lot of goods. The seller may not have dealt with the prospective buyers previously and may not know how to contact them. A broker fills the gap. For instance, a vegetable canner may hire a broker to contact buyers and negotiate the sale of a season's stock. When the entire supply of canned vegetables has been sold, the broker's services are no longer needed.

Selling Agents. **Selling agents** are independent intermediaries who perform the entire marketing task for firms. A producer will hire one selling agent to market the entire output of a company; however, a selling agent will usually perform marketing functions for more than one noncompeting producer. They are frequently hired by producers who cannot afford complete marketing staffs. Selling agents are given the authority to set prices and to decide how products will be promoted. They handle goods such as coal, metal products, timber, food items, and textiles.

Manufacturers' Agents. Producers employ only one selling agent, but they often hire a number of manufacturers' agents. **Manufacturers' agents** are independent intermediaries who sell similar products for several noncompeting manufacturers. They sell these products according to the instructions of the companies they represent. Manufacturers' agents are usually not involved in setting prices or in negotiating the terms of sales. They are restricted to specific sales areas or territories.

The services provided by manufacturers' agents are useful when a company's sales volume is too small to support a sales force. Because these agents already call on a group of customers, they can add another manufacturer's product to their sales lines at a relatively low cost. Manufacturers' agents are used to sell a wide range of items including electrical products, machinery and equipment, and some types of clothing.

THE MARKETING OF SERVICES

Services are tasks that we pay others to do or provide for us. Some familiar enterprises that provide services are laundries, dry cleaners, day-care centers, automobile repair shops, movie theaters, airlines, and motels.

Unlike a product that is manufactured in one city and then transported to another to be sold, a service cannot be separated from its producer or provider. For example, a hairstylist or barber provides a service for customers while they sit in a chair. Since services are provided as they are wanted, there is usually no need for transportation or storage.

The marketing channel for services is often direct from producer or provider to customer. The difference, then, between the marketing of services and the marketing of products is that services are produced and consumed at the same time. No intermediaries are required. The geographic area of the markets that service sellers can reach is limited; however, these sellers are able to personalize their services and get quick and detailed feedback from their customers.

APPLYING MARKETING TERMS

Name _____

Match each term with the statement that best describes an application of that term. Write the letter in the space provided.

a. industrial distributor
b. franchise
c. producer to consumer
d. commission
e. consignment

f. specialty stores
g. manufacturer-owned stores
h. agents
i. truck jobbers
j. mail order retailing

_____ 1. Marketing channel used by a dry cleaner.

_____ 2. The store stocks compact disks and cassette tapes, but can return them to the manufacturer for a refund if they don't sell.

_____ 3. Taylor obtained the right from an ice cream maker to open a shop under its name and to use its operating procedures.

_____ 4. This wholesaler delivers products, such as potato chips and bread, to grocery and convenience stores.

_____ 5. Bookstores and jewelry stores fit in this category of retail business.

_____ 6. A wholesaler who buys lubricating oil from the producer and sells it to a machine shop.

_____ 7. A company that sells the clothing it manufactures through its own stores.

_____ 8. Customers select the computer software they want from catalogs or advertisements.

_____ 9. "You'll be paid five percent of the dollar amount of every sale you make."

_____ 10. These intermediaries don't take title to the products, but they assist in selling them.

MASTERING KEY CONCEPTS

Name _____

Answer each of the following questions in the space provided.

1. What are five common marketing channels for consumer products?

2. Identify four common marketing channels for industrial products.

3. What is the primary difference between merchant wholesalers and agent wholesalers?

4. What are the four major types of retail businesses classified according to ownership?

5. What are the six types of retail businesses classified according to product lines carried?

6. List the four methods used in retailing to reach customers.

7. Explain how full-function wholesalers differ from limited-function wholesalers.

8. What is the main difference between the marketing of products and the marketing of services?

DEVELOPING PEOPLE SKILLS

Read the following description of a human relations situation. Then complete your answer on a separate piece of paper.

Dealing with a Dishonest Co-Worker

Judy and Tim got summer jobs with New Sound Cassette Tape Distributors, a rack jobber that installs and stocks cassette tape display racks in supermarkets, convenience stores, and drugstores. As they arrived for their first day at work, Mr. Joji Eto, the manager, welcomed them to the company and introduced them to Bill Wells. Bill had agreed to teach Judy and Tim how to perform their jobs. Bill had worked for New Sound for more than three years and Mr. Eto thought he was qualified to train the new employees.

The job consisted of going to stores that have New Sound display racks and making sure that each rack was neat, orderly, and fully stocked with cassette tapes. Tapes that had been damaged by customer handling were replaced with new tapes. Occasionally empty cassette boxes were found, indicating that tapes had been stolen. Mr. Eto required that all thefts be reported to him as well as to the manager of the store in which the theft occurred.

After spending a week with Bill, Judy and Tim were confident that they could handle the job on their own. Mr. Eto agreed and Judy and Tim were assigned to their own routes. However, Mr. Eto asked them to meet with Bill at least once a week to discuss any problems they encountered on the job. During one of these meetings, Bill told Judy and Tim how he obtained cassette tapes for his personal use. He takes them and reports to Mr. Eto and to the store manager that they were stolen from one of the racks. Bill said, "It isn't going to hurt the company if I take a tape now and then. The way I look at it, it's not really stealing because it makes up for the times I'm too busy working to take the coffee or lunch breaks I'm entitled to. Besides, shoplifters take more in a week than I do in a year." Bill asked Judy and Tim not to tell anyone what he had said.

1. Is it stealing if Bill takes tapes to make up for the times he doesn't take his coffee or lunch breaks? Explain.
2. Should Judy and Tim have said anything to Bill when they learned that he was taking cassette tapes from the company? Why?
3. Do you believe that most employees report information about employee thefts to company managers? Why?
4. If Bill is caught stealing, how might it affect his future career?
5. What would you do if you were Judy or Tim?

MARKETING PROJECT 14

Use your own paper to complete this project.

Selecting a Marketing Channel

A manufacturer of personal computers has been distributing its products to consumers through the producer to wholesaler to retailer marketing channel. This marketing channel has been used because the company had never developed a strong sales staff. Now the company would like to expand its business by making its personal computers available to industrial users. It is considering two alternative marketing channels to sell to business users: (1) producer to industrial user and (2) producer to industrial distributor to industrial user.

Illustrate the two marketing channels in a drawing. Then recommend which of the two alternative marketing channels the company should use to distribute its personal computers to industrial users. Explain the reason for your recommendation.

MARKETING INSIGHT

Read the following description of real-life marketing practices. Then complete your answers on a separate piece of paper.

Video Rental Stores Innovate to Survive

In 1986, video cassette recorder (VCR) owners rented an average of 3.26 videos per month. That number had dropped to 2.38 by the end of 1989. Video renting drops by twenty-five percent after the first two years of VCR ownership and more than seventy percent of households in the United States already own a VCR.

Those video stores that survive must be prepared to compete for consumers' dollars. In addition to hard work, these competitive efforts will also involve innovation. Innovation, which means introducing new things or finding new ways to do things better, has become the key to survival in the industry. "New gadgets, promotions and attention to customer service," reports *USA Today*, "are on deck as video rental stores stop coasting on the popularity of their product and start working as hard as the rest of the consumer industry."

The large video rental chains are expected to make major financial investments in their innovations. One such firm plans to open mega-stores measuring 5,000 square feet. These stores sell video game cartridges, compact disks, popcorn, ice cream, and tickets for concerts and sports events in addition to renting and selling video movies. Another chain has stepped up its use of television advertising and introduced a game with cash, trips, and merchandise as prizes.

Smaller firms without the financial resources of the chains are becoming innovative in the way they serve their customers. For example, one two-store firm specializes in unusual and hard-to-find video movies and serves out-of-town and out-of-state customers through its mail order service.[3]

1. Why is the average number of videos rented per month decreasing?
2. Other than those mentioned in this Marketing Insight, what other products or services could be sold through video rental stores? Why did you select these products or services?
3. A name other than "video rental store" may be more descriptive of this line of business. After looking at your answer to Question 2, is video rental store still an appropriate name? Explain.

---

[3]Ellen Neuborne, "Video Stores Try to Replay Rental Boom," *USA Today* (30 May 1990), p. 1B.

CHAPTER 15
PHYSICAL DISTRIBUTION

After you read this chapter and complete the activities at the end, you will be able to:

1. **Explain the meaning of physical distribution.**
2. **Describe the five basic modes of transportation.**
3. **Identify the four basic types of storage facilities.**
4. **Discuss the activities businesses perform to support the physical distribution function.**
5. **Identify the causes of various accidents in the workplace and related preventive measures.**

You drive into a service station only to find that the station is out of the unleaded gasoline you need. You are told that a shipment from the supplier is several hours overdue. The jacket you ordered by mail and planned to give as a birthday present did not arrive on the day promised. You wait all day for the moving van to load your furniture and it never comes. You are told it will come tomorrow. Will it?

All of these situations indicate problems the companies are having with physical distribution. As discussed in Chapter 2, physical distribution includes all the activities required to efficiently move finished goods and services from producers to customers. Transportation and storage are the two components of the physical distribution function. The marketing process cannot work unless a proper mix of products and services can be delivered when needed in an efficient manner. Physical distribution links business enterprises with their customers by providing products and services at the right time and place.

Some activities that support physical distribution include controlling inventory, packaging, and materials handling. In addition, employee safety must be considered when physical distribution activities are being planned and carried out.

◢ TRANSPORTATION

Transportation is the movement of goods from where they are produced or stored to where they are sold. In other words, it is the tool that creates place utility. If it is to be effective, the nation's transportation system must be capable of delivering the correct amounts of goods at the right times and at reasonable costs.

Illustration 15-1   The correct amounts of goods must be delivered at the right times and at reasonable costs.

Different methods or ways of moving products from one point to another are called **modes of transportation.** The five basic modes of transportation are (1) railroads, (2) trucks, (3) pipelines, (4) waterways, and (5) air carriers.

Railroads

As shown in Figure 15-1 on page 336, railroads are the major carriers of freight, in terms of ton-miles, between cities in the United States. A **ton-mile** is the movement of one ton (2,000 pounds) of freight for the distance of one mile.

Figure 15-1   Freight transported between United States cities in 1987.

MODE OF TRANSPORTATION	TON-MILES CARRIED (IN BILLIONS)	PERCENTAGE OF TOTAL
Railroad	976	36.5%
Truck	666	24.9
Pipeline	587	22.0
Waterway	435	16.3
Air Carrier	9	.3
Total	2,673	100.0%

Source: Adapted from U.S. Bureau of the Census, *Statistical Abstract of the United States: 1989*, 109th ed. (Washington, D.C.: U.S. Government Printing Office, 1989), p. 589.

Railroads are able to carry large quantities of freight long distances. Products transported by rail are often heavy or bulky and relatively low in value. Examples are goods or raw materials from farms, forests, and mines. Transportation costs account for a large portion of the selling price of these products. As shown in Figure 15-2, the cost of shipping by rail is considerably lower than the cost of shipping by air carrier or truck and is slightly lower than the cost of shipping by waterway.

Figure 15-2   Freight transportation costs in 1987.

MODE OF TRANSPORTATION	COST PER TON-MILE
Air Carrier	97 cents
Truck	20 cents
Waterway	4 cents
Railroad	3 cents
Pipeline	1 cent

Source: Adapted from U.S. Bureau of the Census, *Statistical Abstract of the United States: 1989*, 109th ed. (Washington, D.C.: U.S. Government Printing Office, 1989), pp. 588–9.

Because of their ability to transport a wide variety of products, railroads have an advantage over other modes. For example, trains are able to carry dry cargo, liquid cargo, frozen foods, fresh fruits and vegetables, and equipment of unusual size or shape. Other products moved by rail are paper, automobiles, chemicals, plastics, lumber, iron, steel, metal cans, and canned foods. Railroads are not limited as to the type of freight they can carry; they can handle almost anything. This is not always the case with other modes of transportation

A major disadvantage of railroads is their **low accessibility,** which means that they can only carry freight between a limited number of points. For example, the railroad system is not convenient for a company that is located many miles from a railroad track. The company would have to use another mode of transportation, probably truck, to gain access to rail service.

Other disadvantages of railroads are related to their transit time and frequency of service. **Transit time** is the total time that elapses from pickup to delivery of a shipment. Because of the slow average speed of the equipment and delays on sidings or in terminals, railroad transit time can be long. Since trains travel according to timetables, arrival and departure times are set.

To offset some of their disadvantages, railroads offer additional services. One example is piggyback freight. Goods are loaded on truck trailers which, in turn, are loaded on railroad flatcars. When a train reaches its destination, the truck trailers are off-loaded and connected to truck cabs. The products are then delivered by truck.

Trucks

Trucks are an increasingly significant part of the nation's transportation system. Trucks, which range in size from small pickups to large tractor trailer units, are used throughout business and industry to transport goods.

Trucks can go anywhere there are roads. This means that shippers can reach more customers by truck than by railroads, pipelines, waterways, or air carriers. Trucks clearly enjoy the benefits of our nation's network of well-maintained highways.

The main business of trucks is to transport manufactured items relatively short distances. Items transported by truck are often high in value such as textiles, leather goods, rubber and plastic products, electronics and communication equipment and parts, and photographic and computer equipment. Trucks may also carry other products such as coal, grain, or frozen foods.

As with all modes of transportation, trucks have disadvantages. One disadvantage is that trucks often carry full loads on outgoing trips but usually return empty. This means added costs for shippers. Another disadvantage is that traffic congestion, accidents, and drivers' rest stops increase transit time. Finally, there are some products, such as factory machinery, that are so large they cannot be carried by trucks on the highways.

◤ Pipelines

Although they are rarely noticed, pipelines are one of the basic modes of transportation. As shown in Figure 15-1, they are one of the largest carriers of intercity freight in the country.

Pipelines can transport only a limited number of products including natural gas, crude oil, petroleum products, chemicals, and slurry products. **Slurry products** are dry materials that are converted to liquid form by adding water to permit movement by pipeline. For instance, coal can be ground into a powder, mixed with water, and pumped through a pipeline. The water is removed when the coal reaches its destination. Natural gas and crude oil account for the largest percentage of pipeline shipments; slurry constitutes the smallest percentage.

Pipelines are a unique mode of transportation because they transport products in only one direction. Pipelines are almost completely unaffected by weather. Operating costs tend to be low. Once pipelines are installed, little additional labor is required to keep them in working order.

◤ Waterways

Water transportation can be divided into two broad categories: domestic and foreign. In **domestic water transportation** both the point of origin and the destination of a shipment are within the United States. In **foreign water transportation** either the point of origin or the destination of a shipment is in a foreign country.

Domestic water transportation can be divided into coastwise, intercoastal, Great Lakes, and inland water transportation. **Coastwise water transportation** is the movement of freight by water between points on the same coast of the United States, such as Boston and New York City. **Intercoastal water transportation** is the movement of freight by water from any point in the United States to any other point by way of the Panama Canal. An example of intercoastal water transportation is a shipment from San Francisco to Baltimore through the Panama Canal. **Great Lakes water transportation** refers to the shipping of freight between United States ports on the Great Lakes, such as Cleveland and Buffalo. Moving products between points on the nation's rivers and canals is known as **inland water transportation.**

The major advantage of water transportation is the low cost of shipping those goods that can be efficiently moved by ship or barge.

Illustration 15-2   Ships and barges provide low cost water transportation.

Port Authorities of New York & New Jersey

Generally products that are bulky and relatively low in value can be moved by waterway at very low rates. On the other hand, if delivery time is important, water transportation is not attractive because it is slow. Other disadvantages are that other modes of transportation must be used to complete deliveries and waterways are not accessible to people and businesses in many parts of the country.

Products that can be efficiently transported by water include iron ore, grains, limestone, petroleum, iron and steel, and cement. Also, automobiles manufactured in other countries are brought to the United States on large oceangoing vessels.

Air Carriers

Airplanes mainly transport people, not freight. Although there has been some growth in the use of air carriers for the movement of products, they are still relatively insignificant in terms of the total amount of freight shipped. As shown in Figure 15-1, air carriers account for less than one percent of the total ton-miles of intercity freight.

Air carriers are much faster than any other mode of transportation, but they are also the most expensive. As a result, airplanes are ideal for the shipment of small, lightweight products that are high in value and must be delivered quickly. Examples of items that may be shipped by air carrier are designer clothing, computer components, special dies and tools, and medical supplies.

Because of their speed, air carriers have opened new markets for perishable products. Hawaiian orchids or fresh Maine lobsters can be flown to cities throughout the country.

Combining Modes of Transportation

Various transportation modes can be combined to provide better customer service. Piggyback freight, a widely used method, combines the advantages of railroads and trucks. Trucks can also be used to pick up and deliver trailers that were shipped by waterway or large containers that were transported by air carrier.

STORAGE

Storage means stocking goods for future use. It is an important marketing function because buyers do not always wish to purchase products at the time they are produced. Products must be stored in order to meet the needs of customers. Storage creates time utility. Apples are a seasonal item that must be stored because people want to buy them at all times of the year. A company can manufacture Christmas ornaments year-round and store them until the Christmas selling season begins.

Types of Storage

Different types of products require different types of storage facilities. The four basic types of storage facilities are (1) yard and ground storage, (2) ordinary product storage, (3) special commodity storage, and (4) cold storage.

Yard and Ground Storage. **Yard and ground storage** facilities are used to store products that will not be damaged by exposure to the weather. Coal, bricks, and gravel are examples of products that can be stored without protection from rain, snow, or heat.

Ordinary Product Storage. The storage of products in buildings that will protect them from the weather is called **ordinary product storage.** Products are stored on shelves, in bins, or on the floors of these facilities. Manufacturers, wholesalers, and retailers store products this way; it is probably the most common type of storage.

Special Commodity Storage. Special commodity storage facilities are designed to store farm products such as grain, cotton, and wool. A grain elevator is an example of this kind of facility. Additional functions, such as grading or cleaning, are often provided.

Cold Storage. Cold storage facilities must be provided for perishable food products. For example, grapes and plums must be refrigerated in transit and in storage. The selling season for products such as apples and citrus fruits can be lengthened by storing them at low temperatures. Some frozen foods can also be kept for long periods of time when a low temperature is maintained.

◣ Ownership of Storage Facilities

The two main categories of storage facilities according to ownership are private warehouses and public warehouses. A **warehouse** is a building where products are stored before distribution.

Private Warehouses. Private warehouses are storage facilities that are leased or owned by retailers, manufacturers, or wholesalers for their own use. Retailers, for example, usually have some storage space in their stores. They may also lease space in or own a separate building. Private warehousing is beneficial for companies that must have their products immediately available. Owning and maintaining warehouse space, however, can be expensive.

Public Warehouses. Public warehouses have storage space available for a fee. Business firms that do not want to maintain their own warehouses can rent space in public warehouses.

In addition to renting space to other businesses, public warehouse owners also provide some services for their customers. Products are received, unloaded, and placed in storage. Incoming products may be inspected according to standards set by customers. Public warehouses also provide packing and shipping services and process the necessary paperwork for products that have been sold by their customers.

▲ SUPPORTING THE PHYSICAL DISTRIBUTION FUNCTION

Business firms perform various activities to support the physical distribution function including controlling inventory, packaging, and materials handling.

▲ Controlling Inventory

The products on hand at any given time constitute a firm's **inventory.** An inventory may be composed of raw materials, parts, semifinished products, finished products, or merchandise. Whatever its form, an inventory must be controlled. **Controlling inventory** means maintaining a balance between having too much and having too little on hand.

If an inventory is too large, the costs of carrying it will be higher than they should be. These costs include interest on the money that was borrowed to buy the inventory as well as insurance and storage costs. Damage and theft are more likely to occur when the number of items on hand is excessive.

On the other hand, if an inventory is too small it will run out. This can also be costly for a business. Rush or special orders require special handling and shipping at higher than normal rates. Running out of items needed in a manufacturing process can cause **downtime,** a period during which machinery, a department, or a factory is not in operation. If a business runs out of a consumer good, the results are dissatisfied buyers and lost sales. A firm may also lose customer patronage and goodwill.

Three methods that are used to control inventory are (1) perpetual inventory control, (2) periodic inventory control, and (3) just-in-time (JIT) inventory control.

Perpetual Inventory Control. With a **perpetual inventory control** system, a business can determine the amount of a product on hand at all times. Records show when items are added to inventory or removed. Many companies use computers to maintain these records.

A perpetual inventory control system is beneficial when:

1. Products are so high in value that the cost of recording each sale is relatively small.
2. Products are seasonal or fashion items and the quantity on hand at any time is small.
3. It is difficult to predict the rate at which products will sell.
4. Goods cannot be obtained quickly from suppliers.

Periodic Inventory Control. With a **periodic inventory control** system, the items on hand are counted at regular intervals such as once every month, once every six months, or once a year. A periodic inventory control system is used when the greater expense and detail of a perpetual inventory control system are not justified.

A periodic inventory control system is beneficial when:

1. Products are of low value.
2. Sales transactions are numerous making it costly to record each individual sale.
3. Products sell at rates that are easy to predict.
4. A large quantity of a product is kept on hand at all times.

Just-in-Time Inventory Control. An inventory control method widely used in Japan has been gaining acceptance by businesses in the United States. Known as **just-in-time (JIT) inventory control,** it calls for companies to maintain low inventory levels and to purchase products and materials in small amounts so that they are received just at the time they are needed for production. The main advantage of JIT is that inventory costs are reduced. However, it requires close coordination between producers and suppliers.

Packaging

In order to prevent damage, products must be packaged properly for shipment and storage. There are two broad categories of packaging: consumer and industrial.

Consumer Packaging. The container in which a product is sold is called **consumer packaging.** Consumer packaging holds products and protects them from damage. It is sometimes referred to as the silent salesperson. In addition to protecting a product, appealing consumer packaging attracts shoppers' attention and motivates them to buy. It also provides product information. Plastic egg cartons and cereal boxes are examples of consumer packaging.

Industrial Packaging. While consumer packaging is closely related to advertising and visual merchandising, industrial packaging is associated with physical distribution. **Industrial packaging** is used to protect products that will be shipped and stored and to prevent hazardous products from leaking during shipping or storage.

When selecting industrial packaging, marketing managers should consider the following elements:

Illustration 15-3

Consumer packaging protects products and motivates shoppers to buy.

1. Whether the products can be easily packed and unpacked.
2. The strength of the packaging and its ability to protect the products.
3. Properties that will permit stacking in transit and in storage.
4. The cost of the packaging material compared with the cost of alternative materials.
5. Whether the packaging will be able to protect the environment from the product.

Materials Handling

Materials handling is the short-distance movement of products within a building, between a building and a freight carrier, or from one carrier to another. This function involves transferring products into and out of the warehouse and also moving products to various storage points in the warehouse. Equipment used in materials handling includes forklifts, two-wheel hand trucks, cranes, and conveyors.

One objective of efficient materials handling is to increase the amount of usable space within a storage facility. For example, warehouse space is wasted if items are not stacked as high as safely possible. Another objective is to reduce the number of times products are handled. If boxes of one item must be moved repeatedly to gain access to another item, time is wasted and products are more likely to be damaged.

SAFETY

When an employee is injured on the job everyone loses. The employee may be temporarily or permanently disabled and the company may lose the services of a valued worker. In addition, the firm's facilities or products may be damaged. Accidents also affect the company's image.

Nevertheless, accidents do occur. Figure 15-3 shows the number of job related injuries and illnesses that occurred in transportation occupations in 1986. For every 100 employees holding full-time jobs in the truck, air carrier, and waterway modes of transportation, there was an average of thirteen job related injuries and illnesses. Pipeline workers experienced the smallest number of injuries and illnesses on the job.

Figure 15-3   *Injuries and illnesses in transportation jobs in 1986.*

MODE OF TRANSPORTATION	NUMBER OF OCCURRENCES* PER 100 FULL-TIME EMPLOYEES
Truck	13
Air carrier	13
Waterway	13
Railroad	7
Pipeline	5

*Rounded to the nearest whole number

Source: Adapted from U.S. Bureau of the Census, *Statistical Abstract of the United States: 1989*, 109th ed. (Washington, D.C.: U.S. Government Printing Office, 1989), p. 414.

Causes of Accidents

What causes accidents? Experts who study safety in the workplace cite two main causes: dangerous work habits of employees and unsafe working conditions. Employees can cause accidents through careless practices such as engaging in horseplay, allowing other employees to ride on top of a load on a forklift, improperly stacking cartons, using drugs and alcohol, and speeding while driving trucks or other equipment. Accidents can also be traced to unsafe conditions in the workplace such as inadequate lighting and ventilation, the lack of warning signs, defective equipment, and cramped work areas.

Illustration 15-4

Dangerous work habits such as improperly lifting heavy boxes can cause painful accidents.

Prevention of Accidents

An accident prevention program begins with a review of a company's accident history. This information can be used to establish employee safety training programs and design safer work areas. The cause(s) of any accident should be determined by an investigation. This investigation may provide important information necessitating the redesigning of a work area or an update in employee safety training in order to prevent other accidents of the same type.

Employee job training should include instruction in safe work methods and should emphasize the overall importance of safety. Employees should, for example, be required to demonstrate their ability to operate a forklift before being permitted to use such equipment. Employees should be involved in accident investigations and also in the development of methods to reduce job hazards. They should be encouraged to report unsafe equipment or work practices to their supervisors. Accidents that almost occur should also be reported so that situations can be corrected before someone is hurt.

Thousands of accidents occur every workday because of careless employees or unsafe working conditions. Employees and companies have everything to gain by preventing such accidents. Safety is everyone's business.

APPLYING MARKETING TERMS

Name _____

Match each term with the statement that best describes an application of that term. Write the letter in the space provided.

a. downtime
b. railroads
c. transit time
d. air carriers
e. inland water transportation
f. cold storage
g. coastwise water transportation
h. slurry
i. perpetual inventory control
j. industrial packaging

_____ 1. They account for less than one percent of the total ton-miles of intercity freight.

_____ 2. Helps to lengthen the selling season for apples and citrus fruits.

_____ 3. Tells the amount of a product on hand at all times.

_____ 4. A machine has not been operating for six hours.

_____ 5. Protects a product in transit.

_____ 6. The materials were shipped from New York to Boston by water transportation.

_____ 7. "The shipment we received today left the factory six days ago."

_____ 8. They are not limited by the type of freight they can carry, but their accessibility is low.

_____ 9. Coal that is ground into a powder and mixed with water for transportation.

_____ 10. Shipping on the Mississippi River.

Name _____

Answer each of the following questions in the space provided.

1. What is meant by the term *physical distribution?*

2. Identify the five basic modes of transportation.

3. What is the relationship between transportation costs and the selling price of goods transported by railroads?

4. What makes pipelines a unique mode of transportation?

5. What products are ideally suited for shipment by air carriers?

6. Identify the four basic types of storage facilities.

7. What activities do business firms perform to support the physical distribution function?

8. What are the two main causes of accidents in the workplace?

DEVELOPING PEOPLE SKILLS

Read the following description of a human relations situation. Then complete your answers on a separate piece of paper.

Should Maria Tell the Boss?

Maria has been the manager of a freight company's truck terminal for six months. In a few days she will be having her first performance appraisal interview with her supervisor. Companies use performance appraisals as a basis for making personnel decisions, such as promotions, pay raises, retention, and discharge.

Maria doesn't know how the interview will be conducted. She wants to be ready if her supervisor asks her to describe her accomplishments during the six-month period. Likewise, she wants to be ready if she is asked for suggestions about how to improve the operation of the terminal.

Maria is proud of her accomplishments. Each month since she has been the manager, the terminal has come very close to the goal of delivering every shipment within twenty-four hours of when it is received. Terminals with new managers usually do not come as close to meeting the goal.

The suggestion that Maria wants to make has to do with the handling of shipments of chemicals, pesticides, and similar products. In trying to meet the company's twenty-four hour delivery goal, there may not be enough time to properly inspect containers which appear to have been damaged in transit. The products may become health or environmental hazards if they leak from their containers. Maria thinks the goal should be modified to allow more time to inspect shipments of potentially hazardous products before they are transported to their final destinations.

As the interview draws nearer, Maria is becoming less and less sure that she should offer her suggestion. She is concerned that she might be seen as a complainer. Maria doesn't want to do or say anything that may hurt her chances for advancement in the company.

1. Should Maria follow through and suggest that the company goal be modified to allow more time to inspect shipments of potentially hazardous products before they are transported to their final destinations? Why or why not?
2. Have you ever been in a situation where you wanted to say or do something constructive, but hesitated because you were worried about what would happen if you followed through? Explain.
3. How does industrial packaging relate to Maria's suggestion?

MARKETING PROJECT 15

Use your own paper to complete this project.

Safety Campaign

Assume that as a member of the company's safety committee you have been asked to develop a slogan for this year's safety campaign. You have also been asked to prepare a list of five specific steps that employees in the warehouse can take to prevent accidents on the job. The slogan and the five steps will be included on posters that will be placed in locations throughout the warehouse and should be designed accordingly.

MARKETING INSIGHT

Read the following description of real-life marketing practices. Then complete your answers on a separate piece of paper.

Truck Trailers on the Rails

Railroads carry large quantities of heavy, bulky, and low value freight over long distances and they do so at an average cost per ton-mile that is one-sixth that of trucks. Trucking companies, on the other hand, are not limited to the locations they can serve and have become specialists in carrying high value goods over shorter distances.

Faced with stagnant or declining bulk shipments, and perhaps a threat to their survival, railroads have been looking for new customers, particularly those who now ship short distances by truck. To serve these new customers, however, railroads need to combine their advantages with those of trucking companies.

One way of combining trains and trucks that has been in use for a number of years is piggyback freight. A problem limiting the more widespread use of piggyback freight is the expensive terminals that are needed to load flatcars.

A more recent and less costly innovation is used by the Norfolk Southern Railroad. Called RoadRailer service, a diesel locomotive pulls specially-built truck trailers, with rubber tires retracted, along the tracks on steel-flanged wheels. By lowering their rubber tires and retracting their steel wheels, RoadRailer trailers are ready for the road. Norfolk Southern executive Thomas L. Finkbiner said, "We don't call them trains, because train suggests slow and dumpy. . . RoadRailers are fast and sleek." In addition, RoadRailer trailers are painted white because "We want to tell shippers that this isn't just a dirty old train." With RoadRailer service, the company hopes to become a competitor in the shorter-haul freight routes dominated by trucks.[1]

1. Do you believe that RoadRailer service can overcome the "slow and dumpy" image that Mr. Finkbiner says trains have? Why?
2. How does piggyback freight differ from RoadRailer service?
3. Does RoadRailer service overcome the disadvantages of railroads? Explain.

---

[1]Daniel Machalaba, "Norfolk Aide Bets on Mix of Rail and Road," *The Wall Street Journal* (20 September 1989), p. B6.

UNIT 5
MARKETING AND YOU

16 SPECIAL TOPICS AND TRENDS

17 OBTAINING YOUR FIRST JOB
IN MARKETING

18 GETTING OFF TO THE RIGHT
START IN MARKETING

CHAPTER 16
SPECIAL TOPICS AND TRENDS

After you read this chapter and complete the activities at the end, you will be able to:

1. **Identify how specific demographic trends affect marketing activities.**
2. **Describe how lifestyle patterns are changing.**
3. **Discuss the nature and scope of international marketing.**
4. **Describe how advances in technology have an impact on marketing.**
5. **Discuss the effect the environmental movement is having on marketers.**
6. **Explain how competition affects companies in fast-growth, slow-growth, and declining industries.**
7. **Identify some trends affecting marketing research and decisions on product or service, promotion, price, and place.**

The last decade of the twentieth century promises to be a challenging one for U.S. marketers. They will try to anticipate trends, make plans for dealing with those trends, and then carry out the plans. If you pursue a career in marketing, you will probably be right in the middle of the action, the excitement, and of course, the work. If you choose another career, you will still be affected to some degree because you will be a consumer.

The first six sections of this chapter deal with topics that have a major influence on the way business is conducted. These topics include demographic trends, lifestyle changes, international marketing, technology, environmentalism, and competition. The final section, marketing trends, is concerned with how the marketing of goods and services might change in response to various trends.

◤ DEMOGRAPHIC TRENDS

As discussed in Chapter 8, demography is the study and categorization of the population using such factors as age, sex, and income. Demographic segmentation is the process of dividing the consumer market into target groups using population data. There is no question that changes in demographic trends will influence which products and services companies offer to their customers. However, those companies must not only find out what those trends are, but also decide how to carry out their marketing activities.

Some demographic trends that are expected to have a continuing influence on marketing are in the areas of population growth and distribution, women in the workforce, level of education and income, household size, and influence of minority groups.[1]

Illustration 16-1   Demographic trends that will have a powerful impact on marketing include higher levels of education and more women in the workforce.

Population Growth and Distribution

The U.S. population is growing at a slower rate and the average age is increasing. During the 1980s the population of the United States began to stabilize, growing by an overall rate of less than 1 percent per year. During that same period, the number of 25- to

---

[1]*The Wall Street Journal Reports*, (9 March 1990), p. R12–R13.

44-year-olds increased by 30 percent while the number of 10- to 24-year-olds decreased 12 percent. Looking ahead, over the next twenty years the portion of the population 65 years of age and older will soar 25 percent.

Compared to the stabilizing U.S. consumer market, foreign markets hold increasing opportunities for growth. In addition, companies will be challenged to come up with new products and services that are both useful and attractive to middle- and older-age consumer groups. Possible new product concepts include cars with quick response brakes that allow older people to drive longer, home appliances with large letters, and new food products. Advertising and other promotional efforts will also have to be planned with the goal of reaching an aging American population.

Women in the Workforce

The percentage of women holding jobs outside the home has increased significantly in the past 10 years. Seventy-eight percent of women 35–44 years of age work outside the home. The resulting increase in two-income and single parent families has shifted the time available for household management to evenings and weekends. Firms offering faster checkouts and expanded evening hours should see their business increase. Convenience goods, business clothing, childcare services, house cleaning, and life insurance programs should all experience an increase in demand.

Level of Education and Income

The general level of education is increasing. About ninety percent of men and women between the ages of 25 and 34 have graduated from high school, whereas only half of today's elderly finished high school.

Better educated people often obtain higher paying jobs, which leads to increased purchasing power. Markets with growth potential include luxury cars, leisure activities, and home furnishings. Better informed consumers might also be more critical of advertising, warranties, product quality, and service.

Household Size

The percentage of single-person households is growing; about ten percent of Americans live alone and account for 24 percent of households.

Demand is expected to grow for smaller homes, single serving food products, restaurants, in-home maintenance services, and smaller-sized appliances.

Influence of Minority Groups

The growth rate of various U.S. minority groups is increasing. During the 1980s the Asian population in the U.S. grew by 65 percent and the Hispanic population grew by 44 percent. In 1990, Asians comprised 3 percent of the population while Hispanics accounted for 8 percent, up from 6 percent ten years earlier. During the decade of the 80s, African-Americans comprised 12 percent of the U.S. population.

While minority groups share many values and beliefs with the overall U.S. culture, they also have values and beliefs that influence their preferences in food, music, clothing, and other products and services. Marketers must be sensitive to these preferences and develop appropriate products, services, and promotional campaigns.

LIFESTYLE TRENDS

Lifestyles are the patterns in which people live and spend time and money. Four main lifestyle groups are (1) the outer-directed group, (2) the inner-directed group, (3) the need-driven group, and (4) the integrated group. How these lifestyle patterns might change by the year 2000 and the influence these changes will have on marketing in the future are described in the following paragraphs.

Consumers who buy products and services that will make them fit in with people they admire make up the outer-directed group. The size of this consumer segment is expected to shrink as baby boomers' (people born between 1946 and 1964) interests change.

While this segment may decrease in size somewhat, it will still be the largest of the four groups and will continue to influence consumers to buy products and services that help them gain acceptance by particular social groups. These consumers seem to be more concerned with a product's appearance than its durability. Marketers would be expected, therefore, to emphasize the product's exterior design and closely follow popular fashion trends.

Consumers who value self-expression are in the inner-directed group. This consumer group is expected to increase in size as free expression and self-expression continue to be acceptable. This is a lifestyle group that will choose products that are environmentally safe over those focusing on convenience.

These consumers are more concerned with a product's durability than its appearance. Marketers would be expected, therefore, to emphasize product function and durability when targeting this group. Inner-directed consumers believe in the conservation of natural resources. Sales of insulation and energy-efficient products will continue. Promotional appeals should be rational and retailing should be of the no-frills variety.

Consumers who live at or slightly above the poverty level fall into the need-driven group. The relative size of this group should remain constant in the coming years.

Consumers in this group will buy products and services with prices that are reduced by competition. For example, the price of a digital pager (beeper) service has dropped to where it is more affordable than basic telephone service. According to one report, "The working poor and even the homeless have discovered that putting this communication tool on their hip is relatively easy. A small monthly fee and a fistful of quarters for a pay telephone, and they are hooked into today's sophisticated technology."[2]

Consumers who have qualities of the outer-directed group blended with qualities of the inner-directed group form the integrated group. They are decisive, goal-oriented people who are socially conscious and responsible. This is the smallest of the four groups and it is expected to remain small.

Many companies will not direct their marketing efforts toward this group due to its small size. Instead, they will assume that products and promotional activities designed for the outer-directed and inner-directed groups will meet the needs of the integrated group.

INTERNATIONAL MARKETING

American companies sell their products all over the world. For example, aircraft built by Boeing and Lockheed, chemicals and plastics manufactured by Dow Chemical, and computers produced by International Business Machines are sold in other countries. Citizens around the world are familiar with McDonald's, Disney, Kentucky Fried Chicken, Coca-Cola, and Pepsi-Cola. On the other hand, the names of some imported products have become household words in the United States. Cars produced by Honda in Japan and electric razors from Norelco in the Netherlands can be purchased throughout the United States. These business activities are all part of **international marketing,** the marketing of products or services across national boundaries.

---

[2]David Cannella, *The Arizona Republic*, (25 June 1990), p. A1.

Illustration 16-2   Consumers in Japan are exposed to many American products, including Kentucky Fried Chicken.

Kentucky Fried Chicken

▲ Cultural Differences

International marketing involves more than simply making products available to people in foreign countries. A company will be unsuccessful if it assumes that all markets are the same. Companies must recognize differences in language, meanings of colors, values and customs, and currencies.

Language is the most obvious difference among countries. Business activities require written and spoken communication. In international marketing, a common language cannot be taken for granted. If the parties involved do not understand each other, there is no basis for business transactions. This problem may occur even when people use the same language. For instance, citizens of Great Britain and the United States speak English, but they sometimes attach different meanings to the same word. In the United States, a circus is a form of entertainment featuring performing animals, clowns, and acrobats. In Great Britain, a circus usually is a circular area at an intersection of streets. The translation of some English words into other languages results in unintended meanings. For example, when the term *turtleneck sweater* is translated into the Serbo-Croatian language, it implies that the person wearing the sweater is clothed in a turtle shell. In German, 3M's Scotch® Brand Tape becomes Scotch *schmuck.*

When people who speak different languages attempt to transact business, serious problems may result. Companies might need to hire bilingual or multilingual salespersons and other personnel in order to deal with language differences.

Marketing managers should be aware that colors communicate different meanings to different cultures. In Malaysia, green is associated with illness. Red is a popular color in Chinese-speaking areas but not in Africa.

Values are ideas and principles that people consider correct, desirable, or important. American values are not always accepted or even understood by people in other countries. For example, the value placed on working hard and being successful is not universally accepted. Some people are not as interested in saving time as Americans are. In some cultures, our emphasis on convenience is viewed as laziness.

Customs are practices that are common to a place or a group of people. They define how people act in various circumstances. In the United States, for example, it is a custom to give gifts to people on their birthdays. Knowledge of the customs of other countries is important in international marketing. How a product is used can be determined by custom. Americans who eat cornflakes for breakfast may be surprised to learn that this cereal is considered a dessert in the northeastern part of the Netherlands.

Each nation has its own type of money or **currency.** For example, the United States uses the dollar; France, the franc; Mexico, the peso; and Japan, the yen. Because different currencies are involved, international marketing is more complicated than domestic marketing. If an American company sells products to a French company and wants to be paid in dollars, the French company must exchange francs for dollars. This transaction is handled by a bank. The number of francs needed to buy a dollar may vary from one day to the next because of changes in the supply and demand of the two currencies. On any particular day, fewer francs may be required to buy a dollar than on the previous day. The American company must be aware of this when it agrees to sell its products at a stated price.

◤ Global Events

Twenty-five years ago, foreign competition meant Volkswagen Beetles and Sony transistor radios. Oil was so cheap and plentiful that restrictions were placed on imported oil to protect U.S. oil drillers.

The United States was the dominant business power in the world and could, to a great extent, dictate how business would be conducted.

Things have changed, however, and global events must now be taken into consideration by businesses. Two percent of the U.S. workforce is employed by a foreign-owned company, and the Department of Commerce says one in four jobs is related to foreign trade—so at least a quarter of all jobs are directly related to international business.[3]

Global events are worldwide occurrences having an impact on American firms. Some examples of global events affecting U.S. businesses include political unrest in other countries, a change in the supply of foreign oil, natural disasters, and the rate of population growth in various parts of the world.

Events occurring in another part of the world can affect a business in your community almost immediately. It was only a matter of days after Iraq invaded Kuwait in August of 1990 that the price of gasoline at the local station increased. A poor banana harvest in South America can have a big effect on the price of bananas across the United States.

Trade Barriers

Countries sometimes establish **trade barriers** that restrict the flow of products across their borders. Three types of trade barriers are tariffs, import quotas, and embargoes.

Tariffs are taxes or duties that are levied on certain imported products. Some tariffs are used to raise money for government. Most tariffs, however, are designed to protect domestic producers from foreign competition by limiting imports. When a tariff is added to the price of an import, the product becomes more expensive. This discourages sales.

An **import quota** is a limit set by a government on the amount of a product that can legally enter a country. In many countries, factory workers' wages and production costs are lower than in the United States. For this reason, products made in those countries can be sold at prices lower than the prices charged by American producers. Some people believe that import quotas are necessary to protect American companies and workers from foreign competition. Quotas have been placed on imported products such as clothing and fabrics used to make clothing.

---

[3]Vasil J. Pappas, *Managing Your Career* (Gardena, CA: American Honda Motor Co., Inc., 1990), p. 7.

An **embargo** is a ban placed on the import or export of certain products. For instance, an embargo may be placed on imports of various kinds of animals for health purposes or on exports of military equipment to certain countries. An embargo on ivory has been adopted by many countries around the world to discourage the slaughter of the dwindling population of wild elephants. Hunters kill entire herds of elephants to acquire and sell their ivory tusks.

◢ The European Community's 1992 Internal Market Unification Program

The European Community's 1992 internal market unification program, known as **EC92**, is the merger of the markets of twelve separate countries. For purposes of international trade, Belgium, Denmark, France, Germany, Greece, Ireland, Italy, Luxembourg, the Netherlands, Portugal, Spain, and the United Kingdom will act as a single country. Together they will constitute a single market of 325 million people.[4]

EC92 will present some advantages for U.S. firms doing business with any of the twelve countries. One advantage of EC92 is that U.S. companies can save money due to the use of a single customs document for all twelve countries and the elimination of border checks. The easing of transportation regulations will reduce distribution costs.

While it does not necessarily create any disadvantages, there are some key issues that EC92 does not address. It does not, for example, eliminate language and cultural differences. Many different languages are spoken in Europe. Consumer tastes, unique to each country, will still have to be considered when companies develop their marketing programs.

◢ TECHNOLOGY

Technology is the use of knowledge based on science to solve problems. **High technology** refers to the latest advances in the technology of the product itself or the process used to make the product. Advances in technology, particularly those related to electronics and computers, will have a major impact on how companies carry out their marketing activities. Some of these trends in technology are computer integrated manufacturing, smart cards, and videotex.

---

[4]U.S. Department of Commerce, International Trade Administration, *1990 U.S. Industrial Outlook* (Washington: U.S. Government Printing Office, 1990), p. 29.

Computer-Integrated Manufacturing

Computer-integrated manufacturing (CIM) uses computers to gather and exchange information from all parts of the business to plan, order materials, manufacture, store, and distribute products more efficiently and economically. Included in the CIM network are the production department, the sales department, product engineering, and the shipping docks. CIM gives every employee and machine a way to talk to each other. In other words, the computer is now used to tie together functions that were separate for years.

CIM is still more of a dream than a reality for most companies. However, Motorola, Inc. uses CIM to make and sell its Bravo pocket pagers. A sales rep initiates the procedure by typing an order into a Macintosh computer for 150 black Bravo pagers, specifying the unique code that will cause each pager to beep, and asking for delivery in two weeks. The order zips over phone lines to a mainframe computer in a new factory in Boynton Beach, Florida. The computer automatically schedules the 150 pagers for production in 10 days, orders the proper components, and, on the day after assembly, informs the shipping docks to express mail the pagers to Pacific Telesis Group in California.[5] With CIM, the entire company is working toward the same goal.

Smart Cards

A **smart card** is a device that looks like a credit card and stores information on a memory chip. A smart card can store the user's social security number or other identification number, bank balance, and credit history.

The card may also serve as an electronic checkbook. Deposits to the account are recorded on the card's memory chip by the bank. Instead of writing checks at stores, consumers present their smart cards and cashiers, using computer terminals, deduct the amount of the purchase from the card's bank balance. This also places a record of the purchase into the card's memory. Other potential uses of the card are as a telephone charge card, a vending machine card, and a passport card.

Smart cards are not widely used today even though they were introduced more than ten years ago. However, some experts believe

---

[5]Stephen Kreider Yoder, "Putting It All Together: Computer-Integrated Factories Are Said to be the Savior of Industry," *The Wall Street Journal Reports* (4 June 1990), p. R24.

it is just a matter of time until they become popular with American marketers and consumers.

Videotex

Videotex is a television system that provides information to subscribers and sometimes receives information from them. The television signal can be broadcast through the airwaves or carried by cable.

Two types of videotex are teletext and viewdata. **Teletext** provides information to the viewer. In addition to providing information, **viewdata** allows a message, such as an order for a product, to be sent from a subscriber's home or office to a central point by cable.

A wide variety of information can be provided by videotex including sports, business, and weather news; restaurant guides; travel information; advertising; and book, movie, and theater reviews. In addition, subscribers may be able to use videotex to pay bills, buy and sell stock, and make travel and hotel reservations.

Department store chains are studying videotex to determine if it can be used as an electronic merchandise catalog. Instead of thumbing through a catalog, people will be able to see still pictures of some products and motion sequences showing models wearing the season's fashions or experts demonstrating power tools. Consumers will be able to put their orders directly into the videotex system.

ENVIRONMENTALISM AS A MOVEMENT

Environmentalism, which is the belief or principle that the air, water, animals, plants, and other natural resources must be protected, has developed into a popular movement in the latter part of the twentieth century. For example, 59 percent of the respondents in a recent survey believe their health has been adversely affected by the environment.[6]

Consumers' concern for the environment will affect marketers of a variety of products and services. Companies will have to respond to these concerns by developing more "environmentally friendly" products and services, packaging, and distribution methods. There are indications that many marketers are conducting business with environmental concerns in mind. For example, the terms ozone safe, energy efficient, nonpolluting, and recyclable are being included

---

[6]Kevin Kerr, "Thinking Green Is No Longer Just a Hippie Dream," *Adweek's Marketing Week* (9 July 1990), p. 18.

more frequently in advertising messages, indicating that a number of environmentally safe products and services are already available.

Animal rights groups have become more vocal in recent years. One target of their protests is furriers who use pelts from mink and other animals to make fur coats. Another target is firms that use animals for various types of product testing.

COMPETITION

How competition affects a company depends on a number of factors, including whether the company operates in a slow-growth, fast-growth, or declining industry.

Slow-Growth Industries

In a number of industries in the U.S., the level of competition is expected to remain fairly stable based on both the number of U.S. firms in those industries and consumer demand. Figure 16-1 contains a list of ten industries which are growing at a rate of less than 2.5 percent per year. The majority of these industries deal with either wood products, food products, or beverages.

Figure 16-1   Ten selected U.S. slow-growth industries.

SLOW-GROWTH INDUSTRIES

RANK	INDUSTRY	ANNUAL GROWTH RATE
1	Hardwood dimension and flooring mills	2.27%
2	Millwork	2.08
3	Canned specialties	1.98
4	Fluid milk	1.59
5	Canned fruits and vegetables	1.24
6	Malt beverages	1.02
7	Reconstituted wood products	1.02
8	Wines, brandy, and brandy spirits	0.57
9	Frozen bakery products, except bread	0.23
10	Dry condensed, evaporated products	0.14

Source: U.S. Department of Commerce, International Trade Administration, *1990 U.S. Industrial Outlook* (Washington, D.C.: U.S. Government Printing Office, 1990), p. 26.

Fast-Growth Industries

Competition will increase in industries where fast growth is an incentive for new firms to enter. Organizations will be spending more of each sales dollar on marketing because of increased competition. As shown in Figure 16-2, the fastest growing industries represent a variety of product lines. Surgical and medical instruments, surgical appliances and supplies, and dental equipment and supplies are all involved in health care, a segment of the U.S. economy that is expected to continue a growth trend that started several years ago.

Figure 16-2   Ten of the fastest growing industries in the United States.

FAST-GROWTH INDUSTRIES

RANK	INDUSTRY	ANNUAL GROWTH RATE
1	Surgical and medical instruments	10.0%
2	Surgical appliances and supplies	9.0
3	Footwear (except rubber)	8.0
4	Diagnostic substances	7.0
5	Adhesives and sealants	7.0
6	Welding apparatus	6.8
7	Poultry slaughtering and processing	6.7
8	Dental equipment and supplies	6.1
9	Structural wood members	5.9
10	House slippers	5.9

Source: U.S. Department of Commerce, International Trade Administration, *1990 U.S. Industrial Outlook* (Washington, D.C.: U.S. Government Printing Office, 1990), p. 25.

 ## Declining Industries

A characteristic of declining industries is that competition often decreases as some companies withdraw from the market. In other words, the number of competitors in the industry is reduced. Occasionally a company may be able to generate a volume of business and earn a profit without entering into aggressive competition with other companies because there may only be a few remaining. Ten declining industries are listed in Figure 16-3.

Industries such as those in the household laundry equipment or household refrigerator and freezer business are expected to do poorly because of the slowdown in residential housing construction. This

Figure 16-3 Ten declining industries in the United States.

DECLINING INDUSTRIES

RANK	INDUSTRY	ANNUAL RATE OF DECLINE
1	Household laundry equipment	−5.0%
2	Flat glass	−4.9
3	Semiconductors and related devices	−4.8
4	Cigars	−4.7
5	Household appliances	−4.4
6	Household refrigerators and freezers	−4.2
7	Steel mill products	−4.1
8	Fabricated structural metal	−3.8
9	Carburetors, pistons, rings, valves	−3.7
10	Rubber and plastic footwear	−3.6

Source: U.S. Department of Commerce, International Trade Administration, *1990 U.S. Industrial Outlook* (Washington, D.C.: U.S. Government Printing Office, 1990), p. 26.

slowdown is due in part to a decrease in the number of people who are at the prime home buying age. The decline in the rubber and plastic footwear industry is the result of increased imports of those products.

MARKETING TRENDS

To be successful in the coming years, marketers must be responsive to changing consumer characteristics and to changes in the environment. The rest of this chapter examines the role that marketing research, product or service, price, promotion, and place decisions will play in marketing in the coming years.

Marketing Research

The marketing information that marketers obtain and use is collected through marketing research efforts. There is no question that effective marketing research is an important tool for companies everyday. Not only is the quality of marketing research expected to improve, but it will be used more frequently and consistently. According to one expert in the field, "Successful marketing research in the 1990s will have a direct correlation to the time, effort and concern we direct to evaluate the environment in which we operate now, and will, in the future. Stated another way, the firm that does not think about, plan for, and react to the future, will not have a future."[7]

Product or Service Decisions

Among the new product or service marketing trends that are developing is increased reliance on packaging appeal. The appeal of the product's package can create a competitive edge in many product groups. It is becoming more important for a product to have strong appeal on the store shelf, where standing out from the clutter is an eternal struggle. Some companies, especially smaller ones, are finding that creative package design is less expensive than an advertising campaign. Just Born, Inc., a candy company, found that sales for three of its products soared 25 percent when it changed to colorful packages featuring animated grapes and cherries.[8]

Promotion Decisions

The promotion of products and services will undergo some major changes. One of these changes is the increased use of the line campaign. In a **line campaign,** a line of products, rather than a single product, is featured in a single advertisement.[9] For example, Colgate-Palmolive has featured Colgate regular, Junior, and tartar toothpastes, Colgate anti-cavity mouth rinse, and two types of Colgate toothbrushes in one 60-second television commercial. Johnson & Johnson has promoted CoTylenol cold medicine, Tylenol allergy medicine, and children's Tylenol in one ad.

Line campaigns are seen as a way to deal with the rising cost of television advertising. Furthermore, some marketers believe that the name of the company itself—not just the various brand names—is a powerful selling point and should be emphasized.

The use of telemarketing will continue to grow as a means of promoting and selling products and services. **Telemarketing** refers to

---

[7]Frank D. Walker, "Marketing Research in the 1990s: Facing Expanded Information Inputs, Larger Companies, Self-Centered Consumers," *Marketing Review* (January-February 1986), p. 11.

[8]Alecia Swasy, "Sales Lost Their Vim? Try Repackaging," *The Wall Street Journal* (11 October 1989), p. B1.

[9]Thomas R. King, "Firms Squeeze More Products Into a Single Ad," *The Wall Street Journal* (22 June 1990), p. B1.

selling products and services entirely by telephone. Using the telephone, salespeople do everything that they would do if they were selling to customers face-to-face, but they do it at a lower cost. Without having to take the time to travel from customer to customer, more sales calls can be made over the telephone. The benefits of telemarketing are its low costs and ability to instantly reach potential customers.

▲ Place Decisions

The location from which products and services are sold will also undergo changes in the coming years. According to a report in *Marketing News,*[10] the number of neighborhood shopping centers will decline while the number of community shopping centers will increase at a slow rate. **Neighborhood shopping centers** usually contain a supermarket and/or drug store and several small shops. **Commu-**

Illustration 16-3

Regional shopping centers usually contain 2–3 large anchor stores and draw customers from a wide geographic area.

---

[10]Joan E. Primo and Howard L. Green, "To Mall or not to Mall: Where Retail Opportunities Lie," *Marketing News* (15 February 1988), p. 10.

nity shopping centers draw customers from a larger area than neighborhood shopping centers and usually have a branch of a local department or a discount department store, a supermarket, and some smaller stores in between. Both neighborhood and community shopping centers are known as **strip centers** because they are built as long strings of stores set within a parking area.

Continuing to grow at a modest rate will be **power strip shopping centers** that contain strong retail merchants. These power strip centers' merchants usually specialize in one product line and offer low prices. Examples include off-price apparel stores, promotional department stores, children's stores, major consumer electronics chains, and home centers. Power strips are usually located next to or across the street from **regional shopping centers,** which are designed to draw customers from a wide geographic area and contain 100 to 200 stores.

Price Decisions

Look for marketers to become creative in using **bundled pricing,** which refers to the practice of offering a combination of two or more products or services at a single price. Airlines sometimes create vacation packages by bundling air travel, car rental, and lodging. Some retailers of microcomputers bundle hardware, software, and training into one package.

APPLYING MARKETING TERMS

Name _____

Match each term with the statement that best describes an application of that term. Write the letter in the space provided.

a. global event
b. computer-integrated manufacturing
c. tariff
d. environmentalism
e. smart card

f. customs
g. line campaign
h. international marketing
i. telemarketing
j. bundled pricing

_____ 1. By entering an order for 10,000 of product A, purchasing will order the parts, manufacturing will schedule the machines, and shipping will mail the package to my customer.

_____ 2. A U.S. company sells chemicals to a company in France.

_____ 3. May determine what people in a country eat for breakfast.

_____ 4. Political unrest in another country.

_____ 5. "Our natural resources must be protected."

_____ 6. This marketing technique does not require salespeople to travel from customer to customer.

_____ 7. A company promotes both its charcoal bricquets and lighter fluid in one advertisement.

_____ 8. A 10 percent tax added to the price of imported clothing for the purpose of protecting domestic manufacturers.

_____ 9. Including the price of a service contract in the price the consumer pays for a dishwasher.

_____ 10. Could serve the same function as a checkbook.

MASTERING KEY CONCEPTS

Name _____

Answer each of the following questions in the space provided.

1. Identify five demographic trends affecting consumers.

2. Explain how the four main lifestyle groups might change by the year 2000.

3. List the industries that are ranked first, second, and third in each of these categories: slow growth, fast growth, and declining.

4. Identify and define three types of trade barriers.

5. Name four cultural differences between domestic marketing and international marketing. Give an example of each.

6. What are three advances in technology that will have an influence on how companies carry out their marketing activities?

7. What are two reasons for using line campaigns?

8. How do neighborhood shopping centers differ from community shopping centers?

Read the following description of a human relations situation. Then complete your answers on a separate piece of paper.

Technology in the Supermarket

As the grocery business became more competitive, Metro Supermarket found ways to become more efficient. New conveyor systems were installed in stockrooms so that trucks could be unloaded easier and faster. Electronic scanners were also installed in checkout counters.

Because the Universal Product Code (UPC) is printed on most grocery product packages, the use of scanners meant that shoppers could be processed through the checkout lines more quickly. In addition, employee time was saved because prices did not have to be marked on individual items. Prices, however, were still shown on the shelves.

Customers began to complain as soon as the scanners were put into operation. The main complaint was that it was difficult to compare the prices of unmarked products. One shopper pointed out that he was once able to stay abreast of price increases by examining groceries as he put them away at home. For example, he could compare the price on a new box of cornflakes with the price on the nearly empty box in his kitchen cabinet.

Anticipating questions and complaints, managers were instructed to tell customers that the scanners made the store more efficient and, therefore, helped keep its prices low. The new cash register receipts listed the name of each product and its price. Consequently, shoppers who wanted to compare prices could do so by saving their receipts.

Ben Kanoza is circulating a petition that will be presented to Metro's management requesting that prices be marked on all items.

1. Do you believe that supermarkets should mark the price on each individual item? Why?
2. Assume that you applied for a job at Metro Supermarket. If you sign the petition, do you think this would hurt your chances of getting the job? Explain.
3. Assume that Ben Kanoza, your best friend, asked you to sign the petition and you refused. Based on your experience, would refusal to sign the petition destroy a friendship? Explain.

MARKETING PROJECT 16

Use your own paper to complete this project.

Invitation to Make a Speech

Assume that the Current Events Club at your high school has invited you to make a short speech on international marketing. Go to the library and research this topic. Then write out the main points that you will include in your speech.

MARKETING INSIGHT

Read the following description of real-life marketing practices. Then complete your answers on a separate piece of paper.

Smart Cards Get Smarter

Smart cards, those devices that look like credit cards and perform like little computers, have yet to be widely accepted by businesses or consumers. Hoping to attract more customers, manufacturers of the cards have introduced another version, complete with displays and keypads, that some people are calling super smart cards. Production costs, however, may make these advanced cards too expensive for many applications.

The cost of manufacturing a credit card with a magnetic strip on the back is less than one dollar. When produced in huge volumes, a smart card costs between $2 and $4. Because of the display, keypad, and added memory, the cost of the super smart card is estimated to be between $25 and $30. Nevertheless, some companies believe the new card is just what they need to gain an edge on their competitors.

As part of a pilot test, the Thomas Cook Group, a travel agency, has issued super smart cards to some of its customers. Instead of issuing traveler's checks, travel agents program a super smart card with an amount of money. The traveler can then withdraw funds at any of the agency's locations. With the keypad, users make notes about the trip's expenses. When they return home, they can plug the smart card into a personal computer and print out a detailed accounting of how they spent their money.

Some marketers of consumer products are testing programs that shower super smart card users with coupons. Because the smart card would contain biographical information about the buyer, the companies could collect far more information on buying patterns and better target their marketing efforts.[11]

1. Do you believe that putting biographical information on a smart card violates a person's right to privacy? Explain.
2. What other uses can you suggest for the smart card? Keep in mind the cost of manufacturing the cards.
3. What type of person would be a frequent user of a smart card?

---

[11]Paul B. Carroll, "Smart Cards are Getting a Lot Smarter," *The Wall Street Journal* (26 June 1989), p. B1.

CHAPTER 17
OBTAINING YOUR FIRST JOB
IN MARKETING

After you read this chapter and complete the activities at the end, you will be able to:

1. **Understand the differences between a job and a career in marketing.**
2. **Discuss the job search procedure.**
3. **Prepare a resume.**
4. **Prospect for potential jobs.**
5. **Write a letter of application.**
6. **Conduct yourself properly during a job interview.**
7. **Follow up effectively on job interviews.**

You should approach getting your first marketing position much like you would introduce a new product into the marketplace. You and your qualifications (training, education, and work experience) represent the product you are marketing. You prospect for job leads just like a salesperson prospects for new customers. Your resume represents an advertisement promoting you and your qualifications. In the sales presentation, you will overcome objections as you answer the interviewer's questions, and you will close the presentation by asking the interviewer when you might check back regarding the hiring decision. Your success in marketing yourself is complete when a prospective employer offers you a position. Prospective employers are your customers in the employment process and your major goal is to make sure they are satisfied with what they are buying. When this happens, you know you are following the marketing concept.

DIFFERENCES BETWEEN A JOB AND A CAREER IN MARKETING

When students graduate from high school, many are interested in going directly into the world of work. They usually haven't given much thought to the job they would like to have except the wages they would like to be paid, the benefits they would expect, and the hours they would be expected to work. To these individuals, a job is a way to earn a living as required to support themselves.

Securing employment in a marketing occupation, however, may mean the beginning of your employment career. A career is directly related to your primary interests and allows you to use your talents and education. It also offers the opportunity to grow and advance. Most high school graduates begin their marketing careers in entry-level positions. Entry-level marketing positions are numerous, and opportunities for advancement to positions involving more responsibility are usually available for those who care and perform well.

If, for example, your career goal is in the food marketing field, you might begin with an after school job at a supermarket as a stock clerk. As your experience and knowledge increase, this job may

Illustration 17-1   Most high school graduates begin their marketing careers in entry-level positions. Opportunities for advancement are usually available for those who perform well.

evolve into a full-time cashier position or an assistant store manager position after graduation. With several years of experience and additional training, you may be promoted to store manager position and eventually to the position of regional or district manager. Employers are interested in promoting a person who has performed well, shown sincere interest in the business, displayed enthusiasm and initiative, and expressed a desire to learn.

When you prepare for your first career position in marketing you should develop what is called a **personal marketing plan.** A personal marketing plan is just that—a plan that presents you, the product, to a prospective employer, the customer. A well-written resume should be part of your personal marketing plan. Your personal marketing plan should also include prospecting for potential marketing jobs, writing letters of application, conducting yourself properly during job interviews, and following up effectively on job interviews.

◣ PREPARING A PERSONAL RESUME

Most products require advertising. If people do not know these products exist, they cannot buy them. A personal resume advertises the most important product of all—you! The purpose of a resume is to get potential employers interested in hiring you. The resume you develop should be designed to attract and hold the attention of prospective employers by providing a positive overview of your background and job qualifications.

A **personal resume** is a one- or two-page typed document that presents your abilities, qualifications, accomplishments, and career goals. A resume will help you organize and better understand your qualifications and skills. If properly completed, it will also help you fill out employment applications quickly and accurately. Most importantly, a resume shows prospective employers that you are organized, prepared, and serious about your career. It may make the difference between getting or not getting an interview. A personal resume contains several major sections.

◣ Heading

The heading includes your name, address, telephone number, and social security number. (A social security number is required to apply for a job.) This section usually appears at the top of a personal resume. Figure 17-1 shows a completed personal resume.

Figure 17-1 A complete personal resume should be part of a personal marketing plan.

Samuel J. Mantel, Jr.
123 East State Street
Pasadena, CA 91106
(818) 555–7247

CAREER OBJECTIVE
   A sales or customer service position with a progressive marketing organization that would lead to a sales management position.

EDUCATION AND TRAINING
   Mountain View High School, Pasadena, CA, 1989–92.
   Related Course Work: Marketing I, Retailing, Business Management, Accounting, Microcomputer Applications, and Business Law.
   Special Training: Attended Sales Training Seminar sponsored by Sales and Marketing Executives Chapter in January, 1991.

WORK EXPERIENCE
   Southern California Electronics Warehouse
   Dates Employed: August 1990 to present
   Job Title: Sales Associate
   Job Responsibilities: Making sales presentations to customers on all the electronic items sold by the store, operating the cash register, writing up charge sales, and dealing with customer problems

EXTRACURRICULAR ACTIVITIES
   Secretary of Mountain View High School DECA Chapter
      Varsity football for two years
   Mountain View High School Student council

HONORS AND SPECIAL ACHIEVEMENTS
   Second place, 1991 State DECA Conference, Chapter Public Relations Project
   Advisory Committee Marketing Student of the Year, 1991

PERSONAL REFERENCES
   Ms. Cynthia Stewart, Principal   Mr. Ralph Curritos, Manager
   Mountain View High School   Southern California
   1002 Mountain View Drive   Electronics, Inc.
   Pasadena, CA 91106   1989 Industrial Way
   (818) 555–9809   Pasadena, CA 91106
                                            (818) 555–1444
   Ms. Robin Huffman,
   Marketing Teacher
   Mountain View High School
   1002 Mountain View Drive
   Pasadena, CA 91106
   (818) 555–9809

Career Objective

A **career objective** is a statement that describes the type of position you are currently applying for and your ultimate career goal. The position you are applying for should be closely related to your career goal. For example, if your career goal is to attain a management position in the hotel (motel) industry, you may state your career objective as follows: An entry-level position in the hotel (motel) industry that will lead to a front office management position. If you are qualified for several positions and are preparing an all-purpose resume, list your job objectives in order of preference.

Education and Training

This section of the resume describes your education and any training you have received that relates to the position listed in your career objective. List your most recent education and training first. Be as precise as possible. Identify specific skills you have acquired as a result of your education and training.

Work Experience

All full- and part-time work experience should be recorded in this section. List your most recent employer first. For each employer, provide the dates of employment, your job title, and a brief explanation of your specific responsibilities.

Extracurricular Activities

In this section you should identify all extracurricular activities in which you are involved such as membership or participation in school athletics, band, clubs, or community service groups.

Honors and Special Achievements

Be sure to list any honors you have received in school or from the community and list any special achievements. For example, prospective employers are interested in learning about your participation in local and state DECA competitive events.

References

This section is often considered optional. If you decide to list references, you should include the name of a previous employer as well as the names of two or three other references who have direct knowledge of your abilities and competencies. You should obtain their permission before you use them as references. Provide their names, positions, addresses, and telephone numbers. If you do not wish to list references, you may state that they will be furnished on request.

PROSPECTING FOR POTENTIAL MARKETING JOBS

One of the keys to your success in obtaining a marketing job is your ability to prospect for appropriate job openings. A prospect list will help you keep track of job opportunities. A **prospect list** includes the names of employers who may offer jobs that correspond to your interest and educational background. As shown in the following sample entry, you should include the name of a business, its address and telephone number, the names and titles of persons to contact, and background information on the business.

Name: Modern Office Suppliers
Address: 1640 South Main Street, Littleton, CO 80120–3619
Telephone number: (303) 555-4532
Contact person: James Godfrey, Manager
Background information: Specializes in selling all types of office supplies and some minor office equipment. Twenty employees, twelves in sales and eight in support activities. Possible sales position opening.

Your prospect list should not be composed solely of businesses with existing job openings. Companies frequently have positions for which they are not yet recruiting. Some business firms will even create openings, especially for trainees, when a well-qualified person applies. Many also keep an active file of job applicants in order to fill future available positions.

There are a number of sources of employment information that will help you develop a good prospect list. These include (1) the classified section of the newspaper, (2) state employment agencies, (3) private employment agencies, (4) friends and relatives, (5) school placement offices, and (6) cold canvassing.

Classified Section of the Newspaper

One source of job leads is the classified section of the newspaper. Competition for good positions advertised in newspapers, however, is extremely keen. Companies that advertise in the classified section often receive over one hundred inquiries for each available position. Some examples of classified advertisements appear in Figure 17-2.

Figure 17-2

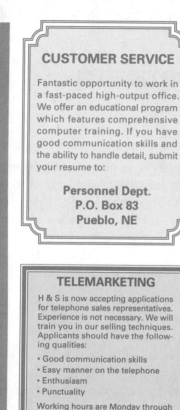

CUSTOMER SERVICE

Fantastic opportunity to work in a fast-paced high-output office. We offer an educational program which features comprehensive computer training. If you have good communication skills and the ability to handle detail, submit your resume to:

**Personnel Dept.
P.O. Box 83
Pueblo, NE**

ROUTE SALES

Position out of Crescent City. Route sales personnel wanted to join team of national ice cream distributor. Salary plus commission. Health benefits plus 401K. Send your resume to:

**Tim Craven
P.O. Box 1219
Crescent City, VT**

TELEMARKETING

H & S is now accepting applications for telephone sales representatives. Experience is not necessary. We will train you in our selling techniques. Applicants should have the following qualities:

• Good communication skills
• Easy manner on the telephone
• Enthusiasm
• Punctuality

Working hours are Monday through Friday 5 p.m to 10 p.m., Saturday, 9 a.m. to 1 p.m.

Salary is $5.50/hour plus commission To apply, contact Lee Smith, weekdays between 1 p.m. and 5 p.m. at 555-2349.

We are an equal opportunity employer

**DIRECT MAIL
COORDINATOR**

Fast-growing direct mail printer has immediate opening.

If you can:
• select mailing lists
• work with copywriters
• work under pressure
• use a PC
We need you!

Call 555-0454 for an appointment

Sample classified advertisements.

State Employment Agencies

All states maintain a number of offices that provide placement services, job counseling, and aptitude testing for persons seeking employment. Their services are free, but these agencies usually deal with entry-level positions that require minimal job skills.

Private Employment Agencies

These agencies can be found in most medium-sized and large cities and are usually profit oriented, which means that they often charge a fee for their placement services. This fee is often paid by the job seeker; it is usually a percentage of the first month's wages earned after placement. Sometimes an employer who is searching for a uniquely qualified individual will offer to pay the placement fee. Positions such as these are referred to as **fee paid.** Private employment agencies, like state employment agencies, offer job counseling and aptitude testing.

Friends and Relatives

Friends and relatives are good sources of information about job leads. They may know of advertised or unadvertised job openings. A friend or relative may be able to give you information about a job before it is advertised or becomes available. Gaining the assistance of relatives and friends in the job search process is known as **networking.**

School Placement Offices

Most high schools offer some type of placement service for their students. Often the school has a designated individual who channels job announcements to students who register for this service. Some large companies even visit schools in order to recruit qualified job candidates for full-time positions. Most of the job opportunities available through high school placement offices are part-time or entry-level positions.

Cold Canvassing

Cold canvassing is a technique for finding job openings rather than employment with a specific organization. It requires that a job seeker contact by phone, letter, or in person a large number of prospective employers. This technique can be very effective. Telephone and business directories can help you identify the different types of marketing businesses you might be interested in contacting.

◢ WRITING A LETTER OF APPLICATION

The ability to write a good letter of application is an important job search skill. A **letter of application** is sent with your personal resume to a prospective employer. A letter of application should not be long, but it must get the employer's attention and convince the prospective employer that you are the person for the job.

The first paragraph of a letter of application should arouse interest and indicate the job for which you are applying. If you have had previous work experience in marketing, this should also be mentioned. An example of an opening paragraph follows:

> Are you interested in employing a hardworking person who has training and experience in marketing and sales and who is willing to start at the bottom and work up? My background includes two years of high school marketing plus on-the-job experience as a salesperson at All Seasons Spas. I believe that this background qualifies me for consideration for the sales position that you advertised in Friday's *Herald Journal.*

The second paragraph of a letter of application should explain your background and personal qualifications in more detail. Personal qualifications should relate to your ability to perform the duties of the job. You should include information about school activities or memberships in organizations that demonstrates your ability to work with other people. For example, if you participated in your school's DECA competition, this information should be included here. If you have previous work experience in marketing or a related field, you should explain the job duties and responsibilities that were involved. Have you supervised other workers? Were you the top salesperson? What skills did you acquire that would be valuable to your prospective employer?

The third paragraph should inform the employer that you are enclosing a copy of your resume for review. The final paragraph of your letter should resemble a close in a sales presentation. You may ask for action on the part of the prospective employer and include your telephone number or address so that the employer can contact you. Examples of closing statements include the following: I will call on Friday to determine the best time for an interview. May I have an interview at your earliest convenience? I can be contacted by telephone at (515) 555–3454 or by mail at P.O Box 282, Des Moines, IA 50305–0282.

A letter of application should be typed. It is a good idea to have someone else, perhaps a teacher or parent, check your letter for clarity, accuracy in spelling and grammar, any typographical errors, and general tone.

CONDUCTING YOURSELF PROPERLY DURING A JOB INTERVIEW

A **job interview** is an opportunity for you to market yourself and your talents. During an interview, an employer will judge your qualifications and appearance, and determine whether you fit the job opening. You must convince the employer that you can make a contribution to the business. Also, the interview gives you a chance to size up the job and the employer. You can determine if the job meets your career needs and interests and whether you will enjoy working for the employer. You should assume, however, that the job you are applying for is precisely the one you really want and prepare for the interview accordingly. This will help you develop a positive attitude that will be reflected in the first impression you give the employer. Figure 17-3 on page 390 identifies job search and interview tips for job hunters.

Preparing for the Interview

A job interview is similar to a sales presentation (see Chapter 10). Before you go to an interview, have a thorough understanding of your career goals and your qualifications for the job. You should also do some research on the business and acquire a basic knowledge of its products or services. Be prepared to answer standard questions such as "How will you contribute to the success of our business?" or "Why do you want to work for us?" Even though the prospective employer may have already seen and reviewed a copy of your resume, it is always wise to take another copy with you to the interview. You may have to complete an application form, or the interviewer may ask you specific questions that you can answer by referring to your resume.

Allow as much time for the interview as it may require. For example, avoid parking your car in a limited time space. Select what you will wear to the interview in advance. Your appearance is extremely important. Dress conservatively. Do not underdress or overdress. If you are uncertain, ask your parents or a teacher for advice. Men should wear a dress shirt, a tie and sports coat, clean and well-

Figure 17-3   Job search and interview tips.

JOB INTERVIEW TIPS

Preparation:
- Learn about the organization.
- Have specific job or jobs in mind.
- Review your qualifications for the job.
- Prepare to answer broad questions about yourself.
- Review your resume.
- Arrive before the scheduled time of your interview.

Personal Appearance:
- Be well groomed.
- Dress appropriately.
- Do not chew gum or smoke.

The Interview:
- Answer each question concisely.
- Be prompt in giving responses.
- Use good manners.
- Use proper English and avoid slang.
- Convey a sense of cooperation and enthusiasm.
- Ask questions about the position and the organization.

Test (if employer gives one):
- Listen carefully to instructions.
- Read each question carefully.
- Write legibly and clearly.
- Budget your time wisely and don't dwell on one question.

Information to Bring to an Interview:
- Social Security number.
- Driver's license number.
- Resume. Although not all employers require applicants to bring a resume, you should be able to furnish the interviewer with information about your education and previous employment.
- Usually an employer requires three references. Get permission from people before using their names. Try to avoid using relatives. For each reference, provide the following information: Name, address, telephone number, and occupation.

Source: *Occupational Outlook Handbook*, 1990–91 ed., U.S. Department of Labor, Bureau of Labor Statistics, April 1990, Bulletin 2350, Washington, D.C., p. 6.

pressed trousers (not jeans), and dress shoes. If you need a haircut, have one before the interview. Women should wear a dress or suit and stockings. Do not wear sandals. Be sure your hair is properly groomed and avoid the overuse of makeup. Wear a minimum of jewelry.

Illustration 17-2   Select what you will wear to an interview in advance. Your appearance is extremely important.

◣ The Interview

A good first impression is important. Interviewers often make their hiring decisions during the first three minutes of a job interview. Be friendly and pleasant but businesslike. Be prepared to shake hands with the interviewer, smile, and say, "Hello, I am (your name)." Wait to be seated until you are invited to do so. If you did not send your resume in advance, give it to the interviewer early in the interview. During the interview, avoid being too aggressive; let the employer control the interview. Your answers to questions should be brief, honest, and to the point.

During the interview, stress your qualifications for the job. If you have work experience in the field or in a related area, make sure that it is brought into the discussion. Show interest and enthusiasm for the job you are seeking. Demonstrate your knowledge of the business, and express a desire to learn and a willingness to work.

Keep your side of the interview positive. Avoid criticizing former employers or co-workers. Avoid dogmatic statements that may offend the interviewer. Avoid discussion of personal, family, or financial problems. Asking questions during the interview is acceptable, but avoid asking them at the beginning of the interview. Later in the interview, the interviewer may ask if you have any questions. You should have several questions prepared.

Although salary is important, wait until the interviewer brings up the subject. Be prepared to state the salary you expect. Be realistic when discussing salary. Prior to an interview, it is helpful to research the salary range for positions similar to the one for which you are applying. The local job service office, your teacher, or the *Occupational Outlook Handbook* may provide background information.

You should be prepared to ask closing questions. **Closing questions** request action on the part of the interviewer. Questions such as "When may I call to learn of your decision?", "May I call on Friday?", or "When do you expect to fill this position?" are appropriate. Always thank the interviewer for the interview. Preplan final statements such as "Thank you for your time" or "I enjoyed our discussion." If the interviewer asks you to call or return, make a note of the time, date, and place.

◣ FOLLOWING UP EFFECTIVELY ON JOB INTERVIEWS

Because an employer needs time to check the information on your resume and application, an interviewer usually cannot tell you whether you will be offered the position. Thus, an effective follow-up is an important part of your personal marketing plan.

You should evaluate the interview and analyze what took place. Were you able to answer the interviewer's questions? Were you able to complete the application completely and accurately? Were you able to ask the questions you wanted to ask? Did you take your personal resume with you? Did you conduct yourself properly? Were you suitably dressed?

The following list provides examples of reasons why employers reject job applicants after their interviews. To help you evaluate your interview, compare your experience with the items in this list.

1. Poor personal appearance.
2. Lack of interest and enthusiasm.
3. Failure to look at the interviewer.
4. Failure to ask questions about the job.
5. Late for the interview.
6. Too aggressive or overbearing.
7. Inability to express self clearly.

8. Use of poor grammar and diction.
9. Know-it-all attitude.
10. Lack of career planning and/or clearly stated career goal.

After you have analyzed the interview, contact the company by telephone or in person to find out if a hiring decision has been made. In most cases, you should wait several days before contacting the business. If you decide to follow up with a telephone call, ask to speak to the person with whom you interviewed. Reintroduce yourself and explain why you are calling. For example, you might say, "Mrs. Johnston, this is Cynthia Allred. I am calling to ask if you have made a decision regarding the part-time sales position I interviewed for last week." If no decision has been made, you should call back, usually after another week. A third call is probably unwise. If you decide to follow up your interview in person, ask to see the person who interviewed you. Greet the interviewer and say, "I stopped by to find out if you have filled the part-time sales position that I interviewed for on April 15."

Another good follow-up strategy is to send a thank you letter or note to the interviewer. This letter should be sent as soon as possible after the interview. A well-written thank you letter should be brief and to the point. Express your gratitude for being given the opportunity to interview, reemphasize your interest in the position, and remind the interviewer that you are waiting for the decision. It is important that your thank you letter be neat and accurate. Figure 17-4 on page 394 provides an example of a typical thank you letter.

Figure 17-4   A sample thank you letter.

September 6, 1990

Mr. Larry Wilson, Manager
All Seasons Spas
120 North 100 West Avenue
Dallas, TX 75203-3616

Dear Mr. Wilson

Thank you for taking time out of your busy schedule to
interview me for the part-time sales position at All Seasons Spas.

As you know, I am very much interested in getting a head start on my career in the home improvement business. I was most impressed with your store as well as with the people I met there prior to the interview. I am very much interested in becoming a part of the sales staff.

Thank you again for your time and interest. I look forward to hearing from you in the near future.

Sincerely

Rebecca Evans
Rebecca Evans

APPLYING MARKETING TERMS

Name _____

Match each term with the statement that best describes an application of that term. Write the letter in the space provided.

a. prospect list
b. personal marketing plan
c. closing question
d. resume
e. career objective

f. fee paid position
g. job interview
h. cold canvassing
i. networking
j. letter of application

_____ 1. A direct way of contacting prospective employers.

_____ 2. "When will you be making a hiring decision?"

_____ 3. The part of a personal marketing plan that is the same as the "presentation step" in the sales process.

_____ 4. Included as an early part of every resume.

_____ 5. When an employer pays the placement fee for a private placement agency.

_____ 6. A plan that presents you, the product, to a prospective employer, the customer.

_____ 7. A written communication sent along with a resume to a prospective employer indicating your interest in the available position.

_____ 8. A list of potential employers who may have a career opportunity in a field of interest to you.

_____ 9. Locating job leads through friends and relatives.

_____ 10. A typed document that presents your career goals, abilities, qualifications, accomplishments, and usually references.

MASTERING KEY CONCEPTS

Name _____

Answer each of the following questions in the space provided.

1. Explain the difference between a job and a career in marketing.

2. Identify three ways in which a well-written resume can help you obtain a position.

3. Name the seven major sections that are usually included in a resume.

4. What is the major purpose of a prospect list?

5. Identify four major sources of employment information that could help you locate potential employers.

6. Why is a job interview similar to a sales presentation?

7. Why is it important to make a good first impression during a job interview?

8. The following questions are typically asked by interviewers. You are interviewing for a job in your career field. How will you respond to each of these questions?

   a. Where would you like to be in your career in five years?

   b. What kinds of courses did you like in school? What courses did you dislike?

   c. What are your greatest strengths and weaknesses?

9. What are three things you can do to follow up on a job interview?

DEVELOPING PEOPLE SKILLS

Read the following description of a human relations situation. Then complete your answers on a separate piece of paper.

High Expectations—Low Salary

Jim Jackson spent the summer before his senior year working for the Interstate Construction Company. Interstate is a construction and paving company that specializes in road building, bridge, and highway construction. During the summer he earned almost twice as much per hour as his other friends who worked in nonconstruction summer jobs. He found, however, that his job did not result in much job satisfaction. Working at dull repetitive jobs has always been difficult for Jim. Jim is an outgoing person and has effective interpersonal skills. He enjoys speaking and working with people, and most of this last summer was spent in various forms of manual labor, requiring very little conversation or interaction with other workers or the public.

During his senior year, Jim was enrolled in an advanced marketing class at his school and he has decided to make business and marketing his career field. As graduation draws closer, Jim has been interviewing for summer jobs. He has been offered a number of entry-level positions in retail stores and telemarketing, but has turned them down because the pay he would receive would be much lower than what he made the previous summer. All of the jobs he has been offered involve working extensively with people. Additionally, they would provide an opportunity for career growth and advancement. The salary offered to him, however, is really bothering him. He has told several of his friends that he won't accept a full-time job offer for less than he made last summer. He has even indicated that he might go back to his old job in construction.

1. What do you see as the major problem facing Jim Jackson?
2. What factors do you think Jim should consider before he makes his final decision?
3. If you were in Jim's position what decision would you make? Why would you make this decision?

MARKETING PROJECT 17

Use your own paper to complete this project.

Preparing a Resume and a Letter of Application

Prepare a resume and a letter of application for a marketing position that you would like to have. Follow the instructions in this chapter. Show a draft of your resume and letter of application to your marketing teacher in order to acquire constructive criticism. Revise and type the two documents.

MARKETING INSIGHT

Read the following description of real-life marketing practices. Then complete your answers on a separate piece of paper.

What Do Employers Want in an Employee?

Employers seeking to fill entry-level positions in sales and marketing are more interested in communication skills and personal traits than in grade point averages, school reputation, or membership in organizations, according to a survey of 114 companies.

Responses to the question, "If you had to select a candidate for an entry-level marketing or sales position on the basis of only three criteria, which ones would they be?" indicated employers want motivated communicators with interpersonal skills and related work experience. The five criteria listed most frequently were as follows: oral communications skills (36 percent), interpersonal skills (31 percent), enthusiasm/motivation (23 percent), written communication skills (22 percent), and related work experience (18 percent).

The importance of communication skills has been confirmed in numerous studies. Writing coaches say communication weaknesses include difficulty in organizing thoughts, the inability to make a point quickly, and the failure to be concise. This lack of communication skills is listed as the major weakness in today's graduates.

Entrepreneurship as a hiring qualification also ranked high. This is to be expected because of the increased emphasis on entrepreneurship in the economy. However, computer literacy was not ranked in the top third, which was unexpected. The *National Business Employment Weekly* believes the ability to use computers for everyday tasks will be the most important job skill in the 1990s and beyond.[1]

1. What are the top three criteria for selecting a candidate for an entry-level marketing or sales position?
2. How would you rate your own effectiveness on the following criteria? Write a statement for each.
   a. Oral communication skills
   b. Interpersonal skills
   c. Enthusiasm/motivation
   d. Written communication skills
   e. Related work experience

---

[1]Ralph M. Gaedeke and Dennis H. Tootelian, "Employers Rate Enthusiasm and Communication as Top Job Skills," *Marketing News* (27 March 1989), p. 14. Courtesy of American Marketing Association.

CHAPTER 18
GETTING OFF TO THE RIGHT START IN MARKETING

After you read this chapter and complete the activities at the end, you will be able to:

1. **Discuss what employers expect from marketing employees.**
2. **Describe what new marketing employees can expect from their employers.**
3. **Identify and explain some of the factors involved in developing and practicing good human relations skills.**
4. **Identify and explain the five steps of the problem-solving or decision-making process.**
5. **Identify factors that influence promotions.**
6. **Discuss the educational and training opportunities that are available.**
7. **Identify poor personal habits that can lead to job dismissal.**
8. **Explain why practicing good safety habits on the job is important.**

As you learned in Chapter 3, there are a large number and variety of opportunities for employment in marketing. Marketing is a huge field employing close to 30 million workers in the United States. Marketing job opportunities exist in nonprofit organizations such as hospitals, retail and wholesale businesses, advertising agencies, marketing departments of production businesses, and service firms such as insurance and real estate agencies. When you obtain your first position in marketing you should look at this as your first step on a career ladder. Almost all marketing executives (managers and owners) got their start in a beginning marketing career where they learned first hand what makes the business successful. So when you begin your career in marketing you should look at what you can learn, how you can develop yourself, and how the tasks you perform influence the success of the organization where you work. Most employers recognize the difference between a person who is just working and one who is interested in a career. The success you have on your first marketing job is important to your future in the field. You will develop work habits, attitudes, and traits that will stick with you for the remainder of your career.

WHAT EMPLOYERS EXPECT FROM YOU

Wages and salaries represent one of the largest expenses a business must pay. Thus, the profitability or success of an organization is often directly related to the quality of the people it employs. Employers are interested in hiring marketing employees who can make a contribution to the success of their business. No matter where or at what level you begin your first marketing job, your employer will expect you to demonstrate the following qualities:

- **Appearance**—Reporting to work neatly and appropriately dressed and well-groomed.
- **Dependability**—Meeting the responsibilities of your job with the minimum of supervision. Following through on assignments without having to be reminded by your supervisor.
- **Punctuality**—Arriving at work on time. Completing work by the deadline. Returning from breaks and lunch on time.
- **Poise**—Displaying confidence when fulfilling the duties of your job. Being at ease among fellow workers, customers, and supervisors.
- **Interest and Enthusiasm**—Displaying keen interest and excitement about your job and job responsibilities.
- **Initiative and Industriousness**—Starting a task or assignment on your job without receiving instructions from your supervisor.
- **Cooperation**—Taking an interest in the people with whom you work. Being tolerant of the ideas of others. Avoiding gossip on the job and criticism of fellow workers or your supervisors. Being helpful to others when the need arises.
- **Courtesy**—Showing appreciation for things that others do for you. Being respectful to everyone, even those who report you. Acknowledging mistakes and listening to others. Thanking those who give you a helping hand.
- **Judgment**—Showing common sense on the job. Thinking before acting when a problem arises.
- **Honesty**—Always telling the truth. Following through on promises made. Not using company products, supplies, or equipment for personal use.

Illustration 18-1   Employers are interested in hiring employees who demonstrate certain qualities.

- **Loyalty**—Supporting company policies and procedures. Speaking well of your company, employer, and fellow workers. Not discussing confidential material outside of your place of employment.[1]

A recent study of 500 college juniors and potential employers examined employers' and students' perception of the most desirable job attributes. Figure 18-1 shows that oral communication skills is ranked first by students and fourth by employers. Enthusiasm/motivation was ranked first by employers and second by students.

WHAT YOU CAN EXPECT FROM YOUR EMPLOYER

Employment is a two-way street. Your employer has certain responsibilities to you as an employee. When considering employment

---

[1]William Stull and Robert Zedlitz, *The Work Experience Planner* (Cincinnati: South-Western Publishing Co., 1990), pp. 57–58.

Figure 18-1   Employers' and students' perceptions of most desirable job attributes.

IMPORTANCE OF EMPLOYEE ATTRIBUTES

EMPLOYEE ATTRIBUTE	STUDENT RANK	EMPLOYER RANK
Oral communication skill	1	4
Enthusiasm/motivation	2	1
Self-confidence	3	8
Ambition	4	6
Entrepreneurship	4	7
Initiative	6	3
Interpersonal skills	7	2
Ability to articulate goals	8	9
Assertiveness	9	11
Written communication skills	10	14
Maturity	11	5
Problem-solving skills	12	9
Leadership skills	13	12
Related work experience	14	15
Personal experience	15	16
Major area of concentration	16	13
Creativity	17	17
Quantitative skills	18	18
Acknowledging limitations	19	19

Source: Ralph M. Gaedeke and Dennis H. Tootelian, "Employers Rate Enthusiasm and Communication as Top Job Skills," *Marketing News* (27 March 1989), p. 14.

with a particular company, you should look for qualities that will provide long-term career satisfaction.

As you begin your marketing career, there are certain things you can expect from your employer. You expect to be paid for your work, provided with regular employment, and treated fairly. In addition, you should expect your employer to provide a clean and safe working environment. It is also your employer's responsibility to explain to you the rules, regulations, and policies of the business as well as your job duties and any changes that may occur in these tasks. Figure 18-2 on page 406 lists wage and salary ranges for marketing and sales occupations. These jobs range from entry-level to manager.

Employers should also provide close supervision while you are working. Supervision involves fair and consistent feedback. This feedback should include positive recognition and periodic salary increases. Additionally, employers should provide advancement opportunities when possible as well as training that will encourage your career success and growth.

Figure 18-2   Median weekly earnings of wage and salary workers who usually
work full time in selected marketing occupations, 1987.

OCCUPATION	WEEKLY EARNINGS
Total, all occupations	$373
Marketing-related occupations	
Market research analysts	635
Marketing, advertising, and public relations managers	731
Public relations specialists	500
Purchasing managers	643
Wholesale and retail buyers	434
Sales occupations	
Advertising salespersons	463
Apparel salespersons	203
Furniture and home furnishings salespersons	296
Hardware and building supplies salespersons	269
Insurance salespersons	482
Manufacturers' and wholesale sales representatives	518
Motor vehicle and boat salespersons	424
Parts salespersons	278
Radio, television, hi-fi, and appliance salespersons	322
Real estate salespersons	479
Sales counter clerks	208
Sales supervisors and proprietors	415
Securities and financial services salespersons	624
Street and door-to-door salespersons	296

Source: *Occupational Outlook Quarterly,* Spring, 1989, U.S. Dept. of Labor, Bureau
of Labor Statistics.

▲ DEVELOPING AND PRACTICING GOOD HUMAN RELATIONS SKILLS

Your marketing employer will expect you to get along with your
co-workers, supervisors, and subordinates. Getting along with others
in a work environment requires good **human relations skills.** When
considering an employee for a promotion, the first question asked by
many supervisors is "What qualifications does this person have?"

The second question is "How well does this person get along with others?"

No one is completely effective in their relationships; there is usually room for improvement. You should constantly try to maintain and improve your human relations skills. The following suggestions will help you as you begin your marketing career.

You must show respect for and interest in the people you work with—co-workers, your supervisor, subordinates, customers. Since most marketing jobs involve working with others, a team effort is required to enable a business to reach its goals. Your realization of the **team concept** and active participation as a team member are important.

The ability to get along with co-workers is a very important human relations skill. Remembering that no two people think or act alike will help you get along with those who think differently from you. Praise or compliment co-workers and supervisors when they do well or are helpful to you. Be sincere in your praise. Emphasize the positive things people do, but do not overuse this important tool. Make the people you work with feel important.

You should avoid gossip and never take sides. Everyone makes mistakes. Avoid making excuses and admit your errors without blaming others. Always display a willingness to follow directions, listen, and learn.

◢◣ UNDERSTANDING AND SOLVING PROBLEMS ON THE JOB

Marketing employers look for employees who can think and solve problems on their own; that is, people who can apply sound **decision-making skills.** Problems that occur on the job can be either people-oriented or task-oriented. **People-oriented problems** concern your relationships with your co-workers, supervisor, subordinates, and customers. **Task-oriented problems,** on the other hand, relate to specific marketing tasks and functions. For example, if you were employed as a retail buyer, you would have to continuously resolve task-oriented problems relating to the selection and ordering of merchandise. If you were a salesperson, you might be asked to devise a new selling strategy.

Solving problems of any scope, severity, or nature requires sound decision-making skills. There are five steps in the decision-making process. The first step calls for a clear definition of the problem. Often the symptoms of a problem are confused with the problem itself. For example, if you are having trouble getting along with one of your co-workers, this may be merely a symptom. The real problem may be that you have overlapping duties. Treating the symptom may only temporarily ease the problem. Identifying and treating the problem itself results in a long-term solution.

The second step in the decision-making process is to collect and analyze information and facts concerning the problem. Faulty decision making often occurs because a worker is in such a hurry to resolve the problem that this step is hastened or even bypassed.

The third step is to identify and list on paper as many potential solutions to the problem as possible. These solutions should reflect not only your own experience and point of view but also the views and ideas of other employees, customers, and the company. When developing solutions, be sure to keep the firm's rules, regulations, and policies in mind.

The fourth step in the decision-making process is to weigh the alternatives and select a solution to the problem. You must choose what you consider the best solution. Obviously you should be able to support your decision with sound reasoning. If the solution you choose will have an impact on other workers, it is a good idea to get their input before putting it into effect.

The final step in the decision-making process is to implement your decision. Again, it is a good idea to obtain the support and assistance of your co-workers and supervisor. It is also a good idea to follow up on your decision in order to determine whether the solution you chose was indeed the best one. If your follow-up reveals that the problem has not been resolved, you should repeat the decision-making process.

◤ WINNING PROMOTIONS

Probably the best time to find out about advancement opportunities in a marketing business is at the job interview. During the interview you might ask questions such as "What are my opportunities for advancement if I do well?" or "Where can the available position lead?" Promotions, however, must be earned! When thinking about a promotion, you should ask yourself two questions: "Do I know everything there is to know about my present job?" and "Have I performed all my job duties in the best possible way?"

Advancement opportunities can often be found within a firm. Many companies have a policy of promoting from within that rewards workers for their length of service or seniority and good job performance. Many jobs you aspire to, however, may not be available unless you are willing to acquire additional education and training.

Sometimes it is necessary to change employers in order to gain more responsibility. For example, small owner-managed marketing businesses that employ a small number of workers usually offer few advancement opportunities.

A promotion makes you feel good about yourself. It makes you feel important and lets you know that your efforts are appreciated. A promotion usually involves increased responsibility and a larger paycheck. It may also mean supervision over other workers.

Illustration 18-2

A promotion makes you feel good about yourself; it makes you feel important and appreciated.

When employers make promotion decisions, they frequently take the following factors into consideration. These factors are not listed in order of importance.

1. Length of time on the job or seniority.
2. Technical job knowledge.
3. Quality and quantity of work.
4. Cooperative attitude and ability to get along with others.
5. Willingness to take initiative.
6. Ability to think and solve problems.
7. Adequacy of training.
8. Flexibility.

◣ CONTINUING YOUR MARKETING EDUCATION AND TRAINING

After you finish high school, you have a number of different ways to continue your marketing education and training. Marketing programs and courses are offered by most two- and four-year colleges, by public schools, and by employers.

Two-year community and junior colleges generally offer specialized marketing programs. For example, you can enroll in fashion merchandising, banking and finance, retail merchandising, transportation management, hotel (motel) management, food service management, and many other types of programs at these institutions. You may also enroll in selected marketing courses. Many classes are offered in the evening so that you can work during the day.

Marketing programs are also popular at four-year colleges. Most collegiate business schools offer a bachelor's degree in business with a major in marketing. These programs include core classes in accounting, business law, economics, management, statistics, finance, and production. In addition a variety of specialized marketing classes such as marketing principles, marketing research, logistics, consumer behavior, retail management, sales management, and marketing strategy are offered.

Another way to continue your marketing education is through adult education programs that are offered by local school districts and community colleges. Adult marketing programs do not usually lead to a formal degree, but they do provide a variety of classes designed to help you advance in your career.

Many businesses offer internal training programs. Some of these programs are short and feature training in specific marketing techniques or supply current information about products and services. Other internal training programs are long term and prepare employees for entry-level management positions. These types of programs are often referred to as management training programs.

◣ CHANGING JOBS

The average American worker changes jobs five to seven times during his or her career. People change for a variety of reasons. Some find that changing jobs is a good way to increase their responsibilities and income. Economic conditions force others to find new jobs. Some workers are released from their jobs because they fail to meet the expectations of their employer or have a poor job performance record.

Being released or fired from a job is a traumatic experience for anyone. The best way to avoid this negative experience is to examine and understand the most common reasons why people are dismissed from jobs. The majority of people do not lose their jobs because they lack technical knowledge and skill but because they have developed and practice poor personal habits. Poor personal habits can quickly lead to conflicts with co-workers and supervisors. People who select a marketing career should be alert to these problem-creating habits and eliminate them from their own behavior patterns.

Although there are numerous poor personal habits that can cause job conflicts, the following are frequently considered the most critical:

1. Bringing personal problems to work. Your personal and family problems, although critical to you, should not be brought into your work environment.
2. Misuse of materials and facilities including the personal use of the telephone. Honesty and loyalty are absolutely essential to your employer.
3. Loafing on the job. Failure to do your share of routine duties often means that your co-workers will give you little support.
4. Personal appearance, including personal hygiene, hair, and dress, which falls below company standards.
5. Not obeying the company's rules, regulations, and policies or following only those rules and regulations that you consider necessary.
6. Tardiness and absence, including coming to work late, leaving early, or taking extended lunch hours and breaks.
7. Failure to follow through on the projects and assignments given to you by your supervisor.
8. Talking too much, speaking before thinking, or spreading gossip about co-workers and supervisors.
9. Arguing with your supervisor and co-workers. Honest differences of opinion do occur, but they should never take place in the presence of customers.
10. Personality problems that cause friction with co-workers and supervisors.

PRACTICING GOOD SAFETY HABITS ON THE JOB

Understanding and practicing good safety habits is the responsibility of every worker. Every workday thousands of workers have on-the-job accidents that result in lost work time, reduced productivity, medical bills, and unnecessary pain. Although most marketing jobs are not generally considered hazardous, there are still a number of safety factors that should be considered.

First, you should become familiar with any aspect of your job that may be considered hazardous. Lifting and moving heavy boxes, the misuse of hand and power tools, or improper handling of ladders and scaffolding can result in serious injury. Second, the **Occupational Safety and Health Administration (OSHA)** sets safety and health standards for workplaces. Most employers are required to place safety posters in areas where they can be seen clearly by employees. It is your employer's responsibility to inform you of OSHA standards that apply to your job as well as any other safety rules that have been established by the firm. It is your responsibility to follow these rules and standards.

Third, it is your responsibility to report dangerous work habits or unsafe conditions to your supervisor. Finally, you should exercise caution during work hours and always keep safety considerations in mind. For example, if you are using power tools, be sure to use the protective equipment provided by your employer. If you travel on the job, be sure that your vehicle has been properly maintained and operate it in accordance with safety rules. If you are injured on the job, seek treatment and report the accident to your supervisor right away.

APPLYING MARKETING TERMS

Name _____

Match each term with the statement that best describes an application of that term. Write the letter in the space provided.

a. initiative
b. decision-making skills
c. human relations skills
d. cooperation
e. OSHA

f. poise
g. task-oriented problems
h. people-oriented problems
i. team concept
j. promotions

_____ 1. Sets safety and health standards in the workplace.

_____ 2. Getting along with others on the job.

_____ 3. The cooperative effort necessary from co-workers, supervisors, subordinates, and you to reach the organization's goals.

_____ 4. Problems that relate to your relationship with others in the organization where you are employed.

_____ 5. Identifying what needs to be done and then following through.

_____ 6. Advancement opportunities within an organization.

_____ 7. The ability to think and solve problems by following a logical process.

_____ 8. Being able to keep your composure under pressure.

_____ 9. Skills required to get along with your co-workers and job supervisor.

_____ 10. Problems that relate to specific marketing tasks and functions.

MASTERING KEY CONCEPTS

Name _____

Answer each of the following questions in the space provided.

1. How can you contribute to the success of a business?

2. Why is employment a two-way street?

3. Give four examples of how you can improve your human relations skills.

4. Why is it important to follow up on a solution to a problem after it has been implemented?

415

5. List four factors that are frequently considered by employers when they are making promotion decisions.

6. How can high school graduates continue their marketing education and training?

7. Identify five poor personal habits that can cause job conflicts.

8. How can a marketing worker practice good safety habits?

DEVELOPING PEOPLE SKILLS

Read the following description of a human relations situation. Then complete your answers on a separate piece of paper.

Attitudes Are Critical

Angie Montgomery is a senior at Fort Union High School. She is looking forward to getting out of school and starting "life." Angie is tired of all of the responsibilities and requirements of high school and has no interest in continuing her education at the nearby community college. Angie wants to be a fashion model or designer and make lots of money. She figures if she can make a lot of money then she can take nice vacations, buy expensive clothes, and have her own apartment. Angie is in the second year of marketing classes in her high school, but usually doesn't complete her assignments or participate in class, except to be critical of her teacher and class members who appear "too" serious about everything.

Angie is able to keep a C average in class without much effort but has a real problem in getting to class on time or completing assignments in a timely manner. When she does turn in an assignment, it is sloppy and disorganized, although it usually does contain some creative and interesting ideas. Angie has even volunteered to do a couple of special assignments, but has not completed them when they appeared to be less interesting or exciting than she anticipated. For example, she agreed to help the marketing teacher, Mr. Profit, organize a fashion show for the local mall. When she figured out how much work was involved, she suddenly announced that she wasn't interested in doing a "dumb" fashion show.

Angie's marketing teacher, Mr. Profit, has tried many times to work with Angie to get her to improve her classroom conduct, but she always gets mad and walks out saying, "None of this has anything to do with the real world anyway!"

1. What do you see as the major problem in this case?
2. What factors should Angie work on if she wants to be employable in the long run in a marketing career?
3. If you were Angie's job supervisor and she acted like she did in the marketing class, what would you do to motivate her?

MARKETING PROJECT 18

Use the outline below and your own paper to complete this project.

Task Problems vs. People Problems

Step 1. Using the newspapers handed out in class, select three classified advertisements for positions that you would be interested in applying for.

Step 2. On your own paper, list four task-oriented problems and four people-oriented problems that may be present in each of these three positions. (The following outline may be duplicated for your use in completing this project.) Identify the human relations or decision-making skills you would need to solve each of these problems.

POSITION TITLE:_____

Task-Oriented Problems:
1.
Skills:

2.
Skills:

3.
Skills

4.
Skills

People-Oriented Problems:
1.
Skills:

2.
Skills:

3.
Skills:

4.
Skills:

MARKETING INSIGHT

Read the following description of real-life marketing practices. Then complete your answers on a separate piece of paper.

Employers Rank Specific Job Accomplishments High

"What have you done for me lately?" is likely to be the theme of your next performance review, and your charm and charisma probably won't come up, says a new survey.

According to that nationwide survey, 66 percent of executives rated "specific accomplishments" as the most influential factor in evaluating an employee's performance, while 47 percent said "general work habits and performance" was the number one criterion for success. (Percentages include multiple responses from some managers who said both factors were equally important.)

Among the findings, "personality" and "comments from co-workers" were at the low end of the scale, at 1 percent each. In addition, while seniority may have once been a major factor in employee evaluations, survey respondents downplayed its importance.

"Employees should recognize that during their performance reviews, the conversation is going to center largely on specific results and accomplishments," said Max Messmer, chairman of Accountemps, the world's largest temporary personnel service. "Keeping an ongoing file of tangible contributions to the company will help remind employees of their past achievements," he added.

It was cautioned that "personality," which scored very low, should not be confused with interpersonal skills. The ability to work and communicate effectively with co-workers is essential in today's information-driven economy.

The second most commonly cited factor, "general work habits and performance," illustrates the importance of such attributes as organizational skills, commitment, and work ethic in receiving a high performance rating.[2]

1. Why do you think that personality and comments from co-workers were rated so low in evaluating an employee's job performance?
2. Why do you think specific accomplishments were rated so high in evaluating an employee's job performance?

---

[2]*New Dimensions* (Distributive Education Clubs of America, January/February 1990), p. 19.

GLOSSARY

Accessory equipment Machinery that has a shorter useful life than installations.

Advertising Using nonpersonal paid messages to promote a service, product, image, or idea. Messages are directed at an audience through various mass media by an identified sponsor.

Advertising agency A business that specializes in helping organizations plan, develop, and implement their advertising plans.

Advertising allowance A reduction in the cost or price of merchandise given to dealers in return for the purchase of a certain quantity of merchandise.

Advertising media The different methods that organizations use to send messages, such as newspaper, radio, television, signs, and billboards.

Advertising media mix The combination of advertising media used by a firm.

Advocacy advertising A form of advertising that presents an individual's or organization's viewpoint.

Agents Intermediaries who actively assist in the sale of products without taking title to them.

Antitrust laws Laws designed to protect competition by preventing one company from gaining an unfair advantage over another.

Appeal An underlying message that is designed to arouse a response.

Approach Begins when a salesperson first meets the customer.

Brand A name, sign, symbol, design, or a combination of these elements which identifies a product or service.

Brand extension An existing brand name is used to facilitate new product introductions.

Broadcast media Radio and television.

Broker A wholesaler who negotiates the sale of products without taking title to them, and then allows the seller to accept or reject the prospective buyer's offer.

Bundled pricing The practice of offering a combination of

421

two or more products or services as a package at a single price.

Business cycle Alternating periods of expansion and contraction of economic activities; such as production, employment, and income.

Business route sales personnel Sell and deliver a wide variety of products and services to a predetermined list of organizational users that buy on a regular basis.

Business specialists Engage in creative direct selling to organizational users.

Buying Selecting and obtaining the type, quality, and quantity of products to be sold by wholesale and retail businesses.

Buying motive Anything that prompts a consumer to make a purchase.

Buying signals Words or motions of customers that indicate they are close to reaching a buying decision.

Career objective A statement that describes the type of position you are currently applying for and your ultimate career goal.

Career plan A plan based on your career goal which includes information about your interests, personality, and abilities.

Career-sustaining occupation Jobs that often require more education, training, and experience than entry-level jobs and usually provide full-time employment.

Cash-and-carry wholesalers Wholesalers who sell on a cash-only basis and do not make deliveries.

Cash discounts Price reductions to reward buyers for paying their bills promptly.

Chain stores Groups of retail stores that are centrally owned, centrally managed, and handle the same product lines.

Channel or medium of communication The medium, either personal selling, direct mail, telephone, radio, newspaper, television, or visual display, through which the encoded ideas will be sent to the receiver.

Channels of distribution Systems of individuals and organizations that direct the flow of products and services from manufacturers or producers to customers. Also called marketing channels.

Choice criteria Product or service characteristics used in evaluating the various alternatives.

Classified advertisements Ads that are placed in a separate section near the back of the newspaper. Also called want ads.

Closing questions Questions you ask that request action on the part of the interviewer.

Closing the sale Asking the customer to buy.

Coastwise water transportation The movement of freight between points on the same coast of the United States, such as Boston and New York City.

Cold canvassing A technique for finding job openings with various organizations rather than employment with a specific organization.

Cold storage Facilities provided for storage of perishable food products.

Commercial business activity The marketing of products made by other companies and providing marketing, financing and other services.

Commission A fee that is a percentage of the dollar amount of products sold.

Communication The exchange of information.

Community shopping Shopping centers that draw customers from a larger area than neighborhood shopping centers and usually have a branch of a lo-

cal department or discount department store, a supermarket, and some smaller stores.

Competencies Skills, knowledge, and attitudes that marketing employees must have in order to be successful in their chosen careers.

Competition The effort of two or more businesses acting independently to sell their products and services to the same customers.

Computer-integrated manufacturing (CIM) Using computers to gather, exchange, and use information to plan, order materials, manufacture, store, and distribute products more efficiently and economically.

Computer network or networking Computers that are linked together, making it possible for a marketing manager from a business to gain access to marketing research from various sources.

Consignment An arrangement that allows retailers to carry items either without buying them or with merchandise return privileges.

Consumer buying Buying products or services for personal or family use.

Consumer buying behavior
The decisions people make in buying products and services.

Consumer contests and games A popular type of sales promotion activity. A contest requires some skill on the part of participants. Games consist of chances given to consumers according to their purchases.

Consumer credit Permits people to obtain products and services for personal or family use now and pay for them later.

Consumer decision process
The series of steps taken when deciding what goods and services to buy.

Consumer packaging The container in which a product is sold.

Consumer products Products purchased by individuals for their personal use.

Consumer route sales personnel Sell and deliver goods to a predetermined list of consumers.

Consumers Persons or households that buy products or services for personal or family use. Refers to ultimate consumers.

Consumer sales promotions
All sales promotion activities that are designed to stimulate consumer demand.

Consumer specialists Engage in direct selling by establishing personal contact with consumers. Door-to-door and telephone sales personnel fall into this category.

Contests Trade promotion in which prizes are awarded to those who sell the most products or services.

Controlling inventory Maintaining a balance between having too much and having too little inventory on hand.

Convenience goods Products that are purchased frequently with minimum shopping effort.

Convenience stores Stores carrying limited varieties of food items—bread, milk, ice cream—to meet customers' needs between major shopping trips.

Cooperative advertising
Combines both national and local advertising, with costs split between the manufacturer and the retailer.

Coupons Certificates that allow consumers to save money on a particular food item or to buy one item and get a second item free.

Culture All ideas and structures that a society develops in order to cope with its environment and provide for the control of members' behavior. These include social norms, customary beliefs, and values.

Cumulative quantity discounts Discounts given to the sum of purchases made during a specific period of time.

Currency A nation's money.

Customer benefit The needs a product or service meets for a customer.

Customer concept Doing what customers want, not what the business wants.

Customs Patterns of behavior that are common to a geographic place or a group of people.

Data base Stores, organizes, and helps to manage marketing information.

Decision-making skills The skills required to make decisions and solve problems on your own.

Decline stage Sales begin to drop off and substitute products become available.

Decoding Interpretation of the sender's message.

Delivered cost The cost of a product to a retailer, which includes the amount paid for the product plus shipping costs.

Demand The amount of a product or service people are willing to buy at a given time and at a given price.

Demography The study of population using such factors as age, sex, and income.

Department stores Retail stores which sell a variety of merchandise grouped into well-defined departments.

Depression The lowest level of economic activity in a business cycle; that is, unemployment and the number of business failures are very high, consumers are unwilling or unable to buy, and capital investment is very low.

Derived demand Exists when the amount purchased is determined by the demand for related products or services.

Desk jobbers Limited-function wholesalers who take title to the goods they sell, but do not take physical possession of these goods. Also called drop shippers.

Direct retailing Sellers contact prospective customers in their homes.

Discount houses Stores that offer wide varieties of products at so-called discount or low prices.

Discounts Reductions in the price of a product or service.

Discretionary income The money remaining after taking care of the basic needs of life.

Display advertisements Advertisements that are located throughout a newspaper. They usually include a headline, illustration, body copy, price, and business identification.

Domestic water transportation A category of water transportation in which both the point of origin and the destination of a shipment are in the United States.

Downtime A period during which machinery, a department, or a factory is not in operation.

Drop shippers Limited-function wholesalers who take title to the goods they sell, but do not take physical possession of these goods. Also called desk jobbers.

Durable goods Items made to last for several years.

EC92 Abbreviation for the European Community's 1992 internal market unification program, which is the merger of the markets of 12 countries.

Embargo A ban placed on the import or export of certain products.

Emotional appeal Advertising that appeals to a consumer's wants and needs.

Emotional buying motives Buying motives which influence consumers to make purchases to satisfy emotional needs.

Encoding Using verbal or nonverbal symbols to transmit ideas.

End display An open display of merchandise on a rack, table, or bin at the end of an aisle.

Entrepreneur A person who attempts to earn a profit by taking the risk of starting and managing a business enterprise.

Entrepreneurship The process of starting and managing a business enterprise.

Entry-level occupations Jobs that require little specialized training or experience and involve routine duties.

Environmentalism The belief or principle that air, water, animals, plants, and other natural resources must be protected.

Esteem needs The needs for recognition, achievement, and accomplishment.

Even prices Selling prices that end in event numbers,

such as $40.00 instead of $39.95. Used to give an exclusive or upscale image.

Evoked set A group of brands that a consumer actually considers and gathers information about.

Excuses Not based on facts and difficult for a salesperson to overcome. Often mistaken for objections.

External marketing information Data collected from other sources, such as government reports or professional publications.

Extractors Businesses that grow farm products or remove raw materials from where they are found in nature.

Fact-feature benefit analysis A list of significant facts or features pertaining to a product or service and the corresponding customer benefit.

Fad An item that is popular and sells well for only a brief period.

Family brand The same brand used by a seller on an entire product line.

Family life cycle The series of life stages through which many people pass, including childhood, marriage, childrearing, and death or divorce.

Fashion A style that is generally accepted by a large group of people.

Feedback Message from receiver back to sender.

Fee paid Positions offered through a private employment agency for which the applicant's fee is paid by the prospective employer.

Financing Granting credit to customers so that they can buy the company's products or services.

Foreign water transportation A category of water transportation in which either the point of origin or the destination of a shipment is in a foreign country.

Form utility What a raw material gains when it is changed into a useful form.

Franchise An agreement by which a parent company gives an individual or another company the right to do business in a standardized manner.

Franchisee The person or company that is given the franchise rights by the franchisor (parent company).

Franchisor A manufacturer, wholesaler, or service company with the authority to grant franchise rights to other companies.

Full-function wholesalers The most common type of

merchant wholesaler. They perform a wide range of marketing activities. Also called full-service or service wholesalers.

Full-service wholesalers The most common type of merchant wholesaler. They perform a wide range of marketing activities. Also called full-function or service wholesalers.

Functional discounts List price reductions given by producers to resellers for performing certain marketing functions. Also called trade discounts.

Geographic segmentation Dividing the market into groups by location.

Global events Worldwide occurrences having an impact on American firms.

Goods Tangible items or things you can touch. Also called products.

Great Lakes water transportation The shipping of freight between United States ports on the Great Lakes, such as between Cleveland and Buffalo.

Gross national product A measure of the total dollar value of goods and services produced in the nation being measured.

Growth stage Product sales begin to increase at a rapid rate.

Heavy users Consumers who account for a small fraction of the number of buyers, but a large fraction of sales volume.

Hierarchy of needs Five categories of needs ranked in the order they must be satisfied.

High technology The latest advances in technology used in a product itself or in the process used to make a product.

Horizontal market Exists when a product or service is purchased by many kinds of businesses in different industries.

Household One or more persons who, as a unit, consume products and services.

Human relations skills Getting along well with your co-workers, supervisors, and subordinates.

Import quota A limit set by a government on the amount of a product that can legally enter a country.

Impulse items Convenience goods which are purchased on the spur-of-the-moment.

Independent retail store A small business that is managed by the owner(s).

Individual brand A brand name for each product.

Industrial business activity The production of goods.

Industrial distributors Wholesalers who buy goods from producers or manufacturers and sell them to industrial users.

Industrial market Consists of firms that buy goods and services to be used, directly or indirectly, to produce other goods and services.

Industrial packaging The container used to protect products during shipping and storage.

Industrial products Products purchased by extractors, manufacturers, service firms, and nonprofit organizations for use in running their businesses.

Industrial sales personnel Responsible for sales of expensive products such as heavy equipment, computer and electronic equipment, and machinery.

Inflation A general rise in the prices of products and services.

Information search The step in the consumer decision process that involves the gathering of information related to the problem or need.

Information utility What marketing creates by providing informative messages to buyers and potential buyers.

Inland water transportation Moving products between points on the nation's rivers and canals.

Inner-directed group People who value self-expression.

Installations Major items such as buildings, large machines, or pieces of equipment that are used to produce finished products or provide services.

Institutional advertising Attempts to generate goodwill or bolster a company's image.

Integrated group People who have qualities of the outer-directed group blended with qualities of the inner-directed group.

Intercoastal water transportation The movement of freight by water between two points in the United States by way of the Panama Canal.

Interior displays Displays located within a business, designed to promote merchandise and allow prospective buyers to see and handle merchandise.

Intermediaries Businesses that aid the movement of goods and services through channels of distribution. Also called middlemen.

Internal marketing information Information collected from records of a business, such as sales or inventory records.

International marketing Marketing products or services across national boundaries.

Introduction stage The product has just been developed and introduced to the market place.

Inventory The products on hand at any given time.

Island displays Usually large open tables stacked with merchandise and separated from surrounding displays.

Job description A brief statement listing what an employee does in a specific job.

Job interview An opportunity for you to market yourself and your talents. An employer will judge your qualifications and appearance, and determine whether you fit the job opening.

Just-in-time (JIT) inventory control system Companies maintain minimum inventory levels and purchase products and materials in small amounts so that they are received just at the time they are needed for production.

Letter of application A letter sent with your personal resume to a prospective employer. It should get the employer's attention and convince the prospective employer that you are the person for the job.

Lifestyles The patterns that people follow in their lives.

Lifestyle segmentation Divides consumers into groups according to their activities, interests, and opinions.

Light users Consumers who comprise the largest number of buyers, but account for a small portion of its sales.

Limited-function wholesalers Wholesalers who provide a narrow range of functions or marketing services for their customers.

Line campaign The practice of featuring a line of products, rather than a single product, in an advertisement.

List price The price which is normally quoted to potential buyers and which is sometimes preprinted on the package.

Local advertising Local community coverage usually sponsored by retail businesses.

Loss leaders Items which are sold at very low prices, often below cost, to attract customers who may also buy regularly priced merchandise.

Low accessibility The ability to only carry freight between a limited number of points.

Mail-order retailing Selecting products from catalogs or advertisements and placing orders by mail or telephone.

Mail-order wholesalers Limited-function wholesalers who sell through catalogs that are distributed to their customers, who are mainly small retailers and other businesses in rural areas that are not served by other types of wholesalers.

Managerial/entrepreneurial occupations Jobs that involve (1) the various dimensions of owning or managing a small business or (2) the marketing functions within a large business.

Managers People who get work done through other people.

Manufacturer-owned stores Retail outlets that are owned by the manufacturer, giving the manufacturer complete control over the channel of distribution for their products.

Manufacturers Businesses that combine raw materials and parts to make products for customers' use.

Manufacturers' agents Independent intermediaries who sell similar products for several noncompeting manufacturers.

Marketing The activities that provide products and services for the satisfaction of consumer needs and wants.

Marketing business A business that buys products for resale, for example, wholesalers and retailers.

Marketing channels Systems of individuals and organizations that direct the flow of products and services from manufacturers or producers to customers. Also called channels of distribution.

Marketing concept To satisfy customers and do so at a profit.

Marketing environment Factors (competition, laws and government, the economy, society, and culture) that may affect marketing directly or indirectly.

Marketing functions Activities necessary in the marketing of a product or service. Included are product or service planning, purchasing or buying, physical distribution, promotion and selling, pricing, financing, obtaining and using marketing information, and risk management.

Marketing information Any information that aids the transfer or movement of goods and services from producer to customer.

Marketing information system A system that allows marketing personnel to collect, analyze, and organize their marketing information.

Marketing management Plans, implements, and controls the marketing mix to satisfy the company's chosen target market.

Marketing mix The combination of product or service, promotion, place, and price decisions for a particular firm.

Marketing research An organized way of collecting, recording, and analyzing marketing information in order to make good decisions.

Marketing researchers People responsible for collecting and analyzing marketing information.

Markets Consist of customers—people and organizations—who are both willing and able to buy.

Market segmentation The process of dividing the total market for a product or service into segments based on similarity of demand.

Market segments Groups of customers with similar characteristics within the total market.

Markon The amount that is added to a product's cost (the amount originally paid for it) to arrive at the selling price. Also called markup.

Markup The amount that is added to a product's cost (the amount originally paid for it) to arrive at the selling price. Also called markon.

Mass marketing A marketing program aimed at the entire consumer market.

Materials handling The short-distance movement of products within a building, between a building and a freight carrier, or from one carrier to another.

Maturity stage Product sales slow down and perhaps level off.

Merchant wholesalers Wholesalers that take title to the products they distribute.

Middlemen Businesses that aid the movement of goods and services through channels of distribution. Also called intermediaries.

Modes of transportation Different methods of moving

products from one point to another.

Monopoly When one organization has control of the market for a product or service. The firm is the sole seller of a product or service for which there are no close substitutes.

Motivation An internal force that causes a person to take the action necessary to satisfy a need.

National advertising Sponsored by a manufacturer or other supplier whose products are distributed nationwide or in a large region of the country.

National brand A manufacturer's branded product sold on a nationwide basis.

Need-driven group Consumers who live at or slightly above the poverty level.

Needs Those things considered essential to human existence.

Neighborhood shopping centers Shopping centers that usually contain a supermarket or drug store and several small shops.

Networking Obtaining the assistance of relatives, friends, and acquaintances in the job search process.

News releases Written articles that objectively describe a business-sponsored special event or the achievements of an employee who is making a special contribution to the community.

Noncumulative quantity discount Applies to a single order rather than to the total volume of orders placed during a period of time.

Nondurable goods Items that last only a short time.

Nonpersonal promotion Indirect persuasive communication with consumers.

Nonprice competition Sellers emphasize factors other than price to distinguish their products and services from those of competitors.

Nonprofit organization An organization, either private or public, involved in providing a product or service without using profit as its goal.

Nonusers People who never buy the product.

Objections Honest points of difference between the buyer and the salesperson.

Occupational Outlook Handbook A publication compiled by the U.S. Department of Labor, Bureau of Labor Statistics, that lists future forecasts of occupations.

Occupational Safety and Health Administration (OSHA) A government agency that sets safety and health standards for workplaces.

Occupational specialty areas Different occupations and businesses in the marketing career field as identified by the U.S. Department of Education.

Odd prices Selling prices that end in odd numbers, such as $9.99 instead of $10.00. Used by retailers who believe this will improve sales.

Ordinary product storage The storage of products in buildings that will protect them from the weather.

Organizational buyers Businesses or institutions that buy products and services and resell them, with or without reprocessing, to other organizations or consumers.

Organizational market Market made up of the nation's organizational buyers.

Organizational marketing The marketing of products and services to organizational buyers.

Outer-directed group Consumers who buy products and services that will make them fit in with people they admire.

Outside displays Signs, banners, pennants, and other attention-getting devices that identify a business.

Over-the-counter retailing Selling goods in a store.

Packaging Material designed to physically protect the product, provide product information, and establish a symbolic image.

Parts Manufactured items that become components of other products without modification.

Patronage motives Factors that influence where a consumer will buy.

Penetration pricing Pricing a new product or service below the market.

People-oriented problems Problems that concern relationships with your co-workers, supervisor, subordinates, and customers.

Periodic inventory control Items on hand are counted at regular intervals such as once every month, once every six months, or once a year.

Perpetual inventory control Enables a business to determine the amount of a product on hand at all times.

Personal marketing plan A plan that presents you, the product, to a prospective employer, the customer.

Personal promotion Direct persuasive communication with consumers.

Personal resume A one- or two-paged typed document that presents your abilities, qualifications, accomplishments, and career goals.

Personal selling Personal, persuasive communication from a marketing employee that is designed to convince the consumer to purchase a product or service.

Physical distribution All the activities required to efficiently move finished products from producers to customers.

Physical needs The primary needs for food, shelter, and clothing.

Piggyback freight Goods are loaded onto truck trailers and then shipped on railroad flatcars. When the train reaches its destination the trailer is removed, hooked up to a truck tractor, and driven to the customer's location.

Place decisions The location products and services will be sold.

Place utility What a product or service gains when it is available in a convenient location.

Platform displays Raised stands for displaying merchandise.

Point-of-purchase displays Displays of merchandise placed near the checkout area.

Policies Action guidelines related to attaining the firm's objectives.

Possession utility What a product or service gains when a transaction has been completed.

Postesting Testing performed after the actual promotional campaign.

Postpurchase evaluation The step in the consumer decision process in which consumers consider how satisfied or dissatisfied they are with the product or service purchased.

Power strip shopping centers Strip centers containing strong retail merchants who specialize in one product line and offer low prices.

Preapproach The first step in the sales process that occurs before the salesperson establishes direct contact with buyers.

Premium or push money Cash premiums offered to businesses that buy a specified quantity of merchandise.

Premiums Something received free either in a package or by returning a label, box top, or other proof-of-purchase symbol.

Pretesting Test to determine the effect promotional efforts will have prior to the actual promotion.

Price The exchange value of a product or service stated in terms of money.

Price competition Sellers stress low prices.

Price deals Short-term discounts offered by manufacturers which are designed to increase sales of particular products.

Price decisions Setting prices for products or services that are acceptable to customers and profitable to the company.

Price lining The practice of offering products at a limited number of set prices.

Price skimming Pricing a new product or service above the market.

Pricing The process of determining the exchange value of a good or service. This is the price and it is usually expressed in dollars and cents.

Pricing strategies How marketers price their products and services relative to competing products and services.

Primary marketing information Information gathered with a specific marketing question in mind.

Print media Newspapers, magazines, shoppers' guides, direct mail, the yellow pages, and other printed materials.

Private brand A brand name created by individual retailers which products are sold under.

Private warehouses Storage facilities that are leased or owned by retailers, manufacturers, or wholesalers for their own use.

Problem recognition The step in the consumer decision process in which consumers realize there is a discrepancy between the existing state of affairs (the way things are) and the desired state of affairs (the way they would like them to be).

Processed materials Materials that are the end product of one business but which will undergo further treatment by other manufacturers.

Product A tangible item; it can be seen, handled, or consumed. It is produced, grown, or extracted.

Production The creation of something that can satisfy a need or want.

Production business A business that manufactures, constructs, extracts, or grows products that are marketed in order to achieve the goals of the company.

Product life cycle The four stages every product goes through: introduction, growth, maturity, and decline.

Product or service decisions Development of the right products or services for the target market.

Product or service planning Deciding which products or services the company will develop and offer to its customers.

Product sampling Products or services consumers receive free from manufacturers or retailers.

Product-service mix The sum of all products and/or services offered by a business.

Profit The difference between the revenue generated by a business and the cost of running that business.

Promotion Persuasive communication about products and services.

Promotional advertising Attempts to convince potential buyers to purchase a specific product or service.

Promotional allowances Merchandise discounts that manufacturers or wholesal-

ers give retailers in return for additional retail shelf space or the placement of their merchandise in desirable locations.

Promotional mix A combination of personal selling, advertising, visual merchandising, sales promotion, and public relations.

Promotion and selling Communicating product and service information to influence customer buying.

Promotion decisions Concerned with ways to inform members of a target market about a product or service and influence them to buy it.

Prospecting The process of locating buyers who are capable of purchasing the organizaton's products or services.

Prospect list A list that includes the names of employers who may offer jobs that correspond to your interests and educational background.

Prosperity A period of relatively high economic activity; that is, profits, consumer confidence, capital investment (money invested in a business), and employment are high.

Psychological stages of a sale Five phases of a sale: attention, interest, desire, conviction, and action.

Publicity Information distributed through various media, free of charge, often in the form of news releases.

Public relations The total process of building goodwill toward a business among customers, employees, suppliers, stockholders, creditors, the community, and the government.

Public warehouses Storage space available for a fee.

Pull strategy Promotional efforts undertaken by the manufacturer or supplier to convince the ultimate consumer to purchase certain products or services. The promoter attempts to pull their products or services through the marketing channels.

Purchasing Selecting and obtaining the type, quality, and quantity of products and services in manufacturing and service businesses.

Push strategy Promotional efforts undertaken by the manufacturer or supplier to convince intermediaries such as agents, wholesalers, and retailers to carry certain products or services.

Quantity discounts Price reductions to encourage

buyers to order larger quantities than normal.

Rack jobbers Full-function wholesalers who place their own display racks in stores and stock them with merchandise.

Rational appeal An advertisement that is directed at a consumer's logical thought process.

Rational buying motives Motives involving conscious thought and deliberation which influence consumer behavior.

Raw materials The basic elements of the manufacturing process that are supplied by mines, farms, forestry companies, or other extractive enterprises.

Rebate A portion of the sales price that is returned to the consumer when the consumer completes a form and sends it to the manufacturer.

Receiver Interprets the message sent by the sender.

Recession A marked decline in the level of economic activity; that is, profits, consumer confidence, capital investment (money invested in a business), and employment are lower than during prosperity.

Recovery A business cycle phase in which there is an

increase in business activity and the economy moves from recession or depression towards prosperity.

Reference group Any group of people that influences a person's attitudes or behavior.

Regional shopping centers Shopping centers which are designed to draw customers from a wide geographic area and which contain 100 to 200 stores.

Resale products Items of merchandise bought by retailers and wholesalers and then sold to others.

Reseller market Consists of firms engaged in wholesale and retail trade.

Retailers Businesses that buy products from extractors, manufacturers, or wholesalers and sell them to persons who will use them.

Retailing That part of marketing in which goods and services are sold to ultimate consumers.

Retail sales personnel Responsible for sales at a fixed location.

Risk management The process of analyzing risks to the company and then developing ways to handle them.

Safety needs Needs related to protection from danger, insecurity, illness, and pain.

Sales concept Trying to sell something before learning what customers want.

Sales presentation The heart of the sales process during which the salesperson creates desire for the product or service.

Sales promotion Any activity that supplements advertising, personal selling, and visual merchandising, such as coupons, games, trading stamps, and product demonstrations.

Seasonal discounts Price reductions to encourage buyers to place orders and pay for products in advance of when they will need them.

Secondary marketing information Information that has been collected for some other purpose, but which may be of value to managers in the decision-making process.

Self-actualization needs Needs involving personal fulfillment.

Selling agents Independent intermediaries who perform the entire marketing task for firms.

Sender Puts information into a form that a receiver can understand, with either verbal or nonverbal symbols.

Service Task or activity that is performed rather than produced.

Service businesses Firms that market intangible products to consumers or organizational markets.

Service wholesalers Also called full-function or full-service wholesalers. The most common type of merchant wholesaler. They perform a wide range of marketing activities.

Shadow box displays Small enclosed interior displays that are built into walls or placed on counters or ledges.

Shopping goods Items that are purchased after consumers have compared prices, qualities, styles, and colors at several stores.

Singles market A market made up of people who have never married, separated couples, surviving spouses, and divorced people.

Slotting allowance A direct payment to a retailer, usually a chain of supermarkets or convenience stores, for carrying an item.

Slurry products Dry materials that are converted to liquid form by adding water to permit movement by pipeline.

Smart card A device that resembles a credit card and stores information on a memory chip.

Social class The group which people belong to according to their prestige and power in society.

Social needs Need for love, belonging, and friendship.

Society A community, nation, or broad grouping of people with common traditions, institutions, activities, and interests.

Special commodity storage Facilities designed to store farm products such as grain, cotton, and wool.

Special events A variety of special activities as part of the overall sales promotion program.

Specialized occupations Marketing jobs that require extensive technical knowledge of the products or services.

Special sales Holiday sales, Labor Day Sale, President's Day Sale, and other sales that are used by retailers to generate a large percentage of a year's sales volume.

Specialty goods Items with special features for which consumers are willing to make a major buying effort.

Specialty media Promotional items that carry the firm's name. These are used in an attempt to keep the company name in front of the customer.

Specialty stores Stores that carry a limited variety of goods but a large assortment of each item.

Staple items Basic products—bread, milk, soap, light bulbs—that households try to keep on hand.

Storage Stocking goods for future use.

Strategies Plans to reach the company's objectives.

Strip centers Neighborhood and community shopping centers that are built as long strings of stores set within a parking area.

Suggestion selling Positive suggestions regarding the purchase of additional or supporting products or services.

Supermarket A large retail store that sells a wide variety of food items, some nonfood items, and features self-service.

Superstores Very large stores that carry foods and numerous other products and services that consumers routinely buy.

Supervisory occupations Marketing jobs that require decision making, communication, and supervisory skills.

Supplies Items, such as grease and cleaning materials, that do not become part of the finished product but are used in the daily operation of a business.

Supply The quantity of a product or service that firms provide at a given time and at a given price.

Target market A specific group of customers that a company wants to serve.

Tariff Tax or duty levied on certain imported products.

Task oriented problems Problems that relate to specific marketing tasks and functions.

Team concept Realization that a team effort is required to enable a business to reach its goals.

Technology The use of knowledge based on science to solve problems.

Telemarketing A selling approach that is conducted entirely by telephone.

Teletext A type of videotex that provides information to viewers.

Test marketing When an organization makes a product

or service available to the market in a limited geographic area.

Time utility   What a product or service gains when it is available at the time a customer needs it.

Ton-mile   The movement of one ton (2,000 pounds) of freight for the distance of one mile.

Total company effort   All parts of a business working together.

Trade barriers   Factors that restrict the flow of products across borders.

Trade credit   Financing provided by suppliers, manufacturers, and wholesalers to their customers; that is, to other businesses.

Trade discounts   List price reductions given by producers to resellers for performing certain marketing functions. Also called functional discounts.

Trademark   A brand or part of a brand which has been granted legal protection by the U.S. Patent Office.

Trade premiums and gifts   Items offered to dealers, wholesalers, sales representatives, and retailers to encourage them to buy and sell more of certain products or services.

Trade promotions   Activities that encourage inter-

mediaries—wholesalers, industrial distributors, agents, retailers, and sales representatives—to buy and sell large quantities of products or services.

Trade publications   Specialized magazines for specific industries.

Trade shows   Booths set up by manufacturers and suppliers to display their merchandise or services.

Trading stamps   Stamps given to consumers that can be saved in booklets and redeemed for merchandise at a trading stamp redemption center.

Transit time   The total time that elapses from pickup of a shipment to delivery.

Transportation   The movement of goods from where they are produced or stored to where they are sold.

Truck jobbers   Limited-function wholesalers who sell and make deliveries to retailers from the stocks they carry on their trucks.

Tying agreement   A business has to agree to buy unwanted products in order to obtain wanted products.

Ultimate consumers   Persons or households that buy products or services for personal or family use.

Usage rate segmentation
The practice of dividing the market into segments based on how much of the product or service consumers buy.

Useful life The period of time during which a product can be used effectively.

Utility Usefulness or value added to products and services.

Values Ideas and principles that people consider correct, desirable, or important.

Vending machine retailing
The product is sold through a machine and no personal contact is made between buyer and seller.

Vertical market Exists when a product or service is used by only a small number of industries.

Videotex A television system that provides information to subscribers and sometimes receives information from them.

Viewdata A type of videotex that allows a message to be sent by cable from a subscriber's home or office to a central point.

Visual merchandising The visible presentation of products, services, or a business itself for the purpose of attracting attention,

creating desire, and stimulating consumers to buy.

Wall display A display of clothing and accessories pinned or hung on the wall.

Wants Things we can live without but which make our lives easier or more comfortable.

Warehouse A building where products are stored before distribution.

Wholesalers Businesses that buy large quantities of goods from extractors and manufacturers and sell them to other companies.

Wholesaling Selling products to buyers who are purchasing them for reasons other than personal or family use.

Window displays Displays located in interior windows, designed to attract attention and persuade potential buyers to come into a business.

Yard and ground storage Facilities used to store products that will not be damaged by exposure to the weather, such as coal, bricks, and gravel.

INDEX

A

Ability, examining, 68
Accessibility, 337
Accessory equipment, 158
Accidents, causes and prevention, 345–46
Action, 218–19
Advertising, 148, 201–2, 234–61
   agency, 252–53
   allowance, 274
   appeal, 240–41
   budget, 248–50
   coverage, 240
   critics of, 238
   defined, 236
   ethics, 259
   evaluation of effectiveness, 251–52
   importance and purpose, 236–38
   media, 240–48
   media mix, 242, 250–51
   objectives, 248
   planning process, 248–53
   promotional, 238–40
   purpose, 238–40
   three-dimensional print ads, 261
   types of, 238–41, 260
   video, 285
Advocacy advertising, 240
Age, and demographic segmentation, 176–77
Agency
   advertising, 252–53
   state employment, 386
Agents, 313
   manufacturers', 325
   selling 324–325
   wholesalers, 324–25

Agriculture, 153
Air carriers, 339–40, 345
Allowances, advertising, promotional, slotting, 274
Alternatives, evaluation of, 130
American Cancer Society, 51
American Red Cross, 51
Amtrak, 213
Analysis
   fact-feature benefit, 118, 126
Antitrust laws, 37
Apparel and accessories marketing, 55
Appeal, of advertising, 240–41
Apple Computer Company, 26
Application, letter of, 388–89
Approach, 220
Assumption close, 224–25
AT&T, 35
ATM, 23–24
Attention, 217–18, 219
Attitudes, 417
Automatic teller machine (ATM), 23–24
Avon, 311

B

Boeing, 169, 360
Boss, relations with, 211, 351
Brands, 26
   and brand extension, 108
   classification of, 107–8
   purpose of, 108
   and trademarks, 106–8
Broadcast media, 246–47
Brokers, 324
Budget, advertising, 248–50
Bundled pricing, 372
Bundle of values, 32

Business
    cycle, 37–38
    foundations, 69–71
    industrial and commercial,
      7–9
    marketing, 50
    production, 49–50
    route sales personnel, 216
    service, 50
    specialists, 217
    with spouse and friends, 307
Business Service Center (BSC),
    169
Buyer, 198–99
    differences among, 171–73
    government as, 169
Buying, 25, 26–27, 54
    behavior, consumer, 128–49
    motive, 133, 134, 135
    organizational 150–69
    signals, 224

C

California Raisins, 15
Campbell Soups, 108
Canvassing, 387
Careers. *See* Marketing careers
Career-sustaining occupations,
    61–62
Cash-and-carry wholesalers, 323
Cash discounts, 297
CEO, 15
Chain stores, 315, 316–17
Channels, 198–99
    of distribution, 310
    marketing, 310–33
Chief executive officer (CEO), 15
Choice, 225
Choice criteria, 130
CIM. *See* Computer-integrated
    manufacturing
Classification
    brands, 107–8
    consumer products, 138–42
    products, 106
    selling careers, 216–17
Clayton Act, 37

Closing questions, 392
Closing the sale, 224–26
Coastwise water transportation,
    338
Coca-Cola, 26, 360
Coding, 198–99
Cold canvassing, 387
Cold storage, 341, 342
Colgate-Palmolive Company,
    127
Commercial business activity,
    7–9
Commission, 324
Communication, 33–34, 154,
    198–99
Community shopping centers,
    370–71
Competencies, 69–71
Competition, 34–36, 289–91,
    367
Computer
    and marketing information,
      93–96
    network, 94
Computer-integrated manufac-
    turing (CIM), 365
Concepts
    consumer, 5
    marketing, 4–6
    sales, 4
Consignment, 322
Construction, 153
Consumer
    better-informed, 16
    and buying behavior, 128–49
    classification of products,
      138–42
    concept, 5
    contests and games, 273
    and decision process, 129–32
    influences on, 132–38
    and marketing channels,
      310–13
    markets, segmenting, 174–81
    packaging, 343
    products, 106
    route sales personnel, 216
    sales promotions, 270–73

service, 149
specialists, 217
ultimate, 3
wants and needs, 3–4
Consumer Product Safety Commission (CPSC), 36
Consumer Reports, 114
Contests, 273, 274
Controlling inventory, 342–43
Convenience goods, 138–39
Convenience stores, 317, 319
Conviction, 218, 219
Cooperative advertising, 240
Costs, 290, 299
Coupons, 101, 271–72
Credit, trade, 29
Culture
    and consumer buying behavior, 132, 137–38
    and international marketing, 361–62
    and society, 38–40
Cumulative quantity discounts, 296
Currency, 362
Customers, methods of reaching, 320–21
Customs, 362

D

Data, 366
Data base, and networking, 94
DDB Needham Worldwide, 213
Deadlines, 77
Decision-making skills, 407–8
Decision process, consumer, 129–32
Decisions
    place, 34, 89–90, 370–71
    price, 33, 90, 372
    product or service, 31-33, 88-89, 370
    promotion, 33–34, 89, 370–71
Decline, 105
Declining industries, 368–69
Decoding, 198–99
Delivered cost, 299

Demand, 159–61, 291–93
Demographic segmentation, 176–78
Demographic trends, 356–59
Demography, 176–78
Department stores, 317
Depression, 38
Derived demand, 159–60
Desire, 218, 219, 291
Desk jobbers, 323
Direct close, 226
Direct denial technique, 224
Direct retailing, 9, 320–21
Discount houses, 317, 319–20
Discounts, 295–98
    cash, 297
    functional, 296
    quantity, 296–97
    seasonal, 297–98
    trade, 296
Discovery Toys, 311
Discretionary income, 178
Disney, 360
Displays, types of, 265–68
Distribution
    channels, 310
    physical, 25, 27–28, 54, 334–53
    and pricing, 287–353
Domestic water transportation, 338
Downtime, 342
Drop shippers, 323
Dunhill Personnel System, Inc., 79
Durable goods, 4

E

Economic foundations, 69–71
Economy, 14, 37–38
Education, 358, 410
Effectiveness, 206, 251–52
Emotional appeal, 240–41
Emotional buying motives, 134
Employees, expectations, 401, 404–6

Employers, expectations, 401,
    403–4, 419
Employment, and marketing,
    51–53
Employment agencies, 386
Encoding, 198–99
End displays, 266
Entrepreneur, 15
Entrepreneurial marketing occu-
    pations, 65–66
Entrepreneurship, 15, 401
Entry-level occupations, 59–61
Environment
    and convenience, 127
    marketing. See Marketing en-
        vironment
Environmentalism, 366–67
Equipment, accessory, 158
Esteem needs, 133, 134
Ethics, and advertising, 259
European Community, 364
Evaluation
    of advertising, 251–52
    of alternatives, 130
    postpurchase, 131–32
    and testing, 206
Even prices, 294
Events, special, 272
Excuses, 222
Extension, brand, 108
External marketing information,
    85–86
Extractors, 7

F

Fact-feature benefit analysis,
    118, 126
Fad, 292
Family, and consumer buying
    behavior, 132, 136
Family brand, 107
Family life cycle, 136
Fashion, 292
Fast-growth industries, 368
FCC, 36

FDA, 36
Federal agencies, 36
Federal Communications Com-
    mission (FCC), 36
Federal Trade Commission Act,
    37
Feedback, 198–99
Fee paid, 387
Finance, 154
Financial services marketing,
    55–56
Financing, 25, 29, 54
Floristry marketing, 56
Fluctuating demand, 160–61
Following up
    job interviews, 392–94
    on sale, 226
Follow-up surveys, 103
Food and Drug Administration
    (FDA), 36
Food products marketing, 56
Ford Foundation, 51
Ford Motor Company, 171
Foreign water transportation, 338
Form utility, 10
Foundations
    economic, 69–71
    human resource, 69–71
    marketing and business,
        69–71
Franchise businesses, 315, 317
Freight, piggyback, 27–28, 353
Full-function wholesalers,
    321–22
Full-service wholesalers, 322
Functional discounts, 296
Functions, marketing, 24, 25–
    30, 54

G

Games, 273
General Electric, 108
General Motors, 108
Geographic segmentation, 174–
    75, 181

Global events, 362–63
GNP, 14
Goal
    profit as, 6
    setting, 167
Goods, 4
    convenience, 138–39
    shopping, 139–41
    specialty, 141–42
Government
    as buyer, 169
    and laws, 36–37
    market, 156
Great Lakes water transportation, 338
Gross national product (GNP), 14
Groups
    and lifestyle segmentation, 178–80
    minority, 359
Growth stage, 105

H

Health products and services marketing, 57
Heavy users, 180
Hierarchy of needs, 133–35
Home and office products marketing, 56
Honda, 360
Horizontal market, 161
Hospitality marketing, 57
Households, 176–77, 358–59
Human relations skills, 406–7
Human resource foundations, 69–71

I

IBM, 360
ICC, 36
Image, 291
Import quotas, 363–64
Impulse items, 139
Incentive, 225, 231

Income
    and demographic segmentation, 177–78
    discretionary, 178
    and education, 358
Independent retail stores, 315, 316
Individual brand, 108
Industrial business activity, 7–9
Industrial distributors, 314–15
Industrial market, 151–55, 159–61
Industrial packaging, 343–44
Industrial products, 106
    and marketing channels, 313–15
    types of, 156–58
Industrial sales personnel, 216
Inflation, 38
Information
    product or service, 110–11
    product or service sources, 114–17
    product or service use, 117–20
    search, 130
    utility, 12–13
Inland water transportation, 338
Inner-directed group, 179
Innovation, 333
Installations, 158
Institutional advertising, 240
Insurance, 154, 189
Integrated group, 179
Intercoastal water transportation, 338
Interests, 68, 218, 219
Interior displays, 265, 266–67
Intermediaries, and marketing channels, 310–33
Internal marketing information, 85–86
International Business Machines (IBM), 360
International marketing, 360–64

Interstate Commerce Commission (ICC), 36
Interview, job, 389–94
Introduction stage, 105
Inventory, 342–43
Island displays, 266

J

J.C. Penney Company, 312
JIT, 342–343
Jobs
  changing, 410–11
  description, 60
  in marketing, 380–401
  interview, 389–94
Just-in-time (JIT) inventory control, 342, 343

K

Kentucky Fried Chicken, 360

L

Lands' End, 194, 311
Laws
  antitrust, 37
  and government, 36–37
Letter of application, 388–89
Levi Strauss Company, 108
Life cycle
  family, 136
  product, 105–6
Lifestyle
  and consumer buying behavior, 132, 135–36
  segmentation, 178–80
  trends, 359–60
Light users, 180
Limited-function wholesalers, 321, 323–24
Line campaign, 370
List price, 296
L.L. Bean, 311
Local advertising, 240
Lockheed, 169, 360
Loss leaders, 295
Low accessibility, 337

M

McDonald's, 26, 360
Mail order retailing, 9, 320
Mail order wholesalers, 323, 324
Management
  marketing, 31
Managerial marketing occupations, 65–66
Managers, 31
Manufacturer-owned stores, 315, 317
Manufacturers, 7, 8
Manufacturers' agents, 325
Manufacturing, 153–54, 365
Market
  and segments, 170–91
  singles, 136
  target, 30–31, 171
  vertical and horizontal, 161
Marketing
  defined, 3–4
  and economy, 14
  and employment, 51–53
  and entrepreneurship, 15
  importance, 10–16
  and nonprofit organizations, 6, 50–51
  overview, 2–24
  of services, 325
  special topics and trends, 356–79
  specialty areas, 54–58
  success requirements, 71
  and technology, 364–66
  trends, 369–72
  and utility, 10–13
  world of, 1–79
  and you, 355–419
Marketing areas, specialized, 55–58
Marketing business, 50
Marketing careers, 14–15, 48–79
  beginning correctly, 402–19
  and jobs, 380–401
  planning your future, 67–69

Marketing channels
   and consumer products,
      310–13
   and industrial products,
      313–15
   and intermediaries, 310–33
   selecting, 332
Marketing concept, 4–6
Marketing environment, 34–40
Marketing foundations, 69–71
Marketing functions, 24, 25–30,
   54
Marketing information, 83–86
   and computers, 93–96
   internal and external, 85–86
   obtaining and using, 25, 29–
      30, 54, 82–103
   primary and secondary, 84–85
   system, 94–96
Marketing management, 31
Marketing mix, 30–34, 46,
   88–90
Marketing News, 169, 370
Marketing occupations, 49–58
   career-sustaining, 61–62
   entry-level, 59–61
   levels and diversity, 58–66
   managerial/entrepreneurial,
      65–66
   part-time, 67
   planning your future, 67–69
   researching, 66–67
   specialized, 62–63
   supervisory, 63–64
Marketing research, 86–87,
   369–70
   follow-up surveys, 103
   and marketing mix, 88–90
   and marketing occupations,
      66–67
   process steps, 91–93
Marketing researchers, 86
Marketing segmentation, and
   mass marketing, 170–74
Marketplace, analyzing, 81–191
Market segmentation, 171
   benefits, 182–83
   criteria for, 173–74

Market segments, 171
Markon, 299
Markup, 299
Maslow's hierarchy of needs,
   133–35
Mass marketing, 170–74
Materials handling, 344–45
Maturity stage, 105
MCI Communications, 35
Media
   advertising, 240–48
   broadcast, 246–47
   communication, 198–99
   outdoor, 247–48
   print, 242–46
   specialty, 247–48
Mercedes Benz, 26
Merchant wholesalers, 321–24
Minority groups, 359
Mix
   advertising media, 242,
      250–51
   marketing, 30–34
   product or service, 26, 111–
      14
   promotional, 195, 205–6
Monopoly, 37
Motivation, and consumer buying behavior, 132, 133–35
Motive
   buying, 133
   patronage, 131
Mutual benefit, 215

N

National advertising, 240
National brand, 107
National Retail Merchants Asso-
   ciation, 263–64
Need-driven group, 179
Needs
   consumer, 3–4
   and consumer buying behav-
      ior, 132
   determining, 220–21
   Maslow's hierarchy of,
      133–35

Neighborhood shopping centers, 370
Networking, 94, 387
News releases, 277, 284
Noncumulative quantity discounts, 297
Nondurable goods, 4
Nonpersonal promotion, 196
Nonprice competition, 289–90
Nonprofit organizations, 6, 50–51
Nonusers, 180
Norelco, 360
Norfolk Southern Railroad, 353

O

Objections, customer, 222–24
Objectives, advertising, 248
Occupational Outlook Handbook, 66, 78, 392
Occupational Safety and Health Administration (OSHA), 412
Occupational specialty, 54–58
Odd prices, 294
Ordinary product storage, 341, 342
Organizational buyers, 151
Organizational buying, 150–69
    characteristics, 161–62
    defined, 150–51
Organizational market, 151
    segmentation of, 181–82
    scope, 151–56
OSHA, 412
Outdoor media, 247–48
Outer-directed group, 179
Outside displays, 265, 268
Over-the-counter retailing, 9, 320
Overview
    of marketing, 2–24
    of promotion, 194–213
Ownership, 315–17, 341

P

Pacific Telesis Group, 365
Packaging, 26, 108–10, 343–44

Parts, 156–57
Part-time marketing occupations, 67
Patent and Trademark Office (PTO), 36
Patronage motives, 131
Pay
    and expectations, 399
    for services offered, 283
Penetration pricing, 294
People-oriented problems, 407–8
Perceived value, 309
Periodic inventory control, 342, 343
Perpetual inventory control, 342
Personality, 68
Personal promotion, 196
Personal resume, 282–85
Personal selling, 201, 214–33
    defined, 214–15
    process steps, 219–26
    and professionalism, 215–16
    and psychological stages of a sale, 217–19
Personal service marketing, 55
Physical distribution, 25, 27–28, 54, 334–53
Physical needs, 133–34
Piggyback freight, 27–28, 353
Pipelines, 338, 345
Place decisions, 34, 89–90, 370–71
Placement offices, 387
Place utility, 11
Planning
    and advertising, 248–53
    promotional, 204–6
    and sales presentation, 221–22, 232
    for your future in marketing career, 67–69
Platform displays, 267
Point-of-purchase displays, 267, 285
Population, growth and distribution, 357–58
Possession utility, 11–12
Postpurchase evaluation, 131–32
Posttesting, 206

Power strip centers, 372
Preapproach, 220
Premium money, 274
Premiums, 270, 273
Presentation, 221–22, 232
Pretesting, 206
Price
    competition, 289
    deals, 271
    decisions, 33, 90, 372
    defined, 288
    and discounts, 295–98
    factors affecting, 290–93
    lining, 295
    list, 296
    odd/even, 294
    skimming, 293
Pricing, 25, 28–29, 54, 288–
        309
    bundled, 372
    by manufacturers, 298–302
    by retailers, 299–301
    by service business, 301–2
    by wholesalers, 299
    and distribution, 287–353
    penetration, 294
    policies, 294–98
    promotional, 295
    setting methods, 298–302
    strategies, 293–94
Primary marketing information,
        84–85
Print media, 242–46
Private brand, 107
Private warehouse, 341
Problem recognition, 129–30
Problems, people-oriented and
        task-oriented, 407–8
Processed materials, 156–57
Procter and Gamble, 108, 127,
        199–200
Production, 30
Production business, 49–50
Product life cycle, 105–6
Product or service decisions, 31–
        33, 88–89, 370
Product or service mix, 26
Product or service planning, 25,
        26, 54

Products, 111
    classification of, 106
    consumer, 106, 138–42,
        310–13
    decisions, 370
    industrial, 106, 156–58,
        313–15
    information, 110–11, 114–
        20
    nature of, 291
    packaging, 108–10
    resale, 155
    and sales personnel, 114
    sampling, 270
    segmentation, 181
    and services, 4
    slurry, 338
    understanding, 104–27
Product-service mix,
        111–14
Professionalism, in selling,
        215–16
Profit, as goal, 6
Promotion
    allowances, 274
    and communication, 198–99
    decisions, 33–34, 89, 370–71
    importance, 196–98
    and marketing process,
        195–96
    methods of, 200–204
    mix, 195, 205–6
    nonpersonal, 196
    overview, 194–213
    personal, 196
    planning, 204–6
    pricing, 295
    pull and push strategies, 199–
        200
    and sales promotion, 202–3,
        262, 269–74
    and selling, 25, 28, 54, 193–
        285
Prospecting, 220
Prospect list, 385–87
Prosperity, 38
Psychological stages of a sale,
        217–19
Publicity, 204, 275–77

Public relations, 203–4, 262,
274–77
Public utilities, 154
Public warehouse, 341
Pull and push strategies, in pro-
motion, 199–200
Purchase, 130–31
Purchasing, 25, 26–27, 54
Push money, 274

Q

Quantity discounts, 296–97
Questions, closing, 392
Quotas, 363–64

R

Rack jobbers, 322–23
Railroads, 335–37, 345, 353
Rational appeal, 240
Rational buying motives, 135
Raw materials, 156–57
Real estate, 154
Real estate marketing, 57
Rebates, 271
Receiver, 198–99
Recession, 38
Recovery, 38
Recreation marketing, 57
Reference groups, and consumer
buying behavior, 132, 137
Regional shopping centers, 372
Resale products, 155
Research. See Marketing re-
search
Reseller market, 155
Restate objection technique,
223–24
Resume, personal, 282–85
Retailers, 7, 9, 299–301
Retailing, 315–21
and methods of reaching cus-
tomers, 320–21
and ownership, 315–17
and product line carried,
317–20
Retail marketing, 56

Retail sales personnel, 216
Retail trade, 155
Risk management, 25, 30, 54

S

Safety, 345–46, 411–12
Safety needs, 133, 134
Safeway stores, 107
Salary, and expectations, 399
Sales
closing and following up,
224–26
concept, 4
presentation, 221–22, 232
process steps, 219–26
promotion, 202–3, 262,
269–74
psychological stages of,
217–19
special, 272–73
Salvation Army, 51
Sampling, 270
Samsonite, 116
Santa Claus, 15
Scotch Boy, 107
Search, information, 130
Sears, 107
Seasonal discounts, 297–98
Secondary marketing information, 85
Segmentation
demographic, 176–78
geographic, 174–75, 181
lifestyle, 178–80
and organizational markets,
181–82
product or service, 181
usage, 182
usage rate, 180–81
Self-actualization needs, 133,
134
Seller, 198–99
Selling
agents, 324–25
career classifications, 216–17
personal. See Personal selling
process steps, 219–26

professionalism in, 215–16
and promotion, 25, 28, 54,
    193–285
and psychological stages of a
    sale, 217–19
suggestion, 226
Sender, 198–99
Service, 111
    consumer, 149
    financial, 55–56
    health, 57
    information, 110–11
    nature of, 291
Service business, 7, 9, 50, 301–2
Service marketing, 55
Services, 154–55
    information sources, 114–17
    information use, 117–20
    marketing of, 325
    and products, 4
    and sales personnel, 114
    segmentation, 181
    understanding, 104–27
Service wholesalers, 322
Setting goals, 167
Shadow box displays, 267
Sherman Antitrust Act, 37
Shippers, drop, 323
Shopping centers, 370–71
Shopping goods, 139–41
Shows, trade, 274
Signals, buying, 224
Singles market, 136
Skills, decision-making and hu-
    man relations, 406–8
Skimming, 293
Slotting allowances, 274
Slow-growth industries, 367
Slurry products, 338
Smart cards, 365–66, 379
Social class, and consumer buy-
    ing behavior, 132, 137
Social needs, 133, 134
Society, and culture, 38–40
Special commodity storage, 341,
    342
Special events, 272

Specialists, business and con-
    sumer, 217
Specialized marketing occupa-
    tions, 62–63
Special sales, 272–73
Specialty, occupational, 54–58
Specialty goods, 141–42
Specialty media, 247–48
Specialty stores, 317, 318
Sponsorship, 276
Staple items, 139
State employment agencies, 386
Storage, 28, 340–41
    ownership of facilities, 341
    types of, 340–41
Stores
    and ownership, 315–17
    and product line carried,
        317–20
Strip centers, 372
Success, requirements for, 71
Suggestion selling, 226
Superior point technique, 224
Supermarkets, 317, 318–19, 377
Superstores, 317, 319
Supervisory marketing occupa-
    tions, 63–64
Supplies, 157
Supply, and demand, 291–93
Surveys, follow-up, 103

T

Target market, 30–31, 171
Tariffs, 363
Task-oriented problems, 407–8
Team concept, 407
Technology, 364–66, 377
Telemarketing, 47
Teletext, 366
Testing, pre- and post-, 206
Test marketing, 90–91
Time utility, 11
Ton-mile, 335
Total company effort, 5–6
Tourism marketing, 58
Trade, wholesale and retail, 155

Trade barriers, 363–64
Trade credit, 29
Trade discounts, 296
Trademarks, and brands, 106–8
Trade premiums and gifts, 273
Trade promotions, 273
Trade publications, 114
Trade shows, 274
Trading stamps, 272
Training, 410
Transit time, 337
Transportation, 27–28, 154,
    334–40
Travel marketing, 58
Trends
    demographic, 356–59
    lifestyle, 359–60
    marketing, 369–72
Truck jobbers, 323–24
Trucks, 337, 345, 353
Tupperware, 311
Tying agreement, 37

U

Ultimate consumers, 3
United Way, 51, 276
Universal Product Code (UPC),
    377
UPC, 377
Usage rate segmentation,
    180–81
Usage segmentation, 182
U.S. Army, 134
U.S. Bureau of Labor Statistics,
    51, 66
U.S. Bureau of the Census, 94
U.S. Department of Education,
    54–58
U.S. Department of Labor, 51, 66

U.S. Sprint Communications, 35
Utilities, public, 154
Utility, 10–13.

V

Value(s), 32, 49, 309, 362
Vending machine retailing, 9,
    321
Vertical market, 161
Video advertising, 285
Video rental stores, 333
Visual merchandising, 202, 262,
    263–69
    principles, 268–69
    purpose, 263–65
    types of displays, 265–68

W

Wall displays, 266
Wall Street Journal, 23, 149, 213
Wants
    consumer, 3–4
    and consumer buying behav-
      ior, 132
    determining, 220–21
Warehouses, 341
Waterways, 338–39, 345
Wholesalers, 7, 8–9
Wholesalers, pricing by, 299
Wholesale trade, 155
Wholesaling, 321–25
Window displays, 265, 266
Women, in workforce, 358

Y

Yard and ground storage, 341–41
Yellow Pages, 9
Yes, but technique, 223